The Bedside **Guardian** *40*

A selection from

The **Guardian** 1990-91

edited by John Course

and introduced

by Bob Scott

FOURTH ESTATE · *London*

First published in Great Britain by
Fourth Estate Limited
289 Westbourne Grove
London W11 2QA

The right of John Course to be identified as the compiler of this work has been asserted by him in accordance with the Copyright, Designs and Patents Act 1988.

A catalogue record for this book is available from the British Library.

ISBN 1-872180-14-0

Typeset by York House Typographic Ltd, London
Printed and bound by Clays Ltd, Bungay

Contents

Introduction

The front line: *Bob Scott* ix

Exit Thatcher, pursued by a dead sheep

Winding the crank: *Andrew Rawnsley* 1

Sir Geoffrey's revenge: *Andrew Rawnsley* 3

Hanging up her handbag: *Andrew Rawnsley* 5

Three times a winner: *Hugo Young* 7

That's why the lady was a champ: *Melanie Phillips* 17

The hooligan society: *Alex Brummer* 20

The art of survival: *Howard Brenton* 23

No one left to blame: *Steven Berkoff* 30

John who?: *Andrew Rawnsley* 33

Son of Kong: *Steve Bell* 36

A funny kind of war

No chance: *Matthew Engel* 38

No resistance: *David Beresford* 40

Eclipse: *David Fairhall* 45

No contest: *Martin Woollacott* 48

The Kurdish rising: *Martin Woollacott* 51
The valleys of death: *Martin Woollacott* 53
Fixing a war, fouling a peace: *Edward Pearce* 60
A march on the mild side: *leader* 63

Dispatches from abroad

The reformer informer: *Matthew Engel* 66
East still East: *Michael Simmons* 69
The Chancellor adrift: *David Gow* 73
No joy in Jerusalem: *Ian Black* 75
Solzhenitsyn's circle: *Jonathan Steele* 77
Shevardnadze resigns: *Jonathan Steele* 82
Twenty-two, and still at school: *David Beresford* 86
Nelson's blind eye: *David Beresford* 89

Church and State

Public servants and private lies: *Melanie Phillips* 93
A House built on shifty sand: *Melanie Phillips* 104
Sour sweeteners: *Melanie Phillips* 110
The secret high street: *leader* 113
Can't pay, won't pay, and don't exist: *Peter Hetherington* 114
The indiscreet evangelist: *Peter Lennon* 118
'Twixt Devil and the deep blue sees: *Melanie Phillips* 125
The Lincoln handicap: *Jocelyn Targett* 134

Salesmanship

Money down the tube: *Roger Cowe* 151
Supermarketry: *Ben Laurance* 154
Rough diamonds: *Sarah Boseley* 157
Looking down the plughole: *Judy Rumbold* 159

Justice on trial

Judges' convictions: *Hugo Young* 164
Meddler after the truth: *Peter Lennon* 168
The guilt of the judges: *Ludovic Kennedy* 173
Life without bars: *Paul Hill* 177
Criminal justice: *leader* 178

Strutting players

Return of a legend: *Matthew Engel* 183
Just like old times: *Chris Hawkins* 185
Fading Orchid: *Cynthia Bateman* 187
Kentucky fried: *Matthew Engel* 190
Running on flat batteries: *Frank Keating* 196
Exit Jack's giant killers: *Ian Ridley* 199
Jewel among the Ashes: *Mike Selvey* 202
Blanco's try: *Frank Keating* 205
Master Woosnam: *Matthew Engel* 208
Sweeping death under the carpet: *Matthew Engel* 210
Winners losers: *Bob Fisher* 217
Endgame at Lyons: *Peter Lennon* 220
Kiss of life: *leader* 224

Screen time

Watching with Nancy Banks-Smith 226
A perverse way of doing business: *Derek Malcolm* 239
Walt's golden wonder: *Derek Malcolm* 243
Cannes noir: *Derek Malcolm* 246

People

Lenny the lionheart: *Tom Sutcliffe* 251
Simon Rattle: man of the Millennium: *Michael Henderson* 255
Clever git with a violin: *Jocelyn Targett* 262
The divine Bunnage from Chorlton Rep: *Joan Littlewood* 269

Mother outrage: *Peter Lennon* 272
Freda Jackson's people: *Ian Mayes* 274
Odd genius out: *leader* 277
Dead certainty: *John Ezard* 279
Pornbroker extraordinary: *W. L. Webb* 281
Clipped Wings: *Suzie Mackenzie* 284
Jeremy Beadle – saint?: *Judy Rumbold* 289
King of the crags: *Martin Wainwright* 293
Mr Wainwright and his love letters: *A. H. Griffin* 297
Fellows of the fells: *letter* 300
The voice for the people: *leader* 301
T. E. Lawrence's kid brother: *Erlend Clouston* 303
Putting the skis under the royals: *Charles Nevin* 307

Any other business

Heads you lose, tales you win: *Fred Sedgwick* 315
If this is a good school . . . : *Catherine Bennett* 319
University the Japan-easy way: *Kevin Sullivan* 326
Where the student is always right: *Michael White* 329
Votes on ice: *Martin Walker* 333
Hands off, Donald, they're ma troosers: *Alan Rusbridger* 336
The bottom line: *Joanna Coles* 339
Doves in the midst of war: *Carla Lane* 341
The other woman bites back: *Sarah Johnson* 344
Sperm wail: *Matthew Fort* 349
Aerial tactics: *Mark Morreau* 353
Dove tales and cherry mysteries: *Alan Mitchell* 355
Arguably the worst dish in the world: *Geoffrey Taylor* 358
Very Manchester: *Charles Nevin* 362

Introduction

Bob Scott

The front line

I want to think that my appetite for newsprint is healthy, that it demonstrates a proper thirst for knowledge and an enquiring mind. I am afraid not. I have a hunch that my passion for newspapers is a bit like my need for company, not really liking to be by myself. Mark you, it has given me extraordinary islets of information and an ability to con my way through almost any conversation on remembered snippets. Hence, probably, my guilty addiction to book reviews over the books themselves.

I ought to make clear that I did not read the articles that make up this book as you will – no neat, smallish bound pages. I was sent large photostats of the original *Guardian* pages, inconvenient sheets that had lives of their own. The more I read them the more I felt that this was the right way to enjoy this marvellously varied writing. Column inches in a newspaper are far more urgent than paragraphs in a book; they ask to be read quickly, as if they know they are doomed.

Not surprisingly, I admired the writing hugely. What I

did not expect was to feel a kind of sympathy for the life of a journalist. There is such skill here, such care, such seriousness, that I could not help wondering how the writers could bear to waste it all on something so flimsy as newsprint.

I see the *Guardian* most days and, frankly, I could remember precious few of the articles included here. Even the ones I remembered, like Andrew Rawnsley on the last days of Mrs T., or Martin Woollacott on the Kurdish tragedy, or Frank Keating on 'Blanco's try', I only remembered when I read them again. I have not carried them in my head. This is no criticism of the writing, more an observation on the way we read newspapers – like the theatre they are essentially ephemeral. People often commiserate with actors that their talent is cast to the winds. The journalist, however, is both actor and author and not only his performance but also his words are gone.

Over the years I have developed a reverence for both the actor and the athlete, who seem to me very similar. Forget Ian McKellen's knighthood and Seb Coe's wealth. They are brave. They put themselves up to be shot at, to be criticised and eventually to be written off. I reckon journalists are of this order. We tend not to admire them because they are capable of using words as weapons, and many is the morning that I have dreaded the verdict of a Billington or a Rodda. But they are front-line troops, we sneer when they are proved wrong, and like cricket umpires they do not have long to decide.

Not everyone included here is a journalist. There are playwrights, headmasters and a memorably scorned mistress. Nor is every inclusion an 'article'. There are wonderful obituaries and leaders. What is common is a relish both for ideas and for words.

On reflection, I am certain these qualities will easily survive the move from newspaper page to book page.

Exit Thatcher, pursued by a dead sheep

19 October 1990: Andrew Rawnsley

Winding the crank

Waiting for the arrival of the Prime Minister yesterday, MPs were debating what to do with the poor mad cow. Agriculture Questions were on the menu and Labour's Tony Banks was cooking up a particularly unappetising hors-d'oeuvre.

'A constituent of mine who is a regular eater of that great British institution the lukewarm meat pie, has become very concerned,' Mr Banks told us, serving his question with an ominous flourish. 'Having eaten a number of these pies recently, he has found the world has been dropping out of his bottom.'

Which, at least, is a less painful complaint than that suffered by many MPs, who find that it is words which drop out of their bottoms.

Too late to hear this, Mrs Thatcher came in and sat John MacGregor by her side on the front bench, just to show that having kept him in late at Number 10, John was once again among the teacher's pets. Alternatively, she was just putting the Education Secretary at the front of the class where she could keep an eye on him, before he ran off with any more of the Treasury's money.

From the beginning of the Question Time, the Prime Minister was radiating dangerously high levels of static. But why she blew such a fuse with Neil Kinnock was not clear. Perhaps Denis had overdone the voltage in her early morning electric bath. For when the Labour leader started pressing her about the school vouchers scheme, she short-circuited before our eyes.

Maybe it was because Mr Kinnock called her a 'crank'. But you doubt it; after all some of her best friends are cranks.

Anyway, after his second attempt to get an answer about vouchers, she suddenly started crying 'Nonsense! Nonsense!' at Mr Kinnock – screaming at the Labour leader as if he were a member of the Cabinet.

'Of course, you hate choice. Of course, you hate higher standards. Of course, you hate opportunity.' – and then came the total overload of her rhetorical circuits – 'You are a socialist – a crypto-communist!'

The Labour leader defused her rather well, laughing it off, as if to say he hadn't been one of those for years – a socialist, that is. The worst that can be said of Mr Kinnock these days is that he is a crypto-socialist.

'Mr Speaker,' he came back. 'It is a long time since we have had quite such a tantrum from the Prime Minister.'

By the time Paddy Ashdown rose to have a go, she had calmed down sufficiently to answer the Liberal Democrat leader without calling him a crypto-terrorist. He wanted to know of the crypto-Prime Minister why she disagreed with her Education Secretary – who had been rather forgotten in all the excitement – about vouchers.

'He is sitting next to me and disagrees totally with your interpretation of what he said,' Mrs Thatcher replied, as Mr MacGregor wagged his head in such vigorous agreement that he resembled a nodding dog in the back of a car driving at 100 mph off a cliff.

When the Prime Minister had been returned to Number 10 for some emergency soldering on her circuit boards, Labour MPs besieged the Speaker with demands that she withdraw the remark about their leader.

Dennis Skinner reminded the chair that, for less offensive remarks, which he helpfully repeated, 'I got an early bath.' 'I hope,' replied Mr Speaker, 'the Honourable Gentleman doesn't want another.'

Just keep out of any electric ones, Dennis.

14 November 1990: Andrew Rawnsley

Sir Geoffrey's revenge

Margaret Thatcher now knows that you *can* be savaged by a dead sheep.

Of all the True Confessions from her Cabinet Room, nobody has ever hissed-and-told with such devastating vehemence as Gentle Sir Geoffrey yesterday. The man she had treated as a doormat rose up and kicked her towards the door.

It was an emotional Sir Geoffrey who began to unfold his tragic story, a quaver in his voice as he reminded everybody that this was his first speech from the back benches in a quarter of a century. He told them of his early romance with Margaret, when a shared passion for monetarism had brought them together. He spoke of those blissful days together, the 'privilege' of being her Chancellor, the 'great honour' of being Foreign Secretary.

He made them laugh, by laughing at the notion that his

resignation was just a matter of style. 'If some of my former colleagues are to be believed, I must be the first minister in history to resign because he was in full agreement with government policy.'

Then he made them cry. Sadness crept into his voice as he began to talk openly for the first time about how this woman had ruined his life. The woman who robbed him of the job and the house that he loved. The woman who had wrecked his dreams and the party he loved with her hysterical behaviour about Europe.

'The Prime Minister and I have shared something like 700 meetings of the Cabinet or Shadow Cabinet over the last 18 years,' he said, beginning to detail the full trauma of those years. 'Some 400 hours alongside each other, and more than 30 international summit meetings.'

Now he had everybody on his side, Sir Geoffrey could start putting in the Hush Puppy. And, for once in his life, he was wearing steel tips.

The tale Sir Geoffrey told had everything you could possibly want, particularly if you were Michael Heseltine. Sir Geoffrey offered his shocking revelations. How he and Nigel Lawson – nodding his head by his side – had threatened resignation over the Exchange Rate Mechanism. Then Sir Geoffrey enjoyed his sweet revenge for all those humiliations and handbaggings, snubs and slights of the last eleven years.

He called her 'tragic', 'isolated' and 'extraordinary'. As each sentence drove more sharply into her back than the last, little gasps of shock went up around the place. There was a great 'Ooooo!' when he used Churchill's 'positive vision' of Europe to ridicule her 'nightmare images'. *There* – Sir Geoffrey seemed to say – that one's for taking away Chevening.

The start of the speech was all the more sensational for being delivered in Sir Geoffrey's soft-spoken, sleep-talking way. But as he got into his stride, he began moving about, swinging his shoulders and making little punches in the air, Mogadon Man transformed into Amphetamine Man.

He took her own cricketing metaphor and stumped her with it. Time after time the Cabinet agreed policy on Europe 'only for them to find that the moment the first balls are bowled their bats have been broken before the game by the team captain'.

And his final call – for other Tories to join him in putting loyalty to party before Prime Minister – was a direct appeal to sling out the old bat herself . . .

Sir Geoffrey sat down to a stunned silence. So quiet was the Chamber that you could hear Margaret Thatcher's jaw drop.

The sheep had roared.

23 November 1990: Andrew Rawnsley

Hanging up her handbag

Nothing became Margaret Thatcher's prime ministership as her leaving of it. The last big performance was a command one; a dying aria that played to a packed House. Those bums that could not get on seats sat on their colleagues' laps. In the stalls, Heselteenies crushed in next to Majorettes, who jostled with those following the Hurd instinct. But for an hour yesterday they were all still Thatcherites as the longest-running Prime Minister this century left the stage.

She got a standing ovation before she began, another when she finished. The Tories rose cheering and waving their order papers, many of them the same men and women who had just pulled the lever to send her through the trapdoor of history.

'Hypocrites!' yelled Labour MPs, who are genuinely distressed to see her go.

The premier dry had a wet eye when she first got to the dispatch box. But it soon cleared when she forgot the enemies within and got the opposition across the way firmly back in vision. The grocer's daughter who went on to play so many parts gave us a medley of her most famous roles. The Green Granny, the Finchley Fishwife, Her Maggiesty, the Housewife Superstar, the Duchess of Dulwich and Attila the Hen all made their appearances.

She took them through her favourite routines. The old standard: 'Our policies have brought unprecedented prosperity.' The reliable crowd-stopper: 'We have been steady and staunch in defence.' And one last sentimental rendition of: 'These are the reasons we shall win a fourth election victory.'

For old times' sake, she had a jolly good shout at Neil Kinnock. Before finally hanging up her handbag, she gave it one last swing at a few Labour back benchers who strayed within range.

And then Dennis Skinner engaged her in a double-act. Asked whether, in retirement, she would still oppose a European central bank, Mr Skinner fed her a line, shouting: 'No, she's goin' to be the Guv'nor.'

'What a good idea!' she cried to swelling cheers. 'I'm enjoying this,' she said, doing little bows – 'Thank you. Thank you.'

They have loved her never so much as when losing her. Her own back benchers showered her with bouquets of praise. Neil Kinnock made a pretty display of words about her departing with dignity, although he laced it with barbed wire by asking for an immediate general election – a demand that the whole government pick up a pearly-handled machine-gun.

Paddy Ashdown praised a 'bravura performance', and asked whether she had any advice for whoever was elected to step into her stilettos. 'No,' she smiled. They can learn the hard way.

And following that is not going to be easy. All the rivals

for the role were there. Mr Hurd and Mr Major sat next to each other on the government front bench, the best of enemies.

Mr Heseltine sat below the gangway in a blue suit, flaunting his blond hair. His pitch for the part was clear. If they picked him, they'd hardly have to change the costume. And even Mrs Thatcher's hair dresser could stay on at Number 10.

They said goodbye with more cheers. Mind you, she took care to remind us the show is not quite over yet, hinting that whether she becomes a back bencher from Finchley or a countess from Dulwich – we have not heard the last of that voice. And she expected to be taking Question Time next Tuesday, 'and possibly even on Thursday'.

After 11 years, she is still threatening a few more encores.

23 November 1990: Hugo Young

Three times a winner

She died as she had lived, in battle. It was a quite extraordinary end, but it was in keeping with everything important that had gone before. There was a continuity, not only in the texture of these events but in the circumstances of her long life and swift demise. Just as her triumphs were often rooted in her zest for combat, her refusal to listen to advice and her unwillingness to admit that she could be wrong, so were these the sources of her last predicament. Until yesterday, when all three habits were finally broken.

It is a shocking way to go. Having lost no vote either in the Commons or in the country, she was yet disposed of by the unaccountable will of fewer than 400 politicians.

There has been nothing like it in the democratic era: no verdict apparently so perverse and unprovoked delivered by a governing party against a leader upon whom it had fawned and under whom it had grown fat for so many years. Many Conservatives will be thunderstruck by what they accomplished yesterday; some, even among those who did the deed, will be ashamed. For the first time in her prime ministership she provoked, while not requesting it, the human sympathy reserved for a helpless creature at bay.

The symmetry between the life and the death was none the less compelling. She was a leader of lurid style and risky habits, especially in the field of personal relations. Aggressive to a fault, she spent years scorning not only consensual policies but the consensual demeanour. With nerveless indifference, she was prepared to see the larger portion of her friends as well as enemies in high places depart the scene as a direct result of her behaviour. A kind of rough justice therefore now prevails, its chemistry precipitated by the most enduring victim of these gross habits, Geoffrey Howe. She who lived by fire and insult cannot wholly complain when the ultimate insult repays her.

These have, however, been years that will not be forgotten. The Callaghan era might never have happened, for all that history makes of it. This is less true of the periods to which Harold Wilson and Ted Heath attach their names, but what lingers from them is notoriety more than fame. The Thatcher era will be different, and nowhere more so than in the evidence it offers that personality can be the single most potent contributor to the pattern of events. For better or for worse, this will truly and for ever be called the Thatcher Era. She was a creature of her times. Although as a minister under Heath, she showed an opportunist's capacity to find different times congenial enough, from the mid-Seventies she rode the tide of liberal economics and anti-state politics with missionary aplomb. All reformers need circumstance to coincide with destiny. But character matters more. There were things that happened which would, I think, have happened quite differently without her.

The first was the Falklands War. It was a prime example of ignorance lending pellucid clarity to her judgement. Surrounded by ministers who knew what war was and dithered at its prospect, she understood what the soldiers wanted and shirked neither the military consequences not the huge political risk. This quality of leadership was justly rewarded. She was, in fact, especially decisive in war. But for her it is also certain that American bombers would not have been allowed to bomb Libya from British bases in April 1986.

Second, the conduct of economic policy in the early Eighties owed almost everything to her moral fibre. It may have been a failed policy, but it was hers. She was committed to an economic theory and committed against caring about unemployment. When Lord Hailsham told her, in July 1981, that she would destroy the Conservative Party as surely as Herbert Hoover led the Republicans to oblivion in 1932, she spat in his eye. Blood on the streets did not alarm her, any more than the self-starvation of Irish republicans. She worried not about the jobless masses but the looted shopkeepers: a priority which, nine years later, no longer seems odd.

Third, and for similar reasons, the dethroning of trade-union power would have taken a different course without her. She acted out with utmost seriousness the anti-union prejudice which most other Tories shared but which many of them had not dared to deploy. Public sector strife, culminating with the 1984 coal strike, was permitted to drag out as ministers watched with almost sadistic fascination. But without the gimlet eye of their leader upon them, their record suggests that they would have lost their nerve well before the desired 'demonstration effect', which always mattered more than the money, was achieved.

With Mrs Thatcher's fourth irreplaceable mark, we reach more contentious territory: the region, in fact, where hubris and nemesis met, to ultimately catastrophic effect. Few qualified observers doubt that her stand against the European Community achieved a British advantage in the early days, which was unavailable by other means. By asking reasonable questions in a wholly unreasonable manner, she secured more of 'our money' from Brussels. A decade's combative diplomacy made for a quite different British presence. Arguably, we counted for more in Europe, in a constructive as well as critical role, in 1985 than in 1975.

But here came the first source of her trouble. The mark in Brussels became a kind of curse at home. Her elemental convictions about nationhood and sovereignty were not accompanied by sufficient sensitivity to the opposite feelings of significant colleagues. The issue became an emblem of the style as well as the content at the heart of her difficulties. It showed the falsity of this distinction. With this leader the style *was* the woman.

In modified form, this was also a key to her fifth uniquely personal policy, the poll tax. It is the only tax in the western world to have grown more out of character than reason. Reason, expressed by Nigel Lawson and the Treasury, said that it would be unjust, unworkable and insupportably expensive. Character, sticking blindly with a Thatcher commitment dating from 1974, insisted that it must go forward and enlisted – another consistent trait of these years – the incautious support of enough meekly compliant ministers for the blame to spread.

Policies alone, however, do not define the place she will take in the annals. The intangibles are perhaps more important and may ensure her name a longer life. Thatcherism embodies a style and a set of values that will take a long time to disappear from British politics. At the least, they may be the model of what to avoid: a memory studiously honoured in the breach. More likely, they will endure as an example others cannot neglect.

As a leader, she developed abrasiveness into an art form. She despised, above all, consensus: the goal of most other leaders but not her. She inveighed against it with as much vigour in November 1990 as she did before she became Prime Minister. As a leader, also, she needed to know everything and often seemed to do so. There never has been a leader better briefed, with readier riposte, more scornfully employed against her ignorant enemies. This most formidable capacity was some kind of answer to those who charged her, accurately, with an insatiable desire to interfere in every minister's business. Hardly anything moved in Whitehall without her approval; but for hardly anything that happened did she fail to have a detailed justification.

As well as this ambiguous virtue, however, she had a plainer one. She did not want to be liked. The least likeable of all leaders, according to consistent opinion poll findings, she none the less won three elections. In this she was wholly admirable. She did not pander to the people. They often remarked on how much they hated her, even as they admitted to a grudging respect. This quality, often described as a flaw, did much for the moral calibre of our politics. No other leader in our time, I guess, will be so easily willing to resist the desire to please.

She used this harshness to establish a more prominent British presence in the world. Of all the people bewildered by what has happened, none flounder in deeper astonishment than foreigners from all over. For most of them, Margaret Thatcher has given a passable imitation of the Britannia whom, during the Falklands crisis, she shamelessly sought to personify. Before her, a series of faceless men, usually in grey suits, trod the global stage pretending to an influence that depended on past glories some of them could almost remember. They rarely said or did anything worthy of report on an inside page of the *New York Times*.

In the Thatcher era, the image has been different. During the Reagan years, moreover, image proclaimed more than mere appearance. Through their shared ideology, they formed a society for the mutual support of leaders determined to abolish the post-war consensus. Mrs Thatcher visited Washington often, was invariably feted and, if an election year loomed, nationally drafted for the presidency. She had a very special relationship with Mr Reagan and, as the interlocutor with Mr Gorbachev, a special role in the dialogues that led to the ending of the Cold War. When that ice age broke up, moreover, it was to the Thatcher model that many of the newly free countries consciously turned for guidance on the modalities of the free market. All this was due to her personal charisma. Evangelism and showmanship captured the east, beginning in the Soviet Union shortly before the 1987 election. Some might say that the influence thereby attained was a little illusory. How could a weak country like Britain aspire to change the world, especially when Germany was becoming so manifestly the dominant power in Europe? But that only serves to reinforce the Thatcherite point: without her peculiar quality of conviction, proclaimed by her flamboyant personality, Britain would have continued to take its proper place as an increasingly obscure island off the shore of north-west Europe. It is a destination her successor will have the greatest difficulty in avoiding.

So this defiance of historic inevitability may not last long. There were signs of it waning well before she fell. Developments in both east and west were beginning to relegate Britain back into the second division. What the lady spoke for at home, on the other hand, could expect a longer shelf-life. It was here that her legacy had best chance of surviving, if only because some of it has been seized by her opponents.

She spoke, as no one else did, for business Britain. Not just for big business but, rather more, for small. Detached from her party, she could easily have been a latter day Poujadist, expressing the economic but also the social philosophy of little-England shopkeeping, the world from which she sprang. In entrepreneurship, in profit-making, in market-place success she saw the unalterable foundations of a successful society. She never deviated from this philosophy, and never tired of reiterating its principles as a guide to human conduct. Doubted and even despised during the Seventies, these at last became conventional wisdom in the Eighties.

Nowhere was this more apparent than in the Labour Party. Arguably, the new model Labour Party was one of her most important creations. She often vowed not to leave politics until socialism had been scorched off the face of Britain. One more term, she thought, would finally disabuse the country as well as Labour that the politics of the left had any future. A pseudo-socialist Labour Party has outlived her, which she will deeply regret. But the pseudery is significant. In Labour rhetoric, the virtues of private property and market economics have replaced ancient promises to dismantle the integument of the capitalist system. By departing Mrs Thatcher may have removed Mr Kinnock's favoured electoral target: but she leaves an Opposition more anxious to retain than remove a fair amount of what she has done.

She also leaves an economy which, for all their railing, is stronger than it was. Maybe the most history will be able to say is that the Thatcher years decelerated British decline. Certainly the wondrous miracle, which many of her former colleagues were pointing to in their obituary tributes yesterday, takes its reality only from an assumption about where we might have been without the medicine she administered in the early Eighties. Even so, if we grant that all political careers can be said to end in failure, with their grand promises never fully achieved, this career can none the less be deemed less of a failure than many.

There were failures, however. And of many candidates for consideration, two strike me as reaching close to the heart of the Thatcher experience. Just as there were positive events unattainable without her, so were there the negative: specific and peculiar to her person.

The first concerned her attitude to government itself, and in particular the role of the state. She came into power determined to reduce it. Most Tory leaders have said as much, but she was the first who announced a conscious mission to abandon paternalist aspirations and get government, even benign government, off the people's backs.

This was conspicuously accomplished in only one department, that of state ownership. The privatising of productive business will never be reversed, and even the utilities are likely, under Labour, to remain outside the public sector. Selling council houses and cheap shares in gas switched a few million people from being clients of Labour, as the party of public ownership, to being clients of the capitalist party.

But elsewhere, Mrs Thatcher's relations with the state ended in confusion, futility and contradiction. One of her famous axioms was that no such thing as society existed: which postulated a dismantling of the collective institutions that propped society up. This did not happen. Her sentiment was widely regarded with ridicule and incomprehension, even among her own supporters. Society at large showed no inclination to assume its disintegrating role. Quite the opposite. Every test of public opinion showed that in her didactic task, of persuading people that the state could not be benign, she failed.

But her actions, also, countermanded her ambition. In the Thatcher years, there were many ways in which the central state grew more – not less – powerful. In finance, in education, in health services, the edicts of the centre overrode those of the locality, as local government was substantially undermined. She was aware of this paradox. In schools and hospitals, a species of market choice was supposed to stand substitute for local democracy. But in the end the gentlemen, and un-gentlewoman, in Whitehall knew best. We were told that this would be temporary. But a government of different temper will find a lot of new instruments in place, the tools of Mrs Thatcher's rage for action, conveniently ready for use.

Add to this the curtailments of civil liberties, notably concerning free expression, and the Thatcher era will go down as one in which state power increased. All Tory leaders have been vigilant in defence of the state's policing power. But a special edge was given this trait by this Prime Minister. Her own experience with terrorism, always an underrated aspect of her psyche, made her an unyielding proponent of media curbs which touched upon it. She was in favour of freedom as long as it could be paid for: a less reliable defender of the intangible liberties of man.

The second failure concerned, in the end, her view of what political leaders were meant to be and do. She had the vices of her virtues. This was what finally engulfed her.

She was strong, but put excessive weight on strength. She accumulated more personal power than any peacetime Prime Minister in history; and in that guise will interest the constitutional historians for many years. But she saw too little value in the art of compromise. Leadership, for her, was equated too often with the satisfaction of her will. How often, when challenged with being overmighty, did she deride the notion of a leader who gave precedence to other virtues than strength. She was a conviction politician, but too often scorned the reasoned statement of different convictions, sometimes by her closest colleagues. Argument she relished, as long as she won, but persuasion she neglected. Give-and-take and the other techniques of sweet reason were alien to her nature.

This made for abrasive and often decisive government, but it was fatally disabling for any kind of collective leadership. For surprisingly many years, it wrought no lasting damage.

The collective was willing to put up with its uncomradely supremo because, essentially, it was persuaded that she was going in the right direction: and in any case she kept on winning elections.

But at the end, over Europe, the one issue on which the Conservative Party was prepared to concede that it is most seriously divided, the obedience of the collective – beginning with Nigel Lawson and ending with Geoffrey Howe, and not forgetting the destruction wrought by Nicholas Ridley in between – collapsed.

Behind Mrs Thatcher's political method lay a vision of Britain but, perhaps more importantly, also a vision of herself. Although insecurity was never entirely missing from her makeup, it coexisted with even less confidence in the ability of anyone else to do what she was doing.

For many years she thought she was irreplaceable, a judgement which grew not out of simple vanity so much as an assessment of Britain's plight and what she could contribute to it. When the tumbrels began to roll two weeks ago, she still could not credit that this verdict was being revised. Nor could many other people. Some still cannot. Having broken the rules and beaten the system often in the past, she seemed capable of doing it again. It was almost an offence against nature to suppose that she could not.

But finally the system, which says that this is cabinet and not prime-ministerial government, reacted. There was a point beyond which it declined to be flouted. This point was identified by an age-old reflex: the perception that an election was about to be lost and power surrendered to the other side. No fear exceeds that of politicians faced with the loss of office, not even fear of the avenging virago across the table. So in the end, in a drama whose outlandishness aptly reflected the years before, she went.

23 November 1990: Melanie Phillips

That's why the lady was a champ

And so now they're all chaps together again. The captain has been bowled middle stump while attempting to hit the ball out of the ground. Cricketing metaphors can be rescued from uncomfortable female appropriation. The masculine ethos of public life can reassert itself untroubled by this vexatious business of coming to terms with a woman in power; a woman, moreover, who refused to be a gentleman. For whoever wins the Tory Party leadership, whoever wins the next general election, it will now be men fighting each other by the rules of the game they all understand.

If she'd been a man, she would never have got away with half of it; she understood this and played it for all she was worth. Her gender was the supreme weapon with which she wrong-footed her Cabinet, the Opposition and the media, producing the extremes of drooling sycophancy and spineless wimpishness in a world of public affairs where a woman who stepped outside the role men expected her to play left them effectively emasculated.

The gender card was never afforded the attention it deserved: hardly surprising since the vast majority of political commentators and analysts are men to whom the point would probably not occur at all and, even if it did, they would hardly be well placed to understand how such sexual dynamics served her purpose.

If Robin Day had been a woman, maybe those television

interviews in which he was so clearly labouring under a disadvantage would have run a quite different course. What would have been risible behaviour on her part – the eyelash-batting, the lowered voice – in a world dominated by women interviewers, women Cabinet ministers and women Opposition front-benchers, barely occasioned the slightest comment. Yet it was notable that the people who did succeed on rare occasion in discomfiting the Prime Minister were mainly women: Mrs Diana Gould, for example, who asked the one question during the Belgrano affair that caught Mrs Thatcher off guard, or the young woman local newspaper reporter who, by her well-informed directness, achieved the same effect during a general election campaign.

Against the men who dominated her world, Mrs Thatcher's gender was a devastating weapon deployed in two distinct fashions. In the first, she used it actively and deliberately. She flirted. The seductive appeal of power was never more apparent than in the sexual magnetism between herself and Mr Gorbachev, but it was noticeable that she could turn it on towards any man of affairs, particularly if she felt vulnerable. When she wasn't playing siren and actress she played mother, maybe an even more powerful part. Young men were 'taken under her wing' and she was said to have taken a maternal interest in their private lives.

And if this combination wasn't powerful enough, there was the flattery factor, a phenomenon common to all powerful women in which men tend to feel flattered and grateful when such women bestow upon them merely a little attention.

But she also used the gender weapon in precisely the opposite fashion and to even more devastating effect. This was that Mrs Thatcher simply didn't behave as men thought a woman should behave. She was rude, she shouted, she interrupted, she was tough, she was ruthless – male qualities that she used more effectively than the men who thought all this just wasn't cricket. If a male prime minister had behaved like this, it would have been thought entirely normal and his colleagues and opponents would have had no difficulty in using the same tactics against him.

Indeed, had they complained about a male PM in the way they complained about her, they would have made themselves appear utterly ridiculous. Her Cabinet colleagues, in the early days of her premiership at least, used to say in all seriousness daft things like: 'When she gives you that look of hers, your knees just turn to jelly.' And the men (invariably) in the room with them would nod sympathetically and cluck their tongues. Because she was a woman, they somehow felt they simply couldn't shout back. No wonder she called them wet.

In similar fashion, she wrongfooted the Opposition too. Mr Kinnock, once a noted parliamentary wit, felt inhibited from using against her the one weapon that would have felled her in debate, taking the mickey out of her, because she was a woman. He just didn't know how to handle it without offending feminist sensibilities. Yet a woman in his position would have had no difficulty at all. Maybe, as some of his colleagues fear, Mr Kinnock will come off worse in future contests with Prime Minister Heseltine or Hurd. But he will nevertheless feel, for the first time since becoming party leader, that this is a duel he can handle more comfortably. The playing field has now been levelled.

Yet her gender was also a two-edged weapon. As she said to *The Times* this week: 'If a woman is strong, she is strident. If a man is strong, gosh, he's a good guy.' Ten years ago, a friend commented about her: 'There's something about her I don't like. It's a hardness, a ruthlessness. Ted Heath was a very difficult man but it was more acceptable in him. With Margaret, it's something in her that you can't relate to; you want to relate to her and expect to be able to as she's a woman.'

It is, after all, the paradox about women in power; they are expected to behave like men to earn their place (no nonsense about taking time off work to watch a child in the school play, no sign of emotional or physical weakness permitted) and yet if they are assertive or tough-minded they are condemned as aggressive or hectoring.

The misogyny which greeted her appointment as Conservative leader has not disappeared but has been coated by a thin veneer of respectability. The arguments against Mrs Thatcher's policies and style have been inextricably bound up with the confused hostility provoked by her gender.

It has been said that she was the most extraordinary Prime Minister Britain has had. It is probably nearer the mark to say that the profound effect she had upon national life was due rather more to the extraordinary reactions she provoked among those around her.

24 November 1990: Alex Brummer

The hooligan society

It was a quiet, humid Sunday night when I parked my car at the parade of shops in Putney, south-west London, to buy bottles of mineral water. Ten years earlier it was a journey that would not have been possible or necessary. The generously stocked supermarket would have been bolted, and buying bottled water would have been an affectation. But with horror reports of microbes and worms in the reservoirs and impurities streaming through the pipes, Thames Water's finest seemed as unappealing as the rusty trickle that one coaxed out of the hotel-room tap in Haiti, the poorest nation in the western hemisphere.

While inside, a sleek, silver-grey Honda backed itself

into my passenger door, administering what later was estimated at several hundred pounds of damage. The Honda and its driver made a quick getaway: fortunately there was a Good Samaritan watching who managed to scribble down its number. The Samaritan was insistent that the incident be reported.

Fired up with the knowledge that visiting the police would be a genuine public service, I headed to Putney police station down the road. The shabby six-foot by four-foot vestibule was empty but for one chair. The glass security door to the bench, for my encounter with Dixon of Putney, was locked, while he dealt with another client.

Into the waiting-room marched a tall fellow replete with rippling muscles, earrings and tattoos. One glanced, and there was nowhere else to look.

'What you staring at, mate?' came the growl. 'Do you want your face smashed?'

I looked away, praying that the glass door to the policeman behind the counter would swing open before I was pulverised. It did. Having braved life and limb in the outer room of the police station there was now the chance to trace the missing Honda. The story of the accident was recounted before I was informed by the police officer that he didn't have his book.

'Aren't there any spare books?' I enquired. He repeated tartly, that he hadn't got his book and suggested that I might drive a mile down the road to Wandsworth police station to make my allegations. By this time frustration and anger had set in against the thought of another police station.

This experience was surreal. But it didn't really shock. I had been back in Britain for just over a year, after a ten-year absence – 1979–89 – in the USA as Washington correspondent. I had missed the Thatcher economic, financial and social experiment and was experiencing it for the first time. There were clear and very obvious benefits: telephones that were fitted swiftly and worked;

mobile communications galore; a glorious range of organic foods; and a brilliant sense of design in retailing chains which contrasted with that in the US; and a dozen and one other changes which impressed. But these new efficiencies and services, although a stark contrast with the stultifying attitudes in commerce a decade earlier, were largely offset by the negative: what one has come to call the hooligan society. I'd thought it was only on *Hill Street Blues* that one was in danger of being blown away in the police station. Whatever one did, wherever one was, there was a close awareness of the hooligan society closing in and trapping.

Cars and the roads that serve them, indicators of Thatcherite prosperity, provide a good case in point although there are many other examples of the swing from private prosperity to public squalor symbolised by the waiting in hospitals, the littered streets and parks, and a shambolic education system. Driving was once a relatively civilised activity. No longer. Politeness has taken a back seat. In the US it was customary to talk nostalgically of British drivers who would give way at junctions and roundabouts. On the Thatcher-era roads, when traffic in London is hardly moving anyway, the chances of allowing anyone through have become minimal. If one dares to edge across, a torrent of abuse follows.

What used to be described as 'polite notices' have become 'foul notices'. There is one pinned to my office notice-board, received after parking legitimately in a local car-park with the handbrake off and gears in neutral: 'Don't leave your car in such a stupid place you silly f****** c***. Next time I'll smash the f****** windows. Love the public.' Such warnings have to be taken seriously. Since I rejoined the *Guardian*'s financial team the vehicles of five of my colleagues have been vandalised. Where I sometimes park at Barnes station there is a permanent scree of broken glass on the pavement. A few weeks ago a friend stumbled across a group of youths mindlessly demolishing a wooden bench at the bus-stop near the station; the friend, an American, intervened.

While the quality of cars on the roads has improved immeasurably, with old bangers scarce among the legions of BMWs, Volvos and Rovers, the roads they ride upon are miserable and the risks they run while stationary are considerable. The distortions of a tax system that still favours corporate cars, the availability of easy credit in an era of high interest rates, and the economy of cash limits on public transport have rendered Britain second rate. Indeed, the same short-termism that is complained of by industry about the City is true also of government under Mrs Thatcher. The obsession with 'good housekeeping.' A budget in surplus or balance means that there has been short-termism in public investment in infrastructure, research and development, and education and training.

There is no other Western nation where a potential Prime Minister, John Major, would have had no formal education beyond 16 years of age. Yet Mr Major, as Chief Secretary and Chancellor, has not been known as a robust advocate of longer education, better schools and improved training. He has faithfully executed the Thatcher creed that economy in government is a virtue. As a result, Mrs Thatcher will leave office with government heading back into debt and with a less prepared and trained populace than is required for a European challenge. Farewell to the yob decade.

29 November 1990: Howard Brenton

The art of survival

If there is one insight that comes from the most noted novels, television drama series and plays of the 1980s, it is that during the decade we were overtaken by something malevolent. It may seem exaggerated, but it was as if some kind of evil was abroad in our society, a palpable degradation of the spirit.

On 'enlightenment Thursday', when Thatcher resigned, it was to many of us in the arts as if the curse had been lifted, if only for a day. Parties broke out, the phone never stopped ringing. An eminent theatre director, a very level-headed man, rang me laughing with joy. 'I've just been down to Downing Street,' he said, 'to see her off the premises. It seemed the only place to be.' That afternoon, crossing a South London high street, I was hailed by a painter who has worked for years in obscurity selling hardly anything and who could be, for all I know, our Van Gogh. 'The bastards thought I'd be dead by now,' he cried, sheets of hardboard under his arm for new works, 'but I'm still here.' Roland Rees, whose gallant little touring company Foco Novo was axed by the Arts Council in the mid-Eighties, rang to say, 'Perhaps now we can all get back to normal.'

It was the talk of excited survivors who experienced the Eighties as a philistine hurricane against the idea of culture itself. Theatre workers felt, on that Thursday morning: 'Well! Not all our theatres may be left standing but we still are.'

For these have been very tacky years. There has been a sense of ill-being abroad, which Clare MacIntyre memorably characterised as 'low level panic'. Recently a much overworked social worker, the kind of person who should be honoured as the salt of the earth in our society but whose profession has been calumnied in the past 10 years, described her experience of the Eighties to me as 'feeling inauthentic, feeling that there is nothing you can do because there is nothing *for* you in the country'.

Writers have tried to describe this Eighties 'state of the soul'. I think the record is surprisingly impressive, more so than it seemed at the time, when it was fashionable to say the arts were impotent.

Television gave us Alan Bleasdale's *The Boys From The Blackstuff*, about the loss of the dignity of work, and Troy Kennedy Martin's *Edge Of Darkness*, about our loss of the trust of mother nature. They are two very different works, but they were both shot through with profound anxiety, which, typically of Eighties' writing, the authors could not quite articulate. None of us could: human evil, unlike the glamorous religious evil of Milton's Satan, is banal, grotty and everyday.

For me, two novels brilliantly caught the ethos of the Thatcher years. Martin Amis's *Money*, with its ultimate yuppy hero John Self, duped by the brave new world he so lasciviously embraced, is a modern *Vanity Fair*. Because of the murderous religious hatred it has attracted, it seems to have been forgotten that Salman Rushdie's unruly *The Satanic Verses* is actually an attack on contemporary manifestations of human evil, and an Eighties' classic. It should be re-read, even *actually* read, and extensively reviewed again.

In the theatre, Caryl Churchill's *Serious Money* and, if you will forgive the immodesty, *Pravda* by myself and David Hare dramatised a 'black hole' of amorality in the public world of the day, into which traditional liberal values were sucked away without trace. The most successful dramatist of the past decade, Alan Ayckbourn, is in some ways the poet of the lower-middle classes, whose values have, in effect, been in power throughout it (and I'm not trying to be rude here – that's Alan's bag). But since 1985, his boulevard comedies have begun to take dark turns as if he has begun to smell something putrid behind the privet hedges and net curtains of Thatcher's natural constituency.

Looking at these successes by writers – and there were many more: Clare MacIntyre's plays, Hanif Kureishi's movie scripts, a constant mortar fire of dangerous novels from Fay Weldon – it strikes me that nearly all of them, despite radically different sensibilities, are comic, almost at times to the point of hysteria, and they are wildly inventive, manipulating genres. Writers felt driven to extremes as they tried to describe the banal desolation of what happened in our country in the Eighties. Also, all this work has within it a sense of mourning, of grief for lost opportunities, that something loved between us was being strangled – our culture.

Thatcherism, like all authoritarian dogmas, was brightly coloured. Writers were trying to get at the darkness, the social cruelty and suffering behind the numbingly, neon-bright phrases – 'the right to choose', 'freedom under the law', 'rolling back the state'. It was as if a hyperactive demon was flitting about among us, seeking with its touch to turn everything into a banal conformity, a single-value culture with one creed – 'by their sales returns ye shall know them'.

Trying to define culture has defeated far subtler minds than mine. But as I see it, the arts are only part of 'culture', which could be called 'the good between us'. Malcolm Muggeridge (not a hero of mine, but on this he was interesting) once described culture as a national café of the mind, in which we are all the clientele; a meeting place, which can be raucous at times, both political assembly and place of entertainment, dance floor and theatre, with all kinds of rooms off it. (Muggeridge, in cynical mood, went on to say he was sick of it and leaving. Me, I love to hang out there.) When the café's working, we all take part; the rows, the jokes, the outbursts of singing, the meals we eat together, give us our sense of identity. This was the thinking behind Joan Littlewood's great, but now forgotten, idea for a 'fun palace'. But the café is vulnerable, it can be taken over and become a Bierkeller, with louts thumping out one song over and over again, while the rest of us sit silent and miserable in the corners.

There was bound to be grief when Thatcherite free-market principles met the arts and cultural activity. Theatrical producers and movie people talk of 'product', but we all know that actually the arts are simultaneously worthless and priceless. As a *market* the arts are hopeless, because although the stallholders like money as much as anyone else, their instinct is to give their wares away free, and to go on making them against all financial odds, even if people don't want them. Indeed, all true artists, when they find they can do something that people like, discontinue the line at once, and risk something new. This is the economics of the madhouse of the imagination.

The clash was surreal. The Arts Council – a socialist idea, albeit a mild one – was founded to make modest investments of public money in the arts out of a sense of national pride, to encourage the arts to grow and delight wider audiences – that is to liven up the floorshow in the national café. Under the Thatcher government the Arts Council, became, *de facto*, a politically censorious production agency. Getting any support from them became a nightmare. An Orwellian 'artspeak' developed: theatre companies had to deliver 'assessments of achievement of financial performance targets' and attended brain-melting seminars on subjects such as 'the development of a donor constituency'. I remember a heated meeting with an Arts Council officer. We pleaded for support for a fringe company that produced new plays. The official said, with a cautious tone, 'It *is* Council policy that there is room for idiosyncratic self-expression.' We didn't get the money.

It is extraordinary how deeply the Thatcherites' simplistic, Gradgrindish economic rule of thumb cut into our culture and did such damage. It has just about killed off the British cinema industry. It has all but wrecked the British theatre: reps can no longer perform Shakespeare, unless they cut the sub-plots to reduce the cast. If something is not done quickly by the new government, television will be atomised Skyward. Publishing books, that slow and kindly activity, became a murderous occupation in which publishing houses behaved as if they were the House of Borgia. Cuts in music schools, as Sir Yehudi

Menuhin protested three years ago, are threatening the training of classical musicians – we can no longer make motorbikes or helicopters, soon we may not even be able to make music.

The 'Lego-land', 'dinky' architecture of the period, with its uniform formula arches and 'let's pretend we're in a village' roofs, even though we're in the middle of Birmingham, is a visual expression of conformity. This wave of building was meant to be 'post-modernist', but, I suspect, it will quickly become known as the 'Thatcher style' and be found to be as rotten within as the tower blocks of a previous 'new spirit'.

But culture is, as I've argued, partly about the mental architecture of our shared perceptions and attitudes. Something nasty has happened to British apathy. It used to be commonly assumed in Britain that politics have little or no effect on everyday life, let alone personal happiness and the arts. Now good old British apathy, with its loathing of the pretentious, seems in retrospect to have been a positively healthy attitude.

Thatcherism did something very unBritish to Britain: it managed, in a baleful way, to politicise everything. Apathy became militantly philistine: Norman Tebbit's recent attack on Salman Rushdie was a classic expression of it, full of an unreasoned ire at the unquantifiable imagination.

I think it is not too exaggerated to say that when the crash came in 1987, and in 1988 when the beggars appeared on the streets after Lawson's tax-cutting budget, a curious peeling away from reality set in. What people in public life said on television about the country seemed finally to lose any relation at all to what it was like to live in it, or to walk down any street.

Again and again Thatcher and her ministers claimed success, in torrents of figures. *Everything* was better and 'up by 11 per cent'. This unreality reached a surreal apogee in Thatcher's farewell speech in the House of

Commons. She seemed to think her premiership had established a Utopia that we had been living in for the past 11½ years: surprising news. It was a most fantastical speech.

This characteristic unreality of the late Thatcher years has been countered culturally by flourishing and wildly diverse music scenes. It's unexpected that a really effective 'counter culture' in the late Eighties should begin in music, from opera to the new Manchester rock bands.

David Pountney, the ENO director, tells me the resurgence of interest in opera is not, in his view, merely 'a yuppie thing'; it comes from a desire in the audience to escape from materialism, to be hit in the guts. It's as if the ENO's public has turned to this old-fashioned, almost impossible art form, which works by delivering an emotional pounding, as a reaction against the 'banal unreality' of everyday life.

My 16-year-old son has introduced me to the Manchester bands, Stone Roses, Inspiral Carpets, Happy Mondays, and their fellow bands, Ride, from 'the wrong side of Oxford', and the Charlatans from Northwich ('We're really proud of the Charlatans,' said a middle-aged man in the street on a television pop programme. 'We never thought anything could come from Northwich' – a voice from the cultural desert). Rock 'n' roll, despite the filthy music industry's chewing up of young musicians, seems to be able to regenerate itself endlessly. The Manchester sound is strong stuff, from a flourishing club circuit, true 'garage bands' playing homemade, survival-kit music.

There has, of course, been a lot of schlock in the past 10 years, and, for historians, it is the schlock that speaks of a period as much as the true work. In the novel, Victorian pastiche, the literary equivalent of that 'dinky' architecture, has been all the rage. Much of television's film output has become minimal domestic anecdote, often set in the 1950s by the seaside, reflecting Thatcher's infamous dictum 'there is no such thing as society, only individuals and their families'. Right-wing theatre has found its voice not in new work but in a particular style of reviving Shakespeare's plays, draining their social content and sentimentalising their psychology. And there has been a markedly new virulence in newspaper criticism; discourse in the arts has become something of a brawl in the last 10 years. Even the *Independent*, which claims to be as gently balanced as a seesaw in the park, has taken to kneecapping any of the children at play showing leftish tendencies in their games.

But schlock is always with us and newspaper attacks are part of the hurly-burly. What matters is that we, the artists, are still here and the desire for the 'good between us' is still with our audiences. The country needs someone like the French minister of culture, Jack Lang, who sees no difference between a sense of fun and the public good, a rock 'n' roll fan who is not afraid of Samuel Beckett, who knows that a good school gym with decent gym mats is as culturally important as an opera house, and who would close down the Arts Council and build a national café, with a programme for the delight of all. We won't get such a figure with the new Tory government. Nevertheless, we have learnt, keeping our feet in Thatcherism's philistine hurricane, that there is the possibility of a new counter culture. The fun palace may yet be built.

6 December 1990: Steven Berkoff

No one left to blame

Oooh! what a thrill, Thatcher has gone, so whoops, the left-wing intelligentsia squeal as they phone each other gleefully and pop out to the pub and down a pint of the same stale beer they've been drinking for years with the *Guardian* tucked into their pockets. One 'eminent' and 'level-headed' director actually went to Downing Street to see her off! Wow! What revolutionary zealots – or what a lot of toss-pots. Some were dancing in the streets, and the little cabal of card-carrying consciences patted each other on the back in the media celebrating their vital contribution to the arts of the Eighties.

Of course it was always the same few mates that dined at the same café, and why not indeed? Mr Brenton, the distinguished playwright, puts forth his top of the pops and out come the usual pub mates. If it's not the critics chanting the same old names, like a recipe for the same old stew, it's now the writers themselves recommending their own contributions as dramatising 'a black hole of amorality . . . in which traditional liberal values were sucked away'.

That's so poetic and I'm glad to know that these fine playwrights are such guardians of our morality and values and, of course, traditions. They sit like verbal pitbulls defending the world of goodness and decency from the terrible, Oh, God, Mrs Margaret Thatcher. Gosh, all these anxiety-ridden writers struggling to get on despite Arts Council cuts. Oh, my dear, no more bad Shakespeare in rep, no more funding for all those sets and machines so beloved of your anti-Thatcher directors.

In fact those who most condemn Thatcherism are those who most reflect her aims. What would you do without someone to blame for all the ills and woes of life? What targets will you have to pit your angst against now since it was Thatcher who gave you spice and drama, gave you a dragon for every little St George to dip his little pen into and polish his little anti-Thatcher medal worn alongside the 'I am a good liberal' medal?

When you closed your theatres you could blame Thatcher for philistinism rather than your own incompetence, indulgence and perhaps not very interesting fare. No, it's Thatcher who is to blame and now she's gone perhaps a few whacky fringe companies can try and get some more dough to piss away. Even 'I' (if I may be permitted the arrogance afforded to my colleague to mention myself, immodestly of course) grew in the fringe and watched the creations of my colleagues but I must tell you that it got to be pretty soggy and the ones that didn't cut the mustard bit the dust. Some go to the wall but the better ones survive.

Without Thatcher it will be difficult to blame her for every incompetent and boringly predictable piece of art that is churned out. Anyway, who gave you the self-appointed right to be the moral spokesman of the time? You did have every right to make your case and even drain the RSC coffers with your latest opus.

I believe we all have the right to fail and to experiment and you can always go back to *Pravda* for your credits and forget the ones that I paid for with my tax, since I'd rather pay for your experiments than Cruise missiles.

You've survived largely on Thatcher's money and her tolerance even if the money-box was squeezed a bit. Your fine works didn't have to test themselves in the bleak markets of the commercial theatre but were protected and supported by subsidy, and I, too, am protected by this from time to time. But without the *grande dame* you will have little left to write about or blame and must seek new pastures.

I had a publisher – who shall be nameless – who never paid his royalties until I was reduced to begging and this was before Thatcher and now he easily blames Thatcherism for his monetary ills. Good old Maggie, it's all your fault.

I am sorry she has gone since she showed the face of true-blue Conservatism and this worried even her supporters, who knew that in the age of new Europe such tendencies are anachronistic. She could have been defeated by Kinnock by the sheer contrast between the two since his naked humanism reveals all too well her lack of it. Now it looks as if the Tories, having wised up, are presenting a new mask for the old face, so before you go dancing outside Number 10 have a think. Thatcher was your greatest ally. The future is bleak.

6 March 1991: Andrew Rawnsley

John who?

Hello, caller, House of Commons.

Can you put me through to Peter Lilley's statement on Telecommunications: Setting The Agenda For The Nineties?

Sorry, caller, Peter who?

Lilley. You'll find him listed under Trade and Industry Secretary.

Sorry, caller. That department has been out of order for ages.

Yes, but they still produce white papers from time to time.

OK, caller. Trying to connect you to Mr Lilley now.

'Who can defend a situation where it's legal to sell *Sunday Sport* but illegal to sell the Bible on a Sunday?'

Operator? Hello? Operator? I think you've put me through to John Marshall's Ten-Minute Rule Bill on Sunday trading.

Sorry, caller. Trying for Mr Lilley again.

'Certainly my bathroom cabinet has far, far too many unused drugs in it.'

Operator! Hello! Operator! It was the Trade Secretary I wanted, not William Waldegrave and the true confessions of an Old Etonian Health Secretary.

What was the name again, caller?

Lilley, Peter, Communication and Choice: Telecommunications Policy in the 1990s.

Trying for Mr Lilley now, caller.

'These proposals will stimulate competition, extend choice, cut prices, help to bring down inflation, and give us the most dynamic telecommunications market in the world.'

'Is it not the case that while bills should be falling when British Telecom is making £3 billion a year, bills will still be rising this year and installation and rental charges will be rising even faster than inflation?'

Operator? I think Mr Lilley's got a crossed line with Labour's Gordon Brown.

'The effect of your new formula is that in return for a possible 80p reduction in the international call charge for the typical household, there is still the prospect of an £8 rise in the typical domestic phone bill.

'The long-term prospect . . . **crackle** . . . is remorseless increases . . . **pop** . . . for almost every household!'

'I expect to see 6½ per cent less than inflation . . . **whirr** . . . meaning negative increases . . . **click** . . . in bills in cash terms. The Honourable Gentleman is talking absolute nonsense . . . '

Operator? The Trade Secretary appears to be breaking up. Can you transfer me to John Major?

Sorry, caller. John who?

Major. You should find him under Prime Minister.

Sorry, caller. Only got a listing for Thatcher here.

She was disconnected some time ago.

So she was, caller. Trying for Mr Major now.

'This decision will increase congestion . . . huh-huh . . . increase environmental problems . . . huh-huh . . . damaging . . . huh-huh . . . destroy . . . huh-huh . . . '

Operator! That's John Prescott on the line doing another of his heavy-breathers at Malcolm Rifkind. I wanted John Major.

Sorry, caller. Trying for the Prime Minister again.

'My Right Honourable Friend is in Moscow. I have been asked to reply.'

Sorry, caller. I'm just getting an answering machine on that number.

Yes, that'll be John MacGregor.

Sorry, caller. John who?

The only member of the Cabinet even duller than John Major.

Shall I try him for you anyway, caller?

Might as well, operator. Let's see what he has to say about the future of the poll tax.

Sorry, caller. No reply.

INTRODUCING A TWO PAGE GRAPHIC NOVEL OF OUR TIMES....
SON OF KONG
HOLY MICROWAVED SHITBURGER IN A BOX!! QUEEN KONG'S DEATH THROES LOOK SET TO COLLAPSE THAT PUBLIC SECTOR HOUSING DEVELOPMENT ONTO THAT STRUCTURALLY UNSOUND NEARBY SCHOOL!!
...WHICH IN TURN IS ABOUT TO TOPPLE INTO THE PATH OF THAT ONCOMING TRAIN, SPELLING IN CRUSHING DISASTER FOR THE HUD CARDBOARD CITY DWELLERS BEN RAILWAY ARCHES!!!
TELEPHONE
©Steve Bell 1990-
UNNOTICED BY THE CROWD, A MILD-MANNERED BANK CLERK FROM KENT UNDERGOES A SURPRISING TRANSFORMATION:
TELEPHONE
AT THE THIRD STROKE IT WILL BE ELEVEN FIFTY FIVE PRECISELY.... BEEP-BEEP-BEEP
OH YES!
QUICK! SOMEBODY CALL THE EMERGENCY SERVICES!!
THE TEMPERATURE IN THE CAPITAL IS ONE DEGREE CELSIUS, THAT'S THIRTY FOUR DEGREES FAHRENHEIT....
OH YES! OH YES!
EXCUSE ME!! THERE'S AN EMERGENCY!
I WANT YOU ALL TO LOOK AT THE FIGURES!!
EXCUSE ME - ARE YOU SOME SORT OF PERV... AWWWWWWK!!!
WHO IS THAT MAN WITH HIS UNDERPANTS OUTSIDE HIS TROUSERS?
OH YES OH YES.... ...LOOK AT THE FIGURES!
IS IT A BIRD?
IS IT A PLANE?
I BELIEVE IN REAL SOCIAL MOBILITY.... OH YES!
...TEN MORE DAYS AT THESE TEMPERATURES AND WE WILL DELIVER! OH YES WE WILL!
IS IT ANIMAL, VEGETABLE OR MINERAL?
HE'S HURLED HIMSELF INTO THAT HEDGE!!
GOOD GOD! IT MUST BE...
IK! IK!
LURCH
SMASH
SNIP SNIP
CLUTCH
I BELIEVE IN A CLASSLESS SOCIETY....... SOD THE WORKERS!!
IF IT DOESN'T HURT IT'S NOT WORKING.......IF YOU'RE NOT WORKING YOU OUGHT TO BE HURTING!!
NO QUICK FIX.................. COME TO THAT, NO SLOW FIX EITH
....IT'S HEDGERMAN!!!
HOSPITAL

GERMAN - CAN YOU
E US FROM IMPENDING DISASTER ??
OH YES - JUST LOOK AT MY RECORD - LOOK AT THE FIGURES!...
...LISTEN TO THE FACTS: ONE: YOU REM- -MEMBER THE COLD WEATHER PAYMENTS FIASCO? THAT WAS ONE OF MINE!! TWO: THE INFLATION HIKE? THAT'S ANOTHER ONE OF MINE!!! THREE: E.R.M. ENTRY AT A RUINOUSLY HIGH POUND LEVEL?? YEP! - YOU'VE GUESSED IT!!!
ONE OF YOURS?
EXCLUSIVELY!
FIVE: POLLTAX: I'VE BACKED THAT ONE ALL ALONG!!
BUT THAT'S JUST A CATALOGUE OF COCK-UPS!! HOW DO YOU GET AWAY WITH IT ??
BECAUSE, MY FRIEND, THERE'S LESS TO ME THAN MEETS THE EYE!!
DO YOU
AN??
WHEN THERE'S LESS TO YOU THAN MEETS THE EYE, IT'S HARDER FOR THE SHIT TO STICK!
I STILL DON'T UNDERSTAND, HEDGERMAN - WHAT'S YOUR SECRET??
WITH MY NEATLY CLIPPED LOOKS...
..I LOOK NORMAL, AND WITH MY NEATLY CLIPPED SENTENCES...
...I SOUND NORMAL; AND I SHOULD ADD THAT I ALSO SMELL, TASTE AND FEEL NORMAL!!
YES, BUT WHAT MARKS YOU OUT??
SNIFF
SECRET IS THAT, WHILE
ARING NORMAL IN ALL
PECTS, I AM IN FACT...
...DENSER THAN A SPEEDING TRAIN....
BEEBARP
...MORE BORING THAN A BAG OF SAND...
...STUPIDER THAN A WAGON LOAD OF HEADLESS CHICKENS
DEEP FROZEN
Chunky Chooks
FACT YOU COULD SAY
UTTERLY INVINCIBLE...
CEPT FOR ONE SMALL
THING.....
...CHAIN A LUMP OF BRYXTONITE ROUND MY NECK AND MY SPECIAL POWERS EVAPORATE!!!
© Steve Bell 1990

A funny kind of war

27 February 1991: Matthew Engel

No chance

As ever, the last people to know what is happening in this war are the poor guys meant to be fighting it.

The *Guardian* knew that Saddam Hussein had told his troops to withdraw; no one else had mentioned it to the unit of US Marines we were with in the desert. So we played them the next hourly news on the good old BBC World Service. They listened through a report of the most graceless speech in defeat since Hirohito announced that the war had concluded 'not necessarily to Japan's advantage'. For a while they just grunted. Then they were livid.

'We come all this way to all this sand, getting pissed on with rain and eating this stuff, and we don't get in there,' said one. A few used traditional Marine expressions for situations they dislike. One just whittled away at a stick in frustration.

This unit was part of one of the Marines' proudest

battalions but had been kept back to be the next wave. They were moving forward again last night, withdrawal or no withdrawal.

But right now they were in the middle of nowhere: the only cover was in the foxholes where they had been drenched during the night in a desert storm not controlled by the Pentagon. There was not a bird, not a tree, and what mattered to the Marines, not an Iraqi.

A few miles away the sky was covered in black smoke from one of Kuwait's burning oil wells. Here the Marines stood and watched helicopters come and go, kicking up showers of sand: and they craned their necks to watch planes flash by, trying to identify them but knowing the important detail was not in dispute: they were allied.

Then there was an alert: an unidentified column was heading in our direction. A detachment was sent out. The other platoons huddled, not quite at arms, not quite relaxed.

Then we heard: 13 Iraqi prisoners were being brought this way and many more behind them were trying to surrender but were uncertain of the safe route across their own minefields. Other units' prisoners! It seemed to make matters worse.

The men began to heap their contempt on Saddam Hussein: 'His mines don't work, his missiles don't work. Just his luck if he threw gas, the wind would change and it'd blow back right into Baghdad.'

Another made the most devastating admission any fighting man could make: 'You've got to hand it to the generals. They've planned it right this time. We've done in four days what Iran couldn't do in eight years.'

Another said it was inevitable: 'You couldn't survive weeks of B-52 bombing. I don't care if you are in tanks. It's still gonna rattle your brains out and you're gonna have blood from your nose and your ears and everywhere because you'll be hit by the equipment.' He paused: 'But, hell, it's a shame if we miss it.'

This view was not quite universal in the Marine Corps.

Earlier, we had stumbled on a supply depot where a kindly staff sergeant and corporal had refuelled us with coffee and cake. They were proud Marines and they were happy to leave the routine killing to others. 'There's a lot of guys getting a lot of experience out of this,' said the corporal. 'But then I reckon many of them are going to turn round and they won't ever want to have nuttin' to do with war again.'

Up at the unit that was not even the view of the men with stripes.

'We thought we'd win easily,' said Sergeant Gary Elleman. 'This is incredible. They've just given up. It's kinda frustrating. You're all pumped up and it's all over.' Didn't it beat losing, though? 'Oh, yes,' he said, 'It beats the hell out of losing. Sure beats the hell out of losing.'

His commanding officer, Lieutenant-Colonel Reno Bamford, was a little more measured but the sentiments were the same.

'I don't think anyone likes bullets whistling over their heads but when you've been out here this long you don't like to think you're not going to get a chance to get at them.'

Dusk approached. The men got ready to move. A patch of the desert sky cleared and there was a sunburst of the kind they have in picture bibles above the rainbow signifying the end of the Flood. It portended a better tomorrow: of freedom for the Kuwaitis and, for the Marines, maybe one last chance to kick ass.

28 February 1991: David Beresford

No resistance

'It's a funny kind of war,' said Sergeant James Horton from

Montana. And that is perhaps the best epitaph for it, although there was not much fun.

When the Iraqi prisoners tried to surrender to us and we had to tell them to go away, because we were too busy, it was kind of sad. When they surrendered to the infantrymen in that highway graveyard of burning tanks, pulverised trucks and flattened cars it was just frightening. And there was nothing funny when a Texan medical officer, Charles Russell, shook his head, stopped the heart massage and finally gave up his three-hour battle for the life of the emaciated Iraqi PoW.

But at least it started with a bit of fun: somewhere a tape recorder was playing the Egyptian national anthem and a group of soldiers stood cheering on top of the 20-foot berm marking the Saudi Arabian front when we burst through with the tanks and armoured personnel carriers. On the other side the heavy armour streamed across the desert, the command pennants fluttering from their radio masts in evocation of knights galloping across some ancient battlefield.

Tanks, mobile bridges, tracked recovery vehicles, camouflaged ambulances and even a municipal-style omnibus – to carry the expected prisoners – raced on for nearly 12 miles before the first battle began. From behind, heavy Egyptian artillery guns were thudding their shells high over our heads. In front a few puffs marked Iraqi shells falling short. Batteries of multiple rocket launchers mounted on trucks moved into position and a fearsome four-hour bombardment ensued in a light rain.

'Ten kilometres to Iraqi troops, but no resistance,' called out a captain. It was a phrase that was to characterise the entire ground war for Kuwait: 'no resistance'. The Egyptian 3rd Armoured Division drove on northwards and then turned east, angling towards the Kuwaiti capital. The route provided a study in military wretchedness far removed from the propaganda which allied commanders had been pumping out in the build-up to the war.

The huge Iraqi oil moats, endless minefields, giant sand berms and subterranean trench complexes turned out to be non-existent. As one US Special Forces officer put it: 'The only defensive belt I saw was three strands of concertina wire, two minefields and a trench [of oil] I jumped across.'

The trenches were all hand-dug, frequently pitiful emplacements. Another US Special Forces officer said he had seen the radio antenna of an infantry commander 'which could not have reached [transmitted to] the next trench, much less to his commanders'.

Conditions in the trenches were miserable. They stank of faeces; scattered belongings showed the panic in which they had been abandoned. The inscriptions on ammunition boxes reflected the variety of Iraqi arms suppliers – from Jordan to America, Russia to Saudi Arabia.

The panic was understandable considering the one-sidedness of the fighting. An American tank commander said his men were beginning to feel immortal in their state-of-the-art Abraham tanks. He described one incident when a mine ripped one of his tank's tracks, forcing it to a standstill. An Iraqi tank had fired four main rounds at the sitting target, scoring direct hits with them all. His crew had simply climbed out and walked away unhurt.

This week his men had destroyed 14 tanks in a single action, at ranges of between 1,500 and 3,000 yards. 'They never saw us. All the hits were total kills. They just burned and blew up. To the best of my knowledge not a single shot was fired at us.'

The horrors of life for the conscript Iraqi soldiers over the last few months showed in the faces of hundreds of prisoners sitting in abject groups on the side of the convoy routes, waiting for transportation south. Two prisoners, aged 45 and 50, looked more like men of 70. Both had fought in the Iran-Iraq war. At one stage, when the Egyptian column halted, a group of 11 Iraqis materialised out of the desert driving equally emaciated camels before them.

Again their belongings on the backs of the animals were pitiful, but they did include comprehensive protective clothing against chemical warfare.

The column halted in mid-afternoon some 40 miles west of Kuwait City. Travelling south with three American correspondents we picked up an Egyptian commando unit, including a Saudi Arabian aristocrat, Prince Fahd – serving on attachment as a captain – and were invited to follow them to Kuwait City. Their jeeps careered eastward towards the Gulf across a desert that became increasingly eerie in a fake twilight created by a smog of mist and smoke from burning oil wells.

In the sepulchral light the desert looked surrealistic, littered with the silver canisters of cluster bombs, the green casings of high explosives and here and there in the distance the skewed and broken barrels of Iraqi artillery and tanks.

The commandos joined the front of the Egyptian 4th Division as night fell. The commanders apparently considered driving on to Kuwait City, but decided to halt some 40 miles from the capital on the grounds that the US Marines had dug in on the outskirts of the city and the threat of 'friendly fire' made it too risky to advance through them in the dark. We drove another six miles to the south to a main road running from the south-east into the capital.

The road turned out to be a super-highway and the drive along it belonged to the imagination of Francis Ford Coppola, a blasted landscape limited to the headlamps' angle of light. Every few yards on both sides the grotesquely twisted wreckages of saloon cars, tankers, trucks and armour loomed out of the dark. Two blasted tanks were still burning.

On the other carriageway, figures of Iraqi soldiers could be seen ghosting by. One suddenly ran across the centre island and waved us down, begging by sign language to be allowed to surrender, waving at seven others drifting across behind. We shouted to them to lie down and wait for dawn. The lead soldier suddenly broke into 'thank you, thank you', close to happy tears at having a decision taken from him.

A few miles on we stopped. Out of the dark came the ugly rumble of an armoured vehicle. We dived for the verge away from the car. We could faintly see troops fanning out, and desperately strained to pick up the language of their faint shouts, eventually hearing with relief the cursing of GIs under hair-trigger strain. 'Americans, British,' we screamed.

They were the 'tiger brigade' of the 2nd Armoured Division, General Patton's famous corps. They congratulated us on our survival – explaining we were within a few hundred yards of entering a Marine 'killing sac'.

Waiting for permission to make another try for Kuwait City we met two doctors working with the division. There were three patients in their ambulance – critically injured Iraqi prisoners, including one whose brain had been penetrated by a shrapnel splinter. As we stood in the ambulance the heavily sedated prisoner suddenly rose up on his cot and groaned, in a seizure. Charles Russell, the Texan, began pumping the man's chest in a heart massage. 'Come on,' he urged in a hoarse whisper.

'Heartbeat is almost non-existent,' replied his colleague, Dr Kazamore Yamomoto, and then folded his stethoscope and walked out abruptly in final judgement. An orderly, Raymon Gonzo, moved to the dead man's side, put his head on the cot and began to pray.

In the city some government buildings used by the Iraqi forces were still burning from allied 'smart bomb' attacks, and flames and huge clouds of smoke from blazing oil wells in the region formed a dramatic backdrop to liberation festivities.

Men, women and children clambered on burnt-out Iraqi tanks and crowded the verges of highways to hail the incoming Arab convoys.

But the triumph clearly belonged to the discreet US forces. Huge graffiti slogans praising President Bush were appearing on walls and flyovers. Traffic jams formed outside the US embassy as motorists, hooting and firing AK-47 assault rifles out of their windows, circled past continuously.

'When I joined the army in 1975 the US soldier was scum,' said an enthusiastic GI, Sgt Paul Thomas. 'When we come home we are going to be stinking heroes.'

Most of the atrocity reports were secondhand and there must be a question they were exaggerated or sprang from war hysteria. But ugly traces of the Iraqi occupation were to be seen including crude pillboxes on main roads which controlled movement. Telecommunications had been completely disrupted, and there was no electricity and limited water supplies.

There was some apprehension among the small, domestic Iraqi population and the larger Palestinian community – numbering more than 300,000 – about possible Kuwaiti reprisals. While the celebrations went on, troops on the perimeter were tense, thanks largely to the gunfire coming from the crowds. At one stage a US Marine unit opened fire over our car as a result of a mix-up over whether incoming traffic was allowed. Journalists and television crews began arriving in the city overnight but many were held up by jumpy troops who feared that street to street fighting was taking place.

1 March 1991: David Fairhall in Kuwait City

Eclipse

Not even a smoke-blackened rainstorm, so dark it seemed night had fallen by two in the afternoon, could dampen the carnival atmosphere here yesterday as car loads of jubilant youngsters toured the streets in search of western television crews for whom they could parade their national flag – with a few stars and stripes, Union Jacks and *tricolores* gratefully included in celebration of the ceasefire.

But apart from such superficial exuberance the city centre was empty. There is no electricity, destruction of the desalination plant has cut freshwater supplies and shops are smashed and looted.

After seven months of increasingly brutal occupation, the Kuwaitis who stayed behind are trying to piece their personal lives together again – and apparently settling scores with some of the Palestinians accused of sympathising with the Iraqis. Only afterwards will they begin to contemplate the long process of reconstruction.

One exception was the manager of the five-star SAS Hotel, burnt out by the departing Iraqi troops, who was hoping to set up a generator in a small hotel to cater for the expected influx of foreign journalists and businessmen.

As we drove up the coast road from Khafji it was not so much the mangled trucks and burnt-out tanks that were disturbing. These were the predictable detritus of allied bombing and one of the war's first armoured battles. But writing about the hundreds of oilfield fires had not prepared me for a smoke cloud which quite suddenly transformed a bright desert morning into the equivalent of a gloomy November evening back home.

It was as if the sun had been eclipsed, and in the gloom it became appreciably colder. The army convoys rumbling north beside us needed headlights to pick out the occasional bomb crater. Now I know what a nuclear winter would be like. Kuwait may be a small country, but not that small. The smoke cloud covers thousands of square miles.

It is difficult to have any conversation here at present without hearing of atrocities allegedly committed by the

Iraqis – but inevitably difficult to check. From those I met on the streets yesterday I heard stories of chopped fingers littering the floor, pregnant women raped, girls abducted and 2,000 men aged 13–45 rounded up for deportation to Iraq.

And these were only the most vicious incidents in an occupation regime where theft, extortion and forms of bullying are said to have been routine. Some spoke of the Iraqis with outright hatred. Others excused minor persecutions on the grounds that the soldiers were only obeying orders, on pain of their own execution.

Without visiting every part of the city it was also difficult to assess structural damage done in the Iraqis' final spasm of fear, spite and revenge. They evidently had orders to destroy several symbols of Kuwait's wealth and nationhood, like the big hotels that were burnt and the Danish-designed parliament building whose frontage is pockmarked by gunfire. Outside the entrance stands an abandoned T-62 tank, and across the road are empty trenches and a makeshift pillbox facing seaward to meet the amphibious landing that never came.

But, with Kuwait's vast financial resources, buildings can easily be repaired. It is the infrastructure of petroleum production and public services that will take time to restore – years, not months.

In the long run, it is the personal experiences of wanton damage I heard about that will surely breed more bitterness. Stories of Iraqi troops lodging in a house, setting up a gun position on the roof, even accepting some calculated hospitality, then smashing the place up before they left – though again I cannot tell how widespread this sort of behaviour was.

For the moment though, all is celebration. 'I have seen seven years of work destroyed,' an Indian advertising agent told me. 'But I'm happy. Today we are like birds released from a cage.'

1 March 1991: Martin Woollacott

No contest

Baghdad Radio, whose record of mendacity would have made Goebbels blush, had the gall yesterday to describe the last pathetic engagements of the war as a hard-fought battle which had 'taught the allies some lessons'. The 'battle didn't teach us any lessons, but the propaganda should, for it seems that myths about the conflict are already taking shape on our side that could be as misleading as the nonsense the Iraqis put out.

Foremost among these are the notions that the war required generalship of a high order, and that it demonstrated the superior fighting qualities of Western over Iraqi troops. It is no reflection on Norman Schwarzkopf's qualities as a soldier to say that he did not truly function as a general in this conflict, partly because of the other side's stupidity and partly because of our side's overwhelming technical advantages.

Generalship involves action and reaction: the enemy commander does a, you do b; he does x, you do y. Out of the cumulation of these decisions, a general takes his armies to victory or defeat. But in the Gulf the Iraqi forces were so damaged and demoralised that they neither acted nor reacted. They were, to all intents and purposes, not under command at all. General Schwarzkopf never had to react to a sudden movement of enemy troops, to unexpected resistance, to any impediment other than that offered by the weather or by mechanical breakdown.

General Schwarzkopf may be a good general, but that is not what he has proved himself to be in this conflict. Instead, he has shown himself an able military manager. The essence of the war was that a military machine that had been built to confront the Soviet Union in Central Europe was relocated in Saudi Arabia to deal with an enemy that had not a twentieth of Soviet capacity or offensive power. That machine had to be set up in a very different environment, and oiled and serviced on a grand scale, and this was done with great efficiency. But once set in motion, it simply chewed its way through the Iraqi forces like a ripsaw through logs, requiring only occasional adjustments of tempo and speed.

This is not to say that at certain moments the soldiers, sailors and airmen of the coalition did not have to act with courage. At the beginning of the air war there was real danger, but later the bombing became a production process, in which the very occasional Western casualty was more akin to an industrial accident than anything else. Again, at the beginning of the ground war, who could have known, as our men moved off from their start lines, that it would be as easy as it turned out to be? The fact that courage turned out to be not much required does not mean that it did not have to be summoned. But how can these few moments when our own men were at real risk compare with the horrors Iraqi forces faced? Day after day, night after night, the most sustained and effective aerial bombardment in history killed, maimed and destroyed, with hardly a chance of retaliation.

The Iraqi forces were stripped of everything that makes an army work. At the end, they could no longer see, they could no longer hear, they could no longer communicate with one another. The Iraqi army resembled nothing so much in its last days as a worm when it is chopped by a spade – the segments wriggle, but the creature is already dead.

Of course it is the business of a general to seek advantage. To imagine that war is about fair fights is to misunderstand its nature. It is, in fact, about unfair fights: a general who is in a fair fight – an equally matched encounter – is usually a general who has mismanaged his job. But there comes a point where the advantage achieved is so overwhelming as to change the quality of the event from something like combat to something like execution.

There is surely a horrifying aspect to the utter disparity in the figures of those killed – 150 on our side; 20,000, 30,000, 40,000 estimated on theirs. We can hardly crow about Iraqi surrenders and retreats. These men did not surrender at the first sight of British or American tanks, but after weeks of bitter experience of the utter superiority of allied weapons.

We should remember, too, that the entry of the allied ground troops into Kuwait and Iraq did not give the Iraqis a chance to fight on more equal terms, as President Saddam Hussein had foolishly imagined. If anything, the terms were even more unequal, with our troops' superior firepower, control of the air and unimpeded communications.

Let us admit that there were times when even the experts did not think the war would go as easily as this. Notably, the effectiveness of air power alone in dealing with an inferior opponent was a matter of argument. But the accuracy brought to bombing by electronic guidance systems has changed the calculations that used to suggest that air power alone could never defeat the enemy.

And let us give General Schwarzkopf and the allied armies their due. The general adapted a technology which was untried in war – the air-defence machine built for Nato – to the business at hand, and he and his staffs did it well. He measured the extraordinary damage it did, and came to appropriate conclusions. He judged well the moment when the demoralisation of the Iraqi forces had been completed by President Saddam's offers to withdraw, and put in his troops at that moment. And the troops did the job they were sent to do.

The thing had to be done, even though we may argue about whether this final act was really necessary. But to start trailing clouds of glory is really too much. About this conflict one might well say, adapting the words applied to the Charge of the Light Brigade, '*C'est la guerre, mais ce n'est pas magnifique*.'

25 March 1991: Martin Woollacott in Iraqi Kurdistan

The Kurdish rising

Hajer gestured at the abandoned Iraqi forts and camps that top the hills along the border with Syria and Turkey, then raised his palm to his lips and blew as if wafting away thistledown. It was the big, glossy-bearded guerrilla's way of explaining how a well-equipped Iraqi army was swept out of much of Kurdistan in a few days, and with hardly any serious fighting.

Further south and west, the battles for Kirkuk – and now for Mosul – have been heavier. But the campaigns for the east and north, which preceded these assaults, were based on a long clandestine effort to subvert and 'turn' government forces, and on the seizing of the right psychological moment.

Kamal Kirkuki, the Kurdish Democratic Party commander in north-central Kurdistan, is a quiet-voiced man whose gentleness of manner belies his record as a brave guerrilla fighter. But Mr Kirkuki, wounded twice and a survivor of many engagements, did not have to spill much blood to win a broad swathe of northern Iraq for the revolution.

Earlier, immediately after the end of the war for Kuwait, a similar series of uprisings directed by Massoud Barzani, leader of the KDP and overall military commander, had freed most of the eastern part of Iraqi Kurdistan.

The precursor to the Kirkuk and Mosul battles was an extraordinary campaign in which town after town fell like skittles. It was a turncoat war in which mass defections by Kurdish auxiliary troops cut off and isolated Iraqi regular units in all but major centres. In some cases there was a triple play in which the auxiliaries, 'turned' by the KDP, then turned the regulars as well.

In the headmaster's room of a secondary school in the centre of Zakho, a market town near the border with Turkey, Mr Kirkuki – 'Dr Kamal' in deference to his, uncompleted, medical studies – tells of a war fought to a timetable as precise as the headmaster's roster for classes on his desk. Aged 37, with the face of a weary boy crowned by grey-streaked hair, he speaks in clichés, or in numbers. 'The people, as well as the *peshmerga* [guerrillas], rose at the same time against the government,' he says.

At five o'clock in the morning of 14 March, in 12 towns in a wide, 100-mile arc, the insurgents struck. By that evening all the towns were taken and most of the outlying military positions in the districts around them. In the next couple of days, other Iraqi military positions went as well until, as of yesterday, only two remained untaken in the region.

The key to it all were the *jash* – 'donkeys' – the Kurdish mercenaries on whom the Iraqis depended. The clandestine effort to turn them began as early as last July. On the morning of the 14th Iraqi troops woke to ultimatums from *jash* units alongside them. Some surrendered immediately. Some fought, but not long, well or very effectively.

At the same time, the guerrillas attacked, and the people of the towns poured on to the streets to demonstrate. The guerrillas, however, were vastly outnumbered by the *jash* whose decision to change sides was the critical factor.

At Zakho intermediate school, as dusk closes in, hundreds of armed *jash* and guerrillas mingle together happily. Pistols, grenades, knives and AK-47s hang from the men's shoulders, battle harnesses and belts. On their heads, patterned scarves are wound around embroidered skull-caps. Tall, invariably moustached or bearded, wearing baggy trousers in army shades and complex braided cummerbunds with military belts strapped on top, they talk, smoke and greet one another with kisses and handshakes.

Dfewar Faisal, aged 23, commanded a *jash* unit of 500 men. He joined in 1987 'because it was a living and because we were forced to'. 'When they invaded Kuwait,' he says, 'I knew what I should do . . . That was when the majority of us changed our minds.' Contacts between the KDP and the *jash* began to intensify and, towards the end, Mr Faisal was meeting or exchanging messages with the KDP once a week. 'If the Iraqis had found out I would have been executed,' he says with a glance at Mr Kirkuki, as if to register his credentials.

So, on the 14th, Mr Faisal, the youngest battalion commander in the *jash*, sent an ultimatum to the 300 men of the Republican Guard to whose unit his battalion was attached near Dohuk. They surrendered.

As with many other Iraqi units, they were set free and pointed toward government lines, after giving up weapons, including rifles and side arms.

It was the same story all over. In the whole area, Kurdish casualties, apart from those at Kirkuk and Mosul, may have been no more than a few hundred. The turncoat war worked like a dream, but Kurds know that harder fighting may lie ahead.

3 April 1991: Martin Woollacott's report which first alerted the world to the agonies of the Kurdish refugees

The valleys of death

A monstrous crime is being perpetrated in Kurdistan. As the Kurdish people's brief springtime of freedom ends, they are, and will be, subject not only to the effects of a war waged in their own cities and towns without restraint or morality, but to the reimposition of Saddam Hussein's brutal rule and his revenge on those who have challenged him.

'Let nobody say the Kurdish people is dead,' was spray-painted in English on the end of an oil tanker, its flanks crammed with people, ahead of us in Sunday's chaotic refugee queue out of Salahuddin, the Kurdish headquarters. But the fear must be that Iraqi Kurds are about to suffer blows which could indeed be mortal. Certainly it will be the worst reprisal in 100 years of struggle.

Yesterday Turkey's National Security Council said that more than 200,000 people fleeing Iraq, mostly women and children, were in danger of death near the Turkish border.

'Where is Bush?' was a question we must have heard a thousand times as we toiled on Monday up the slopes of the 8,000ft mountain passes that separate Iraq from Turkey. 'Why did he start if he was not going to finish?' or 'Why has he not finished Saddam?'

Sometimes all the bitterness and despair are compressed into the single word Bush, pronounced with a terrible resignation. The name of a man who was a hero to the Kurds only a few days ago has become almost a curse.

Up the rock-strewn hills, through gorges bristling with dwarf oaks, and over rushing grey streams, a miserable procession of people claws and staggers its way out of Iraqi Kurdistan. There is no road, only a horse track that winds endlessly upward, normally used only by smugglers. Babies cry; old people stand panting by the side of the pass, one pointing wordlessly at his two bottles of pills. The walk, a stiff five-hour hike for fit adults, can be literally killing for the elderly and the sick. Two people died on the path the day before our crossing, the Turks on the other side told us.

But it is one of the few places where people can still escape from the tightening vice of the government forces. Some other crossing points are under artillery fire; Iran is letting in only women and children; sheer chaos on the roads prevents access to other routes. And it will not be too long, the Turks reckon, before Iraqi helicopters poke their guns and rockets into these gorges and valleys.

Turkish villagers whip surefootedly up and down the steep inclines with their wiry horses and donkeys. For a fee they will carry some of the goods which these pathetic people have brought with them.

This is the middle class of stricken towns like Kirkuk and Tuz Kurmatu, joined by families from Irbil as that city came under bombardment. They are the people who have the vehicles and can afford the black-market prices for petrol. 'I've left 100,000 dinars behind, three houses and two cars,' is a typical cry. They are ill-equipped for the trip. High-heeled shoes buckle, badly secured possessions are swept away in the first stream, one woman in a leopard-skin dress walks along with a box containing shampoo, conditioner and hair tint.

A businessman in a grey pinstriped suit and a fur hat, trouser legs caked with mud, says tearfully: 'They killed all the Turkish people in Tuz Kurmatu . . . when they came they started to kill all the Kurdish and Turkish people. Just shoot, shoot, shoot by the government. The United States caused all this, why, why, why?'

He is a Turcoman like many on this crossing, confident that because of their Turkish origins the authorities on the other side will extend some kind of welcome. His family trudges along the path as he speaks, two small children in red and white rompers wailing. His wife gestures angrily with a briefcase: 'Bush is Saddam's friend. Why did he stop?'

These are just a fraction of the hundreds of thousands of people on the move in Iraqi Kurdistan. Many have made it over the borders into Turkey, Iran, and Syria. But many more, reeling from threatened town to threatened town, will not get out.

The Iraqis, at the speed they are advancing, will soon control all the crossings and no one has any doubt that if necessary they will bomb the refugee columns to stop the exodus. They already have bombed refugees on the road from Irbil to Salahuddin. As we left the town the dull thud of helicopter bombing on the other side sent shivers of panic through the refugee traffic snarled on the western side – the way out to Iran and Turkey.

A Kurdish officer, his hands covered in the blood of his children, hit earlier in the day, was frantically trying to open up the blocked road so that they could get to hospital in the next town. An hour afterwards, we were told by refugees who caught up with us later, the helicopters came over to the eastern side of the hill and bombed and rocketed the cars, and Salahuddin itself was shelled. Although there were a few military vehicles in the traffic – we saw one jeep piled with military maps and others with staff files – the column could not conceivably be described as a military target. The fate of those who escape the helicopters, with few possessions and facing months, perhaps longer, in refugee camps, is hard enough, but it is the fate of those who stay which is most tragic to contemplate.

There is no doubt that after he has re-established control, President Saddam will take a terrible revenge on those who rose against him and effaced his image from every corner of their land. This is the man who gassed a whole town and who took hostage thousands of Kurds who disappeared, almost certainly dead, in 1983.

You have only to visit one of the torture palaces which exist in every city and town in Kurdistan to realise how brutal his rule has been. And not just brutal; the tactics of his intelligence services go beyond brutality to the most ingenious refinements of cruelty. There is the raping room, for instance – a sort of hut off the main interrogation room, with a bloodied mattress inside and a pile of discarded women's clothes outside. And there are persistent tales of naked men being thrown to dogs trained to bite their private parts. In other countries you might discount such tales: in Iraq, the chances are that they are true.

The Kurdish response to the revolution was so wholehearted and so widespread that it could be said that virtually everybody has committed offences that would have warranted imprisonment, torture, and execution in the old Iraq. When the security services get back into their burned and blasted headquarters, the list-making will begin and the arrests will soon follow. Their revenge will be the more ferocious because of the evidence that in some towns Iraqi security men were done to death after the fighting was over. In the Sulaymaniyah security centre, the severed forearm of one was still stuck on a hook on the wall.

There were not many such deaths, because on the whole the Kurdish revolution tried to be magnanimous even towards its worst enemies. One middle-class Kurd, who tried to stop the killing of a security man, was shouted at by a woman: 'Have you had a sister who was raped and tortured? If you have, then you can speak. If you haven't, you have nothing to say.'

Another man pushed him away from the scene, telling the story of losing three sons, of whose fate at the hands of the security services he learned only when curt demands for 70 dinars 'burial charges' came through the post. Everybody involved in the revolution, even in a minor way, is potentially on the death list.

In Sulaymaniyah, at a dinner party given by middle-class supporters of the revolution for visiting journalists, the best Kurdish dishes were on the table and the last beer in the town was brought out. Local intellectuals spoke grandly of the problems facing a new reformed Iraqi administration: how to revive agriculture, changes in education, how to instil democratic habits in a people long unused to them.

The news that Kirkuk was in trouble cast a sudden chill on the gathering. The dream castles were already crumbling and the sound of the ambulances and refugee-filled trucks roaring into the town from Kirkuk silenced the happy talk. Everybody in that room – the academics and doctors on the 'Western press reception committee', the young women in their beautiful Kurdish finery, the hostess whose 'pilaff behind a curtain' is famous among the town's gourmets – is marked for death. Even the children.

Later, at the mass grave of the victims of the Halabja gassing, another middle-class man said: 'There are many mass graves in Iraq. If Saddam wins there will be more, and I will probably be in one of them.'

Kurdistan's brief freedom began three weeks ago when a tentative push at the structure of oppression in a town called Rania was so brilliantly successful that it led to a chain reaction throughout Kurdistan. There was an extraordinary euphoria, a feeling that after many betrayals and disasters the Kurdish people's moment had finally come.

It all turned to dust in two days, from the fall of Kirkuk last Thursday to the collapse of Kurdish defences in the last few days. The problem was that the Kurds had won in the north by guile, not by main force. They had persuaded the government mercenaries to change sides, and organised the surrender of President Saddam's unsteady units in many places. The people had done the rest and only in a few towns did the guerrillas have to fight hard battles.

President Saddam proved to have more resources of men and equipment than was believed, and more political control at the centre than had been expected. Only 10 days ago Massoud Barzani, the leader of the Kurdish Democratic Party, was talking confidently of establishing a temporary government for all Iraq in free Kurdistan. The Kurdish military leaders were over-confident, inexperienced in conventional war, and disorganised. They believed too readily that a collapse in Baghdad would come soon and that, if things did by some mischance go wrong, the United States would rescue the situation.

These were their faults. But what of ours? The US, which to the Kurds is shorthand for all of the West, failed to make the intervention that the Kurds are convinced might have tipped the balance their way. Its reconnaissance planes circled lazily over Kurdish towns as Iraqi helicopters bombed the civil population with terrible results. If just one or two of those helicopters had been shot down, like the fixed-wing aircraft that were downed earlier by US planes, it just might have made the difference. It would have had a tremendous effect on Kurdish morale, and it might have convinced President Saddam that further military moves in the north would attract serious American military intervention.

Why didn't the US and the allies do it? God knows, we bent international law and the UN Charter whenever we wanted to in the effort to free Kuwait. We spent millions and killed many thousands to punish President Saddam's aggression and, bluntly, to bring him down. Why then this sudden excess of legalism, this prating about internal affairs, these oh-so-wise thoughts about the undesirability of a divided Iraq?

Saddam Hussein has no more right to Kurdistan than he had to Kuwait. He has forfeited any such right by a vicious record of oppression of the Kurds worse even than his treatment of Iraq's Arab population. When he gets back full control he will kill, and kill, and kill.

It is not too late to intervene, taking up the conditions the Kurds have apparently demanded – a UN-brokered autonomy, demilitarisation, a substantial UN presence – on pain of visiting on President Saddam's forces a punishment from the air as swift and complete as that which we administered over Kuwait.

10 April 1991: Edward Pearce

Fixing a war, fouling a peace

Looking at the performance of George Bush handling the Kurdish matter, as morally anaemic a display of switched off executive apathy as one wants to see, something becomes clear. There are occasions when government knows what it wants and goes for it, taking the electorate on the trip. The stocks are sold, the press is squared, the middle class is quite prepared. Thus it was with the Gulf war. Thus it was not for the things which happened afterwards.

When Mr Bush resolved in late November to settle the Kuwait invasion by war, he was able to call up a subtler coalition than the joining in arms of Syria, Italy, Britain and Saudi Arabia. He was able to delight American conservatives by a touch of swagger and assertion, to charm the British by letting them play with their collection of dinky tanks, and to delight Walter Mittyish editors with a sniff at the glue bottle of power.

But with all this he was able to make a quite separate pitch at a liberal constituency, all the people who used to camp on the White House lawn demanding to know of LBJ how many kids he had killed that day. The ripple of muscle tone was sweetly balanced by a little purr of grief at the dreadfulness of Saddam Hussein, the taking of incubators from Kuwaiti hospitals and yes indeed, the recent gassing of the Kurds.

Incidentally, Mrs Thatcher's sudden excess of concern is in odd contradistinction to her response to the gassing. That event did not prevent the dispatch of a Foreign Office minister to extend credit and talk sales with Saddam himself. But then most political morality improves under lights. The Kurds received highly sympathetic coverage during the build up to the war, they were after all prominent victims of Saddam. Not that they didn't *deserve* such attention, but until they were useful for and coincidental to US war aims they didn't get it.

However such was the nature of Saddam that the normal camp of opposition to colonial adventures and turkey shoots was divided. Hardline disbelievers in the high purpose of aggrandising Western politicians were set against a jumble of war liberals, intellectuals for the invasion, lineal descendants had they known it, of Gilbert Murray and his co-signatories whose press letter argued in 1956 the obvious validity of Eden's action at Suez.

A body of critical opinion was, not to waste time on fine points, suckered. A brisk trade was done in selling the kinder, gentler killing of people. For ends we could all feel proud of, precision bombing would be caringly used in a thoughtful war with Christian undertones.

For the duration of the war including the pocket Dresdens and the strafing of the troops in flight, George Bush occupied the altar-rail of argument. I grew heartily sick of having to explain on TV programmes to the thicker heads of the war party that Saddam was more loathed by the opponents of the Gulf war who tended to have heard of him before August 1990, than by the sudden dispensers of anguished concern in government.

By the time we were counting the dead, arguing about the barbecued civilians in the shelter and looking at the man in the tank turret, the entire Bush operation was complete. Indignation could be folded up and put neatly away until it was needed again, shock at persecution of the Kurds, a rather noble people never previously a big number, could be filed under 'miscellaneous'.

I never quite accepted Noam Chomsky's schematic view of a coherent and composed American conspiracy in the Middle East. Such thinking attributes too long an attention-span in government. The American trouble is not precisely a desire to rule the world as a calamitous inability to either understand or be interested by it.

I will stand by my own definition of the US as a continental parish for whom the people outside, French as much as Waziris, are remote, inexplicable phenomena, devilish or cute according to circumstance or camera angle, and gradable from debenture holders of high culture, to be done as Florence and Oxford are done, all the way down to what are seen candidly as flies on the windscreen.

American arrogance, American ignorance and American requirement of quick results make a splendid tripod. Hence the recurring fondness for utilising the local gangster, the reluctance to be without a Somosa or a Marcos. Hence disastrously, upsetting of the entire Bush package, the belief that some other gangster and/or fascist would do the necessary against Saddam in Iraq after the war.

The Americans have been spoiled by Central America, where General Arturo this rules like General Antonio that. The last thing that Bush wanted was a just rising by an oppressed people fighting a notably chivalrous civil battle to obtain their rightful ends. One can be as high-flown as that about the Kurdish rising and be accurate. But Bush does not give a sucked fruit drop for Kurdish justice. He has been concerned to enjoy a rather long sound bite: American President sustained by superb American fighting men, stands up for the good guys against the bad guys on prime time.

There was no deep policy implication good or bad, merely a short winnable media war that would look good. The President's image requirements having been met in full, ordinary State Department considerations, as brutal and graceless as ever, could obtain again. The Kurds were a nuisance to the Turks, highly useful and apt allies. A Kurdish state or even autonomous region in Iraq would be in the highest degree unhelpful to Turkey. A Shia region in the south would encourage 'Militant Islam', another optional monster on file. In the absence of a satisfactory alternative gangster to rule Iraq, then in the interest of stability why not stick with our former contact?

For all the interest the US showed, Saddam could have machine-gunned the Kurds on that mountain side. Unfortunately for the smooth continuity of government this is an issue where liberal opinion is not divided, where many quite conservative people find themselves in profound empathy with a victim highlighted and circled round for their attention by government agencies.

Speaking of which, the right-wing press could not bring off the adjustment from moral outrage to cool-headed insouciance in the short time allocated by the thoughtlessly dying Kurds. The empty front page of *The Times* will however remain, a dog not barking in the night, what might be mistaken for an editor's loyal omission in the midst of events.

And observe the British government waving its paper stars and stripes, ready to be indifferent and legalistic if that is what the intimators of our opinions require. Governments control none of these events. The Kurds have crashed the commercial, and, dying on camera, have brought upon governments a sudden requirement to demonstrate a concern and readiness to act, also on camera. Policy is being shifted by the media and thank God for that.

22 June 1991: Leader

A march on the mild side

'Rejoice in victory!' we were once adjured. But there was very little of that in the City of London yesterday as the boys from the Gulf got their welcome home. It was a gentle, muted occasion – beneath the sort of lowering skies which suspended missions over the Mansion House just as they had suspended them over Iraq. In every respect, that seemed aptly judged. No tickertapes and weeping Presidents and whooping patriotism. The troops were led by a notably thoughtful soldier, Brigadier Patrick Cordingley. They were glad to have acquitted themselves with high efficiency. But their thoughts were also with those few on their own side who died; the thousands upon still uncounted thousands amongst their out-gunned adversaries who perished; the Kurds in the north and the refugees in the south, huddled in apprehension; the returning strut of Saddam; and, maybe, the squat figure of Kuwait's Crown Prince on the rostrum, saluting the return of freedom with a new law which allows his government to deport without trial any foreigner alleged to have committed a driving offence. A long parade of thoughts.

This was a different kind of war: co-operative effort for a purpose. The narrow aim was to return Kuwait to the Emir. The broader aspiration, pavilioned in adjectives, was to help create a better world. Any present accounting would be of narrow victory and broad failure. There is no glowing Middle East peace process. There is no golden enhancement of UN authority (rather, dismay at its bureaucratic nit-picking). There is nothing yet you could call democracy in the Gulf. There is Saddam. There is uncharitable misery to come for his citizens and his shattered country. Few, in truth, expected a new dawn once the guns fell silent. But even those who expected little must be sadly disappointed.

Nothing of this reflects on the troops who marched yesterday with some dignity. They were professionals assigned to a specific task, and proud in its accomplishment. But the dignity of the occasion, all of a piece with British reflections in the wake of war, makes a creditable study in contrasts. Britain's political leadership, declining to rejoice, gained no lasting garlands: the khaki was already threadbare before the word 'election' could be whispered. America's leaders, meanwhile, are bathed in continuing glory and much triumphalism. They rejoice perpetually: they have defined military victory alone as a line under the affair, seeking to shut out the cries for help of those left behind. That is, to some extent, understandable: exhausted reaction after vast effort. But it is also the line of failure drawn. The Gulf, at this point, is only a defining event in that it defines American attitudes towards the wider role its rhetoric hails. That stance lacks stamina. Its attention span is perilously short; its need to declare an end and move on intense. There is no new world order in any of this. And that, down the damp streets of the City yesterday, was perhaps the abiding memory.

The Gulf was a war which asked to be judged in a wider context. Raking back over might-have-beens is futility: what was done was done, and the troops could hold their heads high. But what was done was supposedly done for greater reasons; and what actually happened thereafter is umbilical – in an age of rapid response – to understanding what such war, for such ends, can and absolutely cannot achieve. That was this time. There will inexorably be a next time – and a vital cue for understanding gained.

Dispatches from abroad

4 October 1990: Matthew Engel

The reformer informer

In the musical *Blood Brothers* two twins are separated at birth and know nothing of each other. One grows up rich, the other poor. Eventually they meet.

Yesterday East Germany actually moved into its rich brother's house bearing the pathetic baggage of a mis-spent life: 496 Olympic medals (mostly tarnished); an economy hardly capable of producing a widget; the world's most concentrated output of sulphur dioxide, carbon dioxide and coal dust; nine million workers of mostly limited skill; 85,000 secret police officers of great skill but no obvious future function; their six million files; and their estimated half-million informers . . .

'Half a million?' asked Salomea Genin incredulously. 'Oh, no. What was the population? 16 million? Then it was far more. It was one in ten.'

Ms Genin speaks with some authority. She admits to

having been one of them, though hardly a typical example. She is 58, a Jewish Berliner who escaped with her family to Australia on the outbreak of war, spent her youth searching for an identity and found one as a committed Communist. She begged to be allowed back into East Germany and succeeded, in 1963, two years after the Ulbricht regime stopped allowing anyone out. In May 1989, six months before the Wall fell, she returned her party card, the final step in a process of disillusionment going back almost 20 years.

Outside, people wandered by bleary-eyed after the celebrations of the previous night. Ms Genin felt clearer-eyed than for many years.

'I regret I took so long to see reality. I became a Communist at a young age and became blind. As a friend once said, I'm a Zionist who went to Israel.'

Of course, she knew even in the early days that everything was not perfect: 'I always put it down to the system being fine but that people had not yet reached the standards of the system.'

She believed in the Wall, accepted Ulbricht's statements that the West planned to invade, that the economy was being destroyed because so many East Berliners were living in cheap houses while commuting to get Western wages, and that socialism could only work without outsiders' interference and sabotage.

'I have to admit I never thought about the shooting and the deaths. The Wall was one of those things that were necessary for the upkeep of the system and the system was the most important thing.'

Nor did she realise how privileged she was. As a victim of fascism, a Communist Party member of long-standing, a returnee and Jewish, she received extra money for light work, teaching and translating, and was able to get a flat in one of the city's few desirable old streets. She never saw the significance of this, or of her two regular visitors. 'I just told them about my daily doings. There was rarely anything concrete. Occasionally, they would ask me about someone or other. They were asking trivial details and I didn't realise the effect they were having. I would say who was saying what to whom. I didn't know they were putting people in jail for ideas, because they weren't doing it to me.'

Her work for the Stasi ceased when she was asked to befriend a couple of writers who were thought to be in possession of an illegal printing machine. She thought about this afterwards and politely declined.

Her life seems to have been occupied with thinking about things afterwards. 'They never put pressure on me. They always treated me with the utmost respect. Because of who I was.'

She was interested not in details but in ideas, or an Idea. And the Idea let her down. She has returned to Judaism. 'I wasted a lot of time and I did things I feel guilty about.' But she confronted herself and, before the end, the system.

Who among the crowds wandering past the jazz bands and the food stalls that lined the road down to the Alexanderplatz yesterday were the one in ten? Will they ever exorcise themselves, or will their guilt poison the new country as it poisoned the old? *Blood Brothers* ends in the death of both twins.

And every day still brings new strangenesses. Yesterday, right outside the Monument to Victims of Fascism and Militarism, there was a giant inflated Pepsi-Cola bottle. A newspaper placard, under the headline about unification, said '40 Years of Peanuts', which turned out to be a reference to the comic strip not to the East German wage structure.

Meanwhile, drivers from the ex-country were having to cope with the loss of their time-honoured prerogative of being able to turn right on red lights.

Salomea Genin struggles to find other things to regret about East Germany's disappearance: 'I was annoyed when you couldn't get milk in plastic bags but only in these cardboard things. And for months there was nowhere to put paper for recycling. We were trained by the GDR to recycle everything, paper, bottle tops, glass. People did that because they had to long before it was fashionable in the West. Now the youth clubs have started to close. They were state-subsidised and very popular. And we are losing our subsidised rents. But these subsidies were so unreal. This economy just wasn't workable. I'm happy that it's all gone. I'm not afraid of the future.' The past, she might have added, is another country.

29 December 1990: Michael Simmons

East still East

Berlin is a city that aches for greatness. It lives in the hope of the big moment, but secretly fears it may finish up on the shelf. Perhaps it is because it has been a bridesmaid several times – for Bismarck, for the Kaisers, for Hitler – but has yet to be a bride. It has lost some of its marvellous brashness; it has become tentative; and it blushes easily.

A year after the breach in the Wall, and a matter of weeks after the first decisive all-German elections for a couple of generations or more, it is also a waiting city. The newly-elected parliament – in the provincial small town of Bonn – will now discuss Berlin's future and will try to quantify the extent to which it may be counted the capital, once again, of a greater Germany. As it waits, there is a sense that it has lost its way, not unlike a giant liner in an uncharted sea with no landfall in sight. The chill smog of winter does nothing to dispel the impression; it is, as it were, the encircling gloom.

But all Berliners are world-weary and many of them have cynicism in their veins. Why, says a large man with a bull neck, straight out of a drawing by George Grosz, we were described in 1939 as the world-city (*Weltstadt*) of the future – and the war broke out. Well, says the despondent former East German Communist, we were described as the capital of the GDR, and then we built that bloody Wall.

Strolling today in the desolate and muddy acres which now surround the Brandenburg Gate, one is reminded of a British judgement in May 1945 – that Berlin was utterly destroyed, completely dead and could never be reconstructed. The ruins, said Air Marshal Arthur Tedder, Deputy Supreme Commander of the Allied Expeditionary Forces, should be preserved – a modern Babylon perhaps, or a Carthage; a monument to militarism and evil.

The Wall has gone, but the estrangement, the unique 'separateness' remains. When it existed, the Wall had brought Berliners together in their resentment of its existence and the pain that it induced. In the end it was the Communists, or some of them, who apologised for it and the West Berliners who endorsed it as 'the basis for a stable East-West relationship'.

Removing it brought rejoicings in the first instance and lots of kisses and hugs for fellow Germans, poor and deprived and so grateful for 'freedom' and small handouts of West German marks. It didn't matter that the East Germans could only gawp at the glittering stores on the Kurfurstendamm – the family was reunited.

Now they've got used to freedom, but the handouts don't come any more. Rather the opposite. The bureaucracy of the GDR has been cancelled and, at a stroke, nearly 200,000 jobs (in a *Hauptstadt* of one million or so) look like ceasing to exist. One of the best prospects for employment now is the demolition of the Communists' huge Palace of the Republic, which may have to be pulled down because of asbestos dangers.

A piercing wind from Siberia cuts across the great swathe of empty land perhaps 500 yards wide which now divides the city where the Wall and adjoining no-man's land used to be. One or two GDR watch-towers remain, usually covered in meaningless graffiti. Even the rabbits which used to frisk around the grassy site of Hitler's last bunker have dispersed to pastures new.

The Brandenburg Gate is still not a gate, but is surrounded by twentieth-century history's most astonishing flea market. Hundreds of Turks, jumping up and down and hugging themselves to get warm, sell bits of Soviet military uniforms, insignia and medals – the trappings of a once great empire on which the sun has now set. What sort of Red Army colonel gave away his badge of rank for a knock-down price?

While Berliners contemplate unemployment, the trestle tables of these market-happy Third Worlders groan under the weight of pieces of the Wall for sale – guaranteed 'authentic' by an illegible signature from an unknown organisation. Two marks for a piece the size of an egg-cup, three marks for the size of a teacup, five marks for the size of a saucer. The Wall, too, was an outpost of empire.

The gulf between East and West is still just as tangible as it was when the Wall was there. The East Berliners, hunched in their anoraks, wearing poor-quality shoes – always a distinguishing feature between East and West – still come over to window shop; the West Berliners, well-shod, in heavy overcoats, still go over to visit relatives, to take photographs. The exploitation by East of West (for hard currency) has diminished; but has the patronage of the East by the West? It's hard to say.

Of course, it is still a racy city, still stark in its old architecture and rather garish in the new; Left-inclined in its politics and able, in almost any situation, to make bitter political jokes to raise a laugh. With the respectable, Right-inclined burgers of Bonn, it has little in common.

But where, assuming Berlin becomes capital, will the poor go next? Until today it has been Kreuzberg, Wedding and the Jewish quarter around the Oranienburg Gate (Brecht country) where the poor hung out. The squatters have been cleared away and Mercedes Benz has already staked a claim to a prime site. Central city properties are central city properties, after all. Prices will climb out of reach, and something, someone, will have to give. Someone will have to go. 'Who?' asked my friend, an incomer called Jochen. 'Who are the new poor of Berlin?'

The coming of the market economy means that the subsidies to ease the pain of living 'on the political front line' will mostly be removed. This in turn means the special characteristics of life which attracted so many creative spirits, draft dodgers and other 'alternatives' who liked uncomplicated living in West Berlin are no longer available. East Berliners have gained what Reagan and Thatcher called 'freedom', but in exchange have lost their jobs, their political self-respect, their motivation, as well as members of their family.

Unemployment is high and getting higher; the pain threshold is disconcertingly lower. Professionals in East Berlin – diplomats, lecturers, teachers, journalists and others – are suddenly without real prospects. Their employer – the State, the Foreign Ministry, this or that institute – has gone under. The old GDR, said Wolfram, a skilled radio journalist, will have the best educated insurance salesmen in Europe.

The lack of restraint has led to new preoccupations with the past as well as the future. Hitler is being scrutinised more closely than ever before.

Talking with people about the Wall coming down, the end of the GDR, the collapse of communism, was suddenly not a political matter at all. It was deeply, deeply personal. 'It takes time to recover from things like this,' said an elderly librarian. 'It is a family matter. Even the West Germans do not understand what we are still going through here in Berlin . . . '

12 April 1991: David Gow

The Chancellor adrift

At the state memorial service on Wednesday for the murdered business executive, Detlev Rohwedder, a cathartic ceremony of soul-cleansing for a divided nation, Johannes Rau, long-standing premier of North Rhine Westphalia, struck the right note: 'It is as if we had completely to rebuild a ship in the middle of the sea.'

He was, of course, referring to the mammoth task of forging a united, coherent society out of the two parts of Germany which formally joined together six months ago, but now stand as far apart as at any period during 45 years of enforced division, separated by mutual distrust, alienation, and even loathing.

The days when western and eastern Germans held aloft the same banner, 'We are one people', are long gone. Now the sad joke – told by Jens Reich, guiding spirit of East Germany's peaceful revolution – runs: the Ossi (easterner) says to the Wessi (westerner), 'We are a people!'; the Wessi to the Ossi, 'So are we!'

Friedrich Schorlemmer, a Protestant pastor in Luther's home town of Wittenberg in eastern Germany and another leading light in the 1989 overthrow of Communism, tried to explain to Chancellor Helmut Kohl on Wednesday night how this division was perceived by a people which, as he put it, had been thrown into deep water without a lifeline. He described the gut feeling of ordinary eastern Germans, faced with an unemployment rate of about 50 per cent by the end of the year and the closure of countless plants and businesses, as a simple one of being unwanted.

Kohl, the captain who will have to oversee the rebuilding of the ship of state, looked chastened. He now accompanies his paternalistic, easy optimism that East

Germany's economic problems will be overcome within at most five years with an awareness that the psychological wounds of division and renewal will take much longer to heal. He may well look chastened.

It is hard now to credit that the man who so surefootedly seized the historic opportunity of unification in the five months available last summer and autumn, could revert so quickly to the faltering, indecisive, provincial politician his critics – even within his own Christian Democratic Union – have reviled. His recognition that the essential nature of the East German crisis is psychological is typically belated: it was obvious to observers months before that the other half of Germany was a social catastrophe. He had already failed, during the Gulf war, to give the new Germany a clear idea of its world role. Now, in the backwater of Bonn's coalition politics, he has again failed to rise to the responsibility of leading east and west, the former suffering a collective breakdown and the latter, made richer by unification, watching with indifference or disgust.

Clear warnings of deep-rooted social unrest were given long before the Leipzig demonstrations, originally against the old Communist regime, began again. The Chancellor is right to stress that these protests can over-dramatise the situation or even create the conditions for unrest, but his critics say he has simply allowed matters to drift. Apart from last Sunday's low-key appearance in Erfurt, he has not visited the east since the general election on 2 December; nor has he made one televised address to the nation. Now, six months after unification and four months after his triumphant re-election, the Chancellor of a sorely divided nation faces a tougher test of survival.

23 October 1990: Ian Black

No joy in Jerusalem

Baq'a is one of the most desirable residential areas of West Jerusalem. Slightly exotic, everyone uses its original Arabic name, instead of the official Hebrew one, Geulim. Narrow leafy streets of gentrified stone Arab houses somehow blend with Jewish ones of more modern design. It is a uniquely Jerusalem neighbourhood, a Hampstead in a harsh and holy city, with little religious presence, a delightful old cinema, a few bookshops and cafés and a fine adventure playground just completed by the residents' association.

Early on Sunday, this peaceful scene was shattered by a teenage Palestinian who coolly bayoneted and killed three Israelis, an unarmed female soldier, a male civilian and an off-duty policeman, in the quiet backwater off the road south to Bethlehem.

There is no reason to doubt the truth of what the killer said afterwards: he was taking revenge for what happened on 8 October, when 21 Palestinians were shot dead and 150 injured by Israeli policemen during riots on the Temple Mount in the Old City.

No city in the world lives without murder, even random, premeditated murder. But when blood is shed here, Jewish or Arab, there are powerful religious, political and historical resonances. And, afterwards, there is nearly always revenge. For this is a city where truth is obscured by wishful thinking and short memories. From the overworked romantic images on the tourist brochures – the golden-domed mosque and ancient churches, the swaying figure of the black-coated Orthodox Jew, the haunting prayer call of the muezzin, the keffiyeh-swathed Arabs – to mundane reality, the distance is almost too great to cover.

Jerusalem is supposed to be one city. The anti-sniper

walls that separated the Jordanian and Israeli sectors came down 23 years ago, yet still no statement by an Israeli politician is complete without a reference to the fact that Jerusalem is the country's 'united and eternal capital'. But it is a hollow claim. On 8 October, I drove from the *Guardian* office, on Hillel Street in central West Jerusalem, up to the Makassed hospital on the Mount of Olives on the eastern side where the dead and injured from the Temple Mount were being brought in. It is a seven-minute journey, but it might as well be inter-galactic travel.

Jewish and Arab Jerusalemites inhabit separate universes. On 8 October, the wife of a Palestinian friend turned back from the busy shopping mall on Ben-Yehuda Street. Black mourning flags were already flying over her home, at Sheikh Jarrah in the east, and the bland, unruffled normality of the western side was simply too much to bear.

No one really wants the city to be physically re-divided, although sometimes – and these are grim, desperate times – there seems to be no other solution. Yesterday in a move designed both to punish Palestinians and to prevent attacks against them, residents of the West Bank were banned from entering Jerusalem. The building sites and the restaurant kitchens were empty. Even the veteran Jewish mayor, the ebullient and ever-optimistic Teddy Kollek, architect and tireless propagandist of Arab–Jewish co-existence, contemplated a drastic, heretical solution: a fence between the two sides of town.

Until the Temple Mount killings, Jerusalem had had a good intifada. A kid-gloves policy by the police and the Shin Bet security service helped maintain a relative calm.

Unlike their compatriots in the West Bank and Gaza, the city's Palestinian residents are Israeli citizens. This week they even began to get free gas masks in the event of an Iraqi rocket attack.

Earthly Jerusalem, not the city of the tourist brochures, but of Muslims and Jews who have confused spirituality with an atavistic tribalism, is a cruel and implacable place. It is a city where violence begets violence and hope does not spring eternal. It is a city where, for Jewish children, Arabs, all Arabs, are frightening, dangerous figures, and where, for Arab children, the Jew is the enemy. And not just in nightmares.

Israel has angrily rejected a UN mission to investigate the Temple Mount killings. Its own inquiry, due to be completed this week, is unlikely to assuage Palestinian fury. A new police commissioner or Border Police reinforcements outside the mosques during prayers will not defuse the ticking bomb that lies at Jerusalem's heart.

'I don't know what our politicians should do,' said one distraught Baq'a woman on Sunday morning, as Arabs cowered and the Jews wept and cursed in rage. 'But there has to be some kind of solution. I don't know whether that means getting rid of the Arabs or giving the West Bank back to them, but something must be done.'

8 November 1990: Jonathan Steele

Solzhenitsyn's circle

Viktor Sereyev was sitting on a stool in the living-room with a strange home-made contraption in front of him. It was a large board with a sliding panel and a diagonal blade set into it. From the pile of cabbages on the bed beside him Viktor would take one, clamp it into the panel, and then rub it backwards and forwards along the blade. A mountain of shreds built up under the machine on a plastic sheet spread over the carpet. 'Winter preparations,' explained Nina Nikolayevna, Viktor's wife. 'We will pickle the cabbage and keep it in jars.'

The scene was quintessentially Russian and what made it particularly memorable was that this was the room where Alexander Solzhenitsyn wrote his most famous works, the final version of *The First Circle, One Day in the Life of Ivan Denisovich* and parts of *The Gulag Archipelago*.

For just over 10 years the reclusive writer lived in the depths of the Russian provinces, in the town of Ryazan. The two-storey wooden house at 17 Ulitsa Uritskovo, where he had a set of three rooms on the ground floor, is little changed except that it now has a plaque on the front wall. Ryazan's most famous former citizen is recognised as a figure of honour at last.

'Come in, come in,' said the Sereyevs warmly when we knocked on the door. They have not yet had enough inquisitive strangers for the experience to become a nuisance. Viktor Sereyev is a department head in the Ryazan Institute of Agricultural Economy which owns the wooden house. Solzhenitsyn's first wife, Natalia Reshetovskaya, also worked at the institute, which is why they were able to find the rooms when he took a job as a teacher of physics and astronomy at High School No. 2.

The Sereyevs produced their treasure, a small piece of plywood inscribed in Solzhenitsyn's hand. They found it under the floor. It was the label which the writer tied round his wife's bicycle when he sent it by train to Ryazan: 'Lady's bicycle. Departure station: Moscow. Destination: Ryazan. Sender: A. L. Solzhenitsyn. Collector: The same.'

For the first two years that Solzhenitsyn lived at 17 Ulitsa Uritskovo he and his wife shared the flat with two gym teachers. Working on highly delicate political topics, Solzhenitsyn took extreme care to destroy his notes and outlines once he had prepared his final version. As Michael Scammell describes in his excellent biography, he typed on both sides of the paper without margins. Late at night after the gym teachers were asleep, the writer and his wife would burn the notes in the communal stove in the kitchen.

He never invited his teaching colleagues to the flat for

fear they would become too friendly and ask about his writing. 'He never invited any of the 13 other families in the house either,' says Vladimir Kharkevich, who still lives upstairs. 'He would always greet us politely in the hall. We would discuss household issues. He wrote to the authorities a lot to complain about a food warehouse opposite where lorries made a great deal of noise unloading.'

In the summer they saw him in the courtyard sitting under a tree from early in the morning, usually writing by hand. They knew he had been in Stalin's camps but never asked about that. 'You couldn't do that at that time. He never mentioned it. We never brought it up.'

On the corner of Lenin Street and Freedom Street is the Ryazan branch of the Writers' Union. It is a modest room in a building of government offices with a typical line drawing of Lenin on one wall and a touched-up photograph of Gorbachev on another. In the bookcase there's no sign of anything by Solzhenitsyn. The writer was invited to the room on 3 November 1969. He rarely attended union meetings and was surprised to be urged to come to a discussion on the 'ideological education of writers' that very afternoon. Suspecting he was the real target, he arrived with a sheath of newspaper cuttings and notes.

After a long and rambling opening report, the branch secretary, Vasily Matushkin, launched into the attack. Solzhenitsyn was accused of 'besmirching our Motherland' with his writings. Four other local writers joined in the chorus – only one of them, Yevgeni Markin, offering any hint of discomfort with the obviously orchestrated onslaught. But he too voted for the unanimous resolution expelling Solzhenitsyn from the union.

None of the six men at the meeting is in Ryazan now. All have died or moved away. Vladimir Kolubov, a branch member chatting with two friends in the gloomy room, says: 'In those days people thought differently. Even then not everyone voted against him'. He mentioned one writer, Ernst Safonov, who did not take part in the vote. It turns out he was in hospital. We all laugh. Now he is the editor of *Literaturnaya Rossiya*, the conservative organ of the Russian Writers' Union.

The issue which everyone is willing to discuss is Solzhenitsyn's latest pronunciamento, his 16,000-word essay, 'How shall we reconstitute Russia?', published in the daily *Komsomolskaya Pravda* and the weekly *Literaturnaya Gazeta*. With its complaints about the desertion of the Russian countryside, the pollution, the destroyed churches and the empty villages, and its praise of the provinces as the real heartland of Russian culture, 'free of the pressure of the capital', Solzhenitsyn must have had Ryazan in mind, although he has not seen the way it has sunk even further in the 21 years since he left.

On a damp autumn day the pot-holed streets and uneven pavements are a mass of puddles. Long queues wait for overcrowded buses. The once attractive façades of the nineteenth high school, market place and other public buildings look as though they have not been painted for decades. The shops are in a miserable state. Virtually everything is rationed.

Beyond Ryazan, Solzhenitsyn's message has had a mixed reception, more critical than supportive. I have yet to hear anyone agree with him wholeheartedly. 'His tone is preachy and condescending,' says Art Troitesky, the energetic entrepreneur of the rock music scene. 'He is no longer in touch with life here.' Irina Sandomirskaya, a young feminist writer, calls the language 'patronising' and the views 'terrible'. When she first read *Gulag Archipelago*, like most of her generation, it was a shock and a liberation, but: 'Since he became the hermit of Vermont he has changed. In the days when we were all one lump with the Red Star above us, we did not think who we were, now we are divided. As a Jew I worry about Solzhenitsyn's Russian patriotism. We know where it can lead.'

The writer's central point, that the USSR should drop its

outlying republics and form a Russian Union with the Ukraine and Byelorussia, has angered people in those two increasingly independent republics. They like this notion that the empire has cost the country dear and that only by abandoning it can Russia redeem itself, but they find his disregard of their own distinct national feelings inconsistent. He is not even calling for a Slavic Union, but a Russian one. His suggestion that northern Kazakhstan, which has a predominantly Russian population, split from the south and join the new Russian Union prompted three days of demonstrations in the capital, Alma Ata.

His criticism of the Russian orthodox hierarchy for timidity wins him few friends there. He rejected an invitation to return as a visitor at government expense. The hard-line nationalists in the Russian Communist Party will have no truck with such a committed anti-communist, nor he with them. An article in their associated paper, *Molodaya Gvardia*, makes the lunatic charge that Solzhenitsyn is the 'continuer of Trotskyism'. Reminding readers that like Trotsky he has holed himself up in a protected villa, in his case in Vermont rather than Mexico, the article's author prays with obscenely false anxiety, that 'God grant there be no repetition' of Trotsky's fate.

Back in the cramped living-room in Ryazan where Solzhenitsyn's single-minded crusade reached its peak on the then secret *Gulag Archipelago* typescript, the Sereyevs express what appears to be the dominant view – gratitude, but . . . 'I think he should come and see Russia. People will relate very well to him. They will thank him. But a great deal has changed. He needs a month or two to see,' Viktor says.

The Sereyevs agree with Solzhenitsyn's prescription (not his alone) that only de-collectivisation and private ownership of the land can save agriculture. By now the cabbage-shredder has been pushed aside and we are sitting round a tiny camping table with folding legs that Viktor has erected by the bed. Potatoes from the Sereyevs' allotment are frying on the stove, home-grown tomatoes appear on a plate. Nina produces a bottle of home-made strawberry wine. Only the mushrooms come from beyond the allotment, but the Sereyevs picked them themselves.

Yet even in this cosy nest of pride in private farming, the desire for a permanent return to the land is muted. The Sereyevs' eldest son graduated from the Institute of Agriculture. So did his wife. Have they considered taking up the chance to start a small farm now that the Communist Party has lifted the ideological ban on this kind of thing? Yes, but they rejected it. Living conditions in the rural backwaters are too tough, no paved roads, no schools, no piped water or indoor plumbing. Like their parents, the younger Sereyevs would rather teach in town.

So, as the Communist Party celebrates Revolution Day in a mood of seemingly inevitable decline, the political authority of the leading Russian anti-Communist in exile is not high either. Meanwhile, the return to Russia's once-productive earth on which he and others, including President Gorbachev, pin many of their hopes is nowhere in sight.

21 December 1990: Jonathan Steele

Shevardnadze resigns

It was long before perestroika began, when Mikhail Gorbachev and Eduard Shevardnadze were the two relative youngsters in an elderly politburo, that the future Foreign Minister told the future President: 'The whole thing is rotten.' The two men were on holiday, strolling in the pine trees in Pitsunda by the Black Sea coast and comparing notes on the state of the nation. This 'walk in the woods' was presumably not the only experience that fired Gorbachev with the idea that only radical reform could change the Soviet Union. By then the country had been stagnating for 10 years under the tired and corrupt leadership of Leonid Brezhnev. But the conversation and the knowledge that he had an ally in Shevardnadze must have been important factors, since the President recalled the walk in a speech last month. At the least it showed how committed Shevardnadze was to reform.

The man whom the world knows as a charming Foreign Minister was a champion of change for most of his previous career. His critics may accuse him of losing touch with Soviet realities as he tirelessly travelled round the world, far more than Gorbachev, who is the butt of the same charges. But Shevardnadze was always conscious of how far the Soviet Union had to go before it could honestly sit down with other developed nations. Far from insulating him from concern about internal Soviet problems, constant rubbing of shoulders with Western colleagues perpetually reminded him of this sad fact.

Shevardnadze was always more outspoken and emotional than his boss, sometimes almost embarrassingly so, about the shame he felt for his country. 'It pained me to watch a television account of how hard currency was collected for a helicopter pilot, a hero of Chernobyl, so that he could go for emergency treatment in the US,' he told his Foreign Ministry staff in May. 'Soviet doctors are unable to help him or thousands of other people with radiation sickness.'

He made it clear he hated the kind of bombastic patriotism that characterises the conservative enemies who have now driven him out. 'The critics of perestroika accuse us of betraying class principles. In the meantime the so-called class enemies supply us with disposable syringes, apparatuses to treat burns, prosthetic appliances, and special vehicles for the handicapped. We are a great nation which should be respected. But what is our greatness? A huge territory? The size of our population? Or the grief of our people? The absence of rights? The low quality of life? What is there to be proud of, when we have almost the highest child-mortality rate in the world? A country arousing fear or a country commanding respect? A country relying on force or a country believing in good?'

Shevardnadze took the brunt of the conservatives' anger over the collapse of Communist rule in Eastern Europe, and particularly the unification of Germany. The conservatives felt he had become too close to the West. Recently, their anger focused on the crisis in the Gulf. They had two points of attack: the first that Shevardnadze was too willing to go along with the United States on the issue of using force against Iraq, the second on whether Soviet troops would be used.

Their case may have had a grain of truth in it. On two or three occasions, most recently during the last visit here by the Iraqi Foreign Minister, Tariq Aziz, Gorbachev seemed to be firmer in ruling out the use of force than Shevardnadze. Gorbachev stressed the need for a political solution. Shevardnadze put his emphasis on maintaining a common US–Soviet front. That at least was the impression. More importantly as far as the conservatives were concerned, Shevardnadze in an interview after the latest UN vote said that if a single Soviet citizen was harmed in Iraq, the Soviet Union might use force without referring to the Supreme Soviet in advance. The Foreign Ministry later sought to modify the statement, but the damage had been done. The overwhelming majority of the Supreme Soviet has said it does not want a repetition of Afghanistan, when a decision to commit Soviet lives was taken by a handful of men.

Colonel Viktor Alknis, a leader of the conservative Soyuz group, called for a parliamentary inquiry. He accused the government of 'not thinking what will happen to the Soviet military and civilian specialists in Iraq if a Soviet contingent takes part'. He also said that Britain and the United States would not be hit by Iraqi rockets armed with chemical and bacteriological weapons. 'They would be directed at our territory, at the Caucasus and Central Asia.' He also said that a prolonged war in the Middle East could spark off severe tension among the Soviet Muslim population.

If there is one thing which Shevardnadze became convinced of in his time in the Foreign Ministry it was that ideology must be totally removed from the conduct of state-to-state relations. This was one of the key points in the 'new thinking'. Shevardnadze was the man who carried it out. Sometimes he went so far that he seemed to allow this pragmatism to outlaw not only ideology but the need to make a moral statement.

Shevardnadze's emotions were fired by viciousness at home rather than viciousness abroad. As party secretary in Georgia, he took a strong stand against the local party mafia during the 1970s. He was very unhappy at the use of troops against a peaceful demonstration in Tbilisi in April last year. Immediately after the clash, which left 20 people dead, he flew to his home region to get the troops withdrawn.

For over a year he has been speaking out against excessive centralisation. He told the Foreign Policy Association in New York a year ago, before Gorbachev decided to create a presidential system, that the 'accumulation of enormous power in the hands of so-called supreme leaders brought misfortune to many people. Centralism at the level of one individual gave rise to the leader's uncontrolled subjectivism.'

If that sounded like a criticism of Gorbachev, Shevardnadze muted it in an interview in March when he first talked of the danger of dictatorship. It seemed he did not have Gorbachev in mind. But he went on to argue that if perestroika failed, 'a dictator would come to power. A great dictator or a comic-opera one, it doesn't really matter'. Yesterday he made it clear he feels his fears are for real.

5 September 1990: David Beresford in South Africa

Twenty-two, and still at school

His name was Lucky – Lucky Mgenge. I didn't ask him why they called him that; it was hardly lucky to be born the son of an unsuccessful gangster, in a tin shack in Alexandra Township. Nor did I ask him about his age – at 22 easily the oldest of the group of kids I met at Realogile High School.

There was lots of giggling as we talked about romance, discotheques and teachers. After a while Lucky offered to show me around Alex.

One of the country's oldest townships, Alex sprawls across about one square mile of hillside, abutting the 'mink and manure belt' of Johannesburg's northern suburbs. The government has spent millions of rands over the last few years trying to clean it up. It's been like bailing out the oceans with a bucket, their efforts cramped by the tide of squatters flooding in from rural areas in search of work. As a result Alex is a curious mix of new blocks of flats and bungalows amid wood and iron shanties surrounded by small hills of garbage on which goats and dogs root for scraps.

Lucky's family of seven live in a three-roomed mud-house on 15th Avenue – or, as the kids would have it, AK47 Avenue. They moved there 12 years ago, from the one-roomed shack where Lucky was born. Lucky sleeps in the kitchen. Fifteen families live in their yard, sharing one communal tap. There is no electricity and the toilets are buckets.

'The crime rate generally is high,' said Lucky off-handedly as we wandered through the township. 'We find six or eight corpses a weekend. Most of those murdered have their private parts taken for *muti*. We have something like 200 *sangomas* in Alex.' Sangomas are witchdoctors and muti their magic potions. Genitals are a favourite ingredient for muti sold to businessmen: R1,000 for a potion which, when buried in the foundations of new business premises, will bring good fortune.

The level of crime acts as a dampener on the social life of youngsters. 'Girls fear to go out at night,' says Lucky. 'The rate of rape is amazing.' But, he confides, 'I have a girlfriend, Lucy. She's white – a Jew.' He met her at a gig in Cape Town, where he was playing the saxophone with a band from Alex. 'She gave me her address and asked me to visit her. We became friends.'

The friendship developed and they became lovers. 'I couldn't believe it. She gave me her photo. I slept with it. I woke up after an hour, looking at the photo,' recalled Lucky. 'When we slept together I had this thing in mind that Whites are very different from Blacks. But it was not so different.'

He brought her to Alex on a visit. 'My parents couldn't accept her. They said, "How can you fall in love with a white girl and bring a white girl here when we're so poor?" I said, "She loves me, she doesn't care if I'm poor." ' She took him home for dinner in Johannesburg's northern suburbs. Her parents would not accept him either. 'They said I could be a friend to Lucy, but not a boyfriend.' He walked out of the house.

'I had a girlfriend before Lucy, but we broke because her parents didn't like me. Her parents said it was because of my commitment to the organisation; I was futureless.'

The 'organisation' was Cosas, the Congress of South African Students, to which the majority of black schoolchildren belong. Lucky joined it in 1985, which was when he got involved in politics and life started getting rough for him. He was no stranger to political violence. In 1976, during the Soweto uprising, he had seen police shoot a cousin dead in Alex. But 1985 was the start of his own political odyssey.

First there was the 'prefects' war'. Lucky was at another school in Alex then. Cosas was fighting for the recognition of students' representative councils. The teachers, feeling threatened by the idea of SRCs, teamed up with the prefects to fight it. 'The prefects used to come into school carrying knives,' recalled Lucky. One day a group of teachers and prefects arrived at his house armed with *sjamboks* (long whips) and thrashed him in front of his parents.

In May 1985 Cosas launched a schools' boycott. The police began hunting down student leaders responsible and Lucky, as a known activist, went on the run. In June the State of Emergency was declared and Cosas was banned. Lucky made the mistake of going by bus to the funeral of four leading activists murdered in the Eastern Cape. When they got back to Johannesburg the police were waiting. They found Cosas T-shirts in Lucky's bag and he spent the next six months in detention.

He came out in 1986 just in time for Alexandra's 'Six-Day War', when the township erupted with gun battles between police, students and rival political factions.

It was at an all-night vigil before a funeral that Lucky last saw his friend and hero, Jingles Mohapo, perform. Jingles was a poet and a singer. 'He recited a poem called "Balaclava Man" about death squad leaders who wear balaclavas. "Balaclava Man shoot me now, kill me now . . . I am waiting for the day when the comrade will be wearing my name on his T-shirt, saying this was a freedom fighter."'

It was Jingles' last poem. Two nights later Lucky and Jingles' girlfriend found his body. He had been shot twice.

On 18 June 1986, Lucky was detained again, this time for two and a half years, which explains why he's still at school now.

The first 14 months were spent in solitary confinement.

'I was beaten on several occasions. They put a tyre on me – a necklace – and said: "Do you know this thing? We are going to pour the petrol and then we are going to set you alight." '

Inevitably the police attempted to recruit him. 'The white cops were beating me and this coloured cop came in and said: "Stop it, you are not allowed to do that." ' He took Lucky into another office and offered him money to inform. 'Informers are a big problem,' said Lucky. 'Four or six have been necklaced in Alex.'

Lucky was released last year, and says life has not changed much in Alex, despite the appearance of change in South Africa as a whole created by recent developments such as the release of Nelson Mandela and the un-banning of the ANC.

Two of his friends have been killed this year, it is suspected by police. But he holds no grudges. 'Whites are also entitled to live in South Africa,' he says. 'I know their bad attitude towards us is because of the education they receive, because of the domination of apartheid in their schools. We will need to do a lot of work to get rid of those ideas.'

As for himself, he hopes to study law. 'Our people are not sure of their rights,' he says. 'I want to contribute something to the community.' Otherwise he wants to be a poet. Like Jingles.

15 May 1991: David Beresford

Nelson's blind eye

It may seem paradoxical to draw comfort from the sight of a woman whose courage has been an inspiration to millions, being sentenced to jail for her part in the kidnapping and beating up of four youths. But with South

Africa seemingly about to fall down around anyone's ears, there was a degree of reassurance to be found in watching Winnie Mandela standing to demure attention in the dock yesterday as sentence was handed down on her.

It was a picture that might well have been captioned, 'White man's justice.' The judge was white, as was his clerk and the stenographer. The state prosecutor was white, as was his assistant and the chief investigating officer who sat with them. Counsel for both of Winnie's co-accused were white and, although the defence included two juniors (one of them, incidentally, a rising star in the Pan Africanist Congress, long-time rivals of the ANC) there was no doubt that her case was in the hands of yet another white, her rotund Rumpole, George Bizos, SC.

The court was in fact the very image, at least superficially, of the legal system that for so long has collaborated with the state in preserving white privilege and in keeping down such 'uppity' Blacks as Winnie herself; and, of course, her husband Nelson. And yet here was the woman who is regarded as the militant face of the liberation struggle – backed by equally militant supporters packed into the public gallery – accepting judgement without so much as a hint of protest. When Mr Justice Stegmann sentenced her to six years – which, at least on the facts of the case, comes close to qualifying as a 'savage' sentence – the only disruption came from the clatter of wire agency reporters stampeding to their phones.

It is two-and-a-quarter years since the *Guardian* broke the scandal surrounding the so-called Stompie Moeketsi affair, with a report substantially summarising the facts on which Judge Stegmann has now delivered judgement. In the intervening period the face of South Africa has changed radically, if not completely; the ideology under which the country was administered for so many terrible years has collapsed, and white power is in disarray and to some extent retreat. Yet amid all the change and the bloodshed accompanying it, the wheels of justice have ground on in a manner which has at least earned the consent of the governed.

But if the Winnie case has seen the judicial system survive that critical test, its impact in the political arena is more difficult to assess. There has been some speculation of a hawkish element in the ANC coalescing around Mrs Mandela, but on present indications that can be dismissed.

As an individual, at least, any political power base that 'the Mother of the Nation' may have enjoyed has been largely destroyed by the scandal, whether or not she actually serves Judge Stegmann's sentence. Crowd scenes outside the Johannesburg Supreme Court may have given a different impression, but they were provided largely by remnants of her former supporters who confuse defiance of injustice with that of justice.

Even if the Appeal Court were to overturn the conviction – and some lawyers give Mr Bizos a good chance – the case has raised many unanswered questions about the evidence, as Judge Stegmann himself suggested, which probably render her reputation irretrievable. The onus of proof on the state in a criminal action is a far heavier one than that of the balance of probabilities with which politicians tend, rightly, to be judged by popular opinion.

In this respect it was significant that the only prominent figure from the ANC leadership who appeared in court to support her this week was her husband. According to those who have observed the whole trial, the previous representative was the ANC chief-of-staff, Chris Hani, who made a brief appearance at the beginning of March.

It is a truism, if an unfortunate one, that the importance of Mrs Mandela lies in her relationship with Nelson, and the trial draws its significance, at least politically, from its effect on him personally. It was therefore almost a relief yesterday that Mandela failed to turn up to hear his wife being sentenced. The sight of him the previous day, the controlled distress which palpably lay behind his poker face, was in itself distressing. To have seen the gross cruelty of fate visited on him yesterday – his wife jailed little more than a year after his own heroic incarceration had come to an end – would have been almost unbearable. Whether it will prove unbearable for him is the crucial question that still has to be answered.

The relationship between Nelson and his Winnie is, perhaps properly, a private matter. But to the extent that the public has been allowed an insight, it apparently remains intense, as was apparent from the passion with which he embraced and kissed her in the well of the court after her conviction on Monday.

It betrayed the feelings of a man who seemingly still nurses the sentiments he expressed 16 years into his own imprisonment, when he wrote to her: 'At my age I would have expected all the urges of youth to have faded away. But it does not appear to be so. The mere sight of you, even the thought of you, kindles a thousand fires in me . . .'

At the age of 73, engaged as he is in negotiations for the future of the nation in what appears at times to be a race against civil war, Mandela self-evidently is a man whose strength is being tested to the utmost. It is in those circumstances that the Winnie scandal could now destroy him; or at least the hopes most people have for his success in bringing a satisfactory conclusion to the cause for which he has already sacrificed so much of his life.

In that respect the sight of Winnie standing, however demurely, before Mr Justice Stegmann yesterday offered naught for South Africa's comfort.

Church and State

9 January 1991: Melanie Phillips

Public servants and private lies

This is an account of corruption at the heart of government. Not hand-in-the-till financial corruption, nor the kind that involves spanking vicars and little boys, but intellectual corruption, the displacement of integrity in public service by routine deception and manipulation of the facts that has become so commonplace that few think twice about it, let alone question or cavil at it.

It is also an account of semantics and sophistry, of secrecy and intimidation, of conscience and cynicism and above all of a club where everyone is only too aware of the rules. It is an account of the dilemmas faced by civil servants who are torn between the universal values to which they subscribe, such as truthfulness, knowledge or serving the public and the demands of their professional role.

Many civil servants are afraid to speak out. (All but one who spoke to the *Guardian* did so on condition that their identities would not be disclosed.) Yet from the testimony of those who have spoken, and from their unions, it seems that a substantial number involved in formulating government policy find what's going on hard to stomach. At its root, their charge is that the civil servant's role has been changed unacceptably. They hark back to a (perhaps apocryphal) golden age when civil servants found a happy harmony between their duties to Crown, government and the public interest, a time when facts were facts and treated with due reverence, when they could present policies neutrally, whatever the politicians may have got up to.

Since the Fifties, goes this theory, such public service integrity has been corroded; with the arrival of television, as the media became more informed and more questioning and as ministers became more nervous about public embarrassment, they got more and more involved in the details of policies and their presentation, which in turn put more pressure on their officials. This process reached its apogee under Mrs Thatcher so that civil servants who had served Parliament and the public interest were now required simply to carry out government policy and bend the facts to suit. The question now is whether it is in the interests of Mr Major (or even Mr Kinnock) to restore the old public service ethic.

Among the most senior civil servants, the Sir Humphreys of Whitehall, this suggestion curls a few lips. There never was such a golden age, they say; their role has remained unchanged. 'Once upon a time, we were all being accused of being too *independent* of government and subverting its policies,' said one Sir Humphrey. 'What these people are saying is wrong-headed and inaccurate,' said Sir Humphrey (retired) from his armchair in clubland. 'It was never true that in the past civil servants had a more neutral role.'

And, indeed, all round Whitehall civil servants still assiduously promote their own discrete policy agenda.

The Criminal Justice Bill, for instance, is a textbook example of a Whitehall-promoted policy to which successive ministers were not only recruited by officials but who furthermore implied misleadingly that this was their own tough and repressive policy to cover up the fact that it was actually dreamed up by liberal civil servants in the Home Office.

Ethical texts in Whitehall are few and far between, but the current ark of the covenant is the memorandum by Lord Armstrong, the former Cabinet Secretary, which laid it down thus: 'Civil servants are servants of the Crown. For all practical purposes the Crown in this context means and is represented by the government of the day . . . in the determination of policy, the civil servant has no constitutional responsibility or role distinct from that of the minister.'

More recently, this was glossed in a speech to the group Christian Responsibility in Public Affairs by Sir Michael Quinlan, permanent secretary at the Ministry of Defence, in this way: 'Our ethic requires that we operate in loyalty to and under any instructions of ministers . . . One may think a particular policy to be a square circle and indeed within the confidence of Whitehall one may argue fervently to that effect; but once the decision is taken it is thereafter a matter both of duty and of professional pride to help make the very best square circle that effort and imagination can contrive.'

Many in Whitehall take issue with the Armstrong/Quinlan interpretation of their role. It takes no account, they say, of the fact that the distinction between politics and public service has become blurred. Sometimes, the blurring is obvious. The fact that during the Conservative leadership election Douglas Hurd and John Major held press conferences at the Foreign Office and the Treasury was a very public symbol of this. One civil servant commented: 'We're very scrupulous that we don't write their speeches for pure party occasions like party conferences but if they appear on TV programmes like *Question Time* they get briefings from all government departments on all issues. But arguably they are appearing there as spokesmen for the Conservative Party, not in their departmental capacity.'

Sir Humphrey's complacency does an injustice to those civil servants whose consciences are deeply troubled. The problem really arises over truthfulness and the suppression or distorted release of information both in policy advice to ministers and to the general public. Is this, as some claim, a process of deliberate deception or is it, as others insist, just rather superior public relations presentation?

Sir Patrick Nairne, a former permanent secretary at the Department of Health, wrote bullishly a few months ago: 'Economy with the truth is the essence of a reply to a parliamentary question.' More junior ranks are sometimes a little more squeamish. Robin Robison, a Quaker whose faith developed while he was a civil servant, was a junior official in the Cabinet Office until he resigned, unable to stomach what he felt was a life of deception. When parliamentary questions were drafted, he would get the information off the computer to give to the statisticians who would send the draft answer off to the relevant section of the Treasury. 'They would say, "Maybe the minister won't like this, can't you change the wording here because this would be politically sensitive, or put the figures in a different way so it doesn't look so obvious or sharp?" It wasn't lying but it was close.

'I felt it was misleading and a politicisation. Where is the dividing line between legitimate loyalty to government and the civil service ethic of neutrality? Armstrong is wrong to say the government of the day represents the Crown. It's dangerous because use of the Royal Prerogative means ministers don't really account to the legislature. The de-unionisation of GCHQ and the Sinn Fein broadcasting ban were both done by Order in Council, so there was no scrutiny by Parliament. That's one reason why it's wrong to identify the Crown with the government of the day.'

Squaring the circle causes untold anguish among conscientious civil servants. Their faithful adherence to instructions has meant giving the public the impression that in the last decade unemployment has fallen sharply, the health service is in the pink of condition and poverty has all but disappeared. In the jargon, this is merely the 'gloss' put on the facts. But gloss involves putting on a shine. What has happened is more a shameless change of colour, and even those officials who are busy slapping fresh paint on the canvas are uneasy.

'Take community care policy,' said one. 'We're instructed to say that it's postponed and will be introduced shortly when it won't be, or that it's working when anyone walking the streets of London knows it's not working.' Or, he said, take last year's Salvation Army survey which said 753 people were sleeping rough one night in London, a figure said to be a substantial underestimate. 'The number was too low, everyone knows there was something wrong with the survey but ministers produce it and quote it when if they were honest they would not. If they were even more honest they would commission their own survey.'

Ah, Sir Humphrey would say, but that's ministers and we all know about them lying their heads off all the time; that's not us. But it's not as simple as that. Government statisticians, who are at the sharpest end of these dilemmas, say they are no longer expected to produce information to further public and ministerial knowledge, only to support government policies.

One former government statistician resigned after an unhappy period in which he was told to produce a set of politically sensitive figures that was biased towards government policy. 'The Government Statistical Service is supposed to be an independent body objectively finding out what's going on and presenting the full picture,' he said. 'We should not be subject to political interference. We've had instructions to put out in press notices the good news, put out the things that present government policies in the best light. It's a selection process that's going on. Putting the best gloss on is deliberately misleading the public because you're not putting out an independent analysis. It's a deliberate intention to mislead and deceive.'

It is the older statisticians, ones who have worked under previous administrations, who tend to be the most uneasy. Yet they're often the ones putting pressure on down the line. Another former government statistician said: 'From my experience, if someone comes up with a creative way of changing something that's politically acceptable it's done; if not, it's not done. I discovered an inconsistency in some figures which meant the poor were worse off but I was told it wouldn't be helpful to do anything about it because it would cost the government money. There is a conflict between statisticians' professional integrity and their conformity. Some just never think about it, some have a social conscience and the majority are deeply cynical.'

How do the Sir Humphreys react to this kind of claim? One recalled an occasion when he was confronted with a junior colleague with an inconvenient conscience. 'There was one man, more ethically minded than I am, who thought the presentation of policy he was asked to do wasn't telling the whole truth. He was an upright man but with rather a thin skin. It was affecting his health and I arranged for him to be transferred to other duties, which meant he had to exercise his conscience less frequently on matters that were deeply troubling him. I was able to put into his job someone who was slightly more robust.'

So how had Sir Humphrey himself felt about this misleading presentation? How robust was his own conscience? 'I was pragmatic. I knew that we had to get on and put this policy out. In many areas of the Civil Service you are Janus-like, you face two ways. As chief finance officer in one department I was highly sceptical of projects within the department because it was my job to be and I would argue against the weak points in their propositions until we went to the Treasury with them, when my other side came out and I was the most eloquent advocate in their favour. I don't think there's so much difference between that and arguing with your minister and then presenting the policy in the most attractive way. But you are asking a lot of a junior civil servant to present information in the way that a minister likes. Some of them of course are able to square their consciences but it's at the top of the Civil Service that this presentational thing should come.'

But, surely, whether this presentational thing was done by a principal or a permanent secretary, it was still a deception on the public? 'The government of the day won't get the policies through otherwise. It's the job of the Civil Service to serve the government of the day. Civil servants have to realise they are doing a professional job and it's only if there is a clear perversion of the truth that they stand up to be counted. There's no intention to deceive with premeditated malice. It's like drinking brimstone with honey round the rim of the cup. Obviously lots of messages that the government has to put across are fundamentally disagreeable. If you put a good gloss on them they are more likely to get them through.

'If you go back to the Roman coinage you will see that Caesar and Augustus struck their coins to present themselves in the best possible light. Caesar used his coinage to get all sorts of messages across like plenty and peace when there was bloody war going on.'

Some civil servants are so attuned to routine economies with the truth they scarcely question them. One former researcher commented: 'Some study gets reported in the media and the private office asks for a briefing so the minister is prepared at question time. It comes down to you and if you're a bright little civil servant you know what the minister wants so you find the piece of good news instead or you rubbish the methodology of the research, which you can do with *any* piece of work. You do it because you want to get on and be noticed and feel worthwhile, which is very human and I was thoroughly overcome by it. Once you're there nobody is so strong they can just stand out against what everyone else is doing. It's routine; you get so used to it you just don't see it as corruption.'

Another official said: 'One might be troubled by it but it's so deep at the heart of the system you can't do anything about it without a change in the system. Serious morality is indivisible but petty morality is divisible. I know that working for the government is going to involve lots of little moral compromises. I've felt uncomfortable but I've accepted that it's a product of the way Civil Service and government is structured.'

Just as worrying to some is the tendency to give ministers only the facts they want to hear. A civil servant said: 'It happened on the rents to mortgages proposal which was something Mrs Thatcher was pushing for several years. Ministers got honest advice from officials to the effect that they couldn't do it. They came back and said, "But we've got to offer the PM something." So it went off to the PM in the form that we would proceed with an experiment, backed up by an estimated take-up at 300,000 to two million people, whereas privately officials would say 300,000 was the absolute maximum over 10 years. Officials are now helping ministers make public statements to that effect. In a sense, telling untruths about the future doesn't matter because it's anyone's guess; telling lies about the present or the past is far more important.'

If they are being candid, officials admit that self-interest lies behind such self-censorship, although they also make a pragmatic calculation based on the degree to which the minister's mind is already closed. One senior civil servant said: 'There have been a fair number of occasions where cheap decisions have been made and I and colleagues have asked ourselves how far should we go in advising against them and risking the minister's good will. Sometimes we do give that advice but not always. You are put under subtle pressure; it gets to be known that this is the view of Number 10 or what the minister wants and if there is a sense of corruption around it is the way this gets to be known which is troubling. The pressure is for self-censorship.'

So how did this official feel on those occasions when he had bitten back neutral advice? 'Miserable. There have been occasions when I have distanced myself in public from the policy. It is done fairly subtly and sometimes it is difficult to understand the code I use but at least I know I have done it. It cannot be in the public interest that civil servants should be moral neuters. That makes it easy for totalitarian governments in the last resort but far beyond that point the quality of government administration has to be something that commands the confidence and commitment of those who carry it out if it is to be administered successfully and honourably.'

The culture of secrecy in itself perpetrates deception, too. Robin Robison worked for the Joint Intelligence Committee, which administers the world of espionage, and helped service the PSIS, the committee of permanent secretaries that oversees their expenditure, the so-called 'secret vote'. 'The JIC doesn't officially exist; we were asked to tell lies about what we did to relatives and friends. We were supposed to say we were working for the Cabinet Office in foreign affairs. It wasn't strictly a lie but it wasn't near enough the truth for my liking. The public isn't told the PSIS exists officially but it's powerful, it takes public expenditure decisions on behalf of the nation by unelected officials; they're supposed to report to the ministerial intelligence committee but that only meets infrequently.

'It's a deception on the public; the pretence is that there's no real expenditure and it's never talked about in Parliament. We're not allowed to tell you the terms of reference of the Cabinet committees, who sits on them, what their deliberations are. Often they are taking key decisions about what is happening in our country without any reference to our legislature or the Cabinet. To me that's a massive deception.'

Like others, however, Mr Robison felt there was no one in the Service to whom he could take his concerns. 'I knew in the JIC there was no point in talking to the people above me. They all believed passionately in what they were doing. And I would never have spilled the beans about, say, the IRA; I'm not in the business of putting people in jeopardy. They knew that so they trusted me. On the other hand it made me profoundly uneasy. They knew I was unhappy and said they would move me. I was being paid to do a job and I had to do it while I was being paid.

'Some intelligence officers and senior civil servants were quite thoughtful but they had been in it too long, steeped in blood too much. It was easier for them to go on than turn back, people with high mortgages and so on. And I don't think any of them were bad people at all. I got on with people I worked with very well. On a human level I had no problems but I got more and more uncomfortable. Either you resigned straight away or you just put up with it. It was easier to stay in, one had to pay the rent, it was a slow process; I'm as human as the rest of them. There was a feeling that it was really rather pleasant to be privy to what was going on. A rather silly feeling of power, seeing minutes no one else ever sees, seeing JIC minutes which very very few people ever hear about. You're leaving behind something rather special, walking past ministers in the corridor. It's the seduction of power, but because of deeper principles I found it repugnant. There was a series of things, a sense that I wasn't in the right place.'

Sir Humphrey says no one who has a moral problem is penalised; the junior ranks disagree profoundly. They say that if they complain and ask for a transfer they lose their chances of promotion and that those who do get promoted, the high-fliers, are people who manage to combine ability with robust consciences. (To which Sir Humphrey retorts that this is a predictable justification of incompetence.)

Those who do raise ethical objections with their superiors say they often come up against a wall of incomprehension. An official said: 'Your permanent secretary himself is deeply and inevitably implicated in the instructions you've been given. If you approach him, he's thinking about his own relationship with the minister and will say, "Don't worry about it," and try to suppress it. The inclination of most top officials is not to ignore issues of conscience but to try to minimise, to say to people, "Isn't it easier just to get on with it?" and most of the time it is. It's almost impossible to maintain an individual ethic of serving the public good in practice. So many of these things are questions of degree and that's why people get drawn half-way in before they are prepared to admit this is a matter of conscience, how did I get drawn so far in, how can I explain it to ministers or senior officials who are almost bound to say, "Is what you're now making an issue of so fundamentally different from what happens all the time?"'

In the enclosed world of Whitehall, insulated as it is from real life and from the consequences of the political decisions it processes, there is an assumption that it's all just a game they're playing. Economies with the truth are justified because officials think no one really takes it all seriously. It's politics as theatre, and officials shelter behind their masks. One said: 'With parliamentary questions and select committees, it's misleading to think of it like giving evidence under oath in a court of law. It's all play acting, a bit of a charade, people realise it is and there are these conventions that govern the way it's done.'

The Quakers are so concerned about standards of integrity in the Civil Service that they've set up a research project under Robin Robison. 'The laws we apply to ourselves at a personal level must apply at a professional level too,' he said. 'Truth is indivisible. We're all party to white lies; that's what government is doing to us, we're dealing in lies in your interest.'

One of the statisticians said: 'There's been a whole change of culture in the civil service. But is your duty to your minister or to your country? I consider my loyalty lies to my country.'

Another put it more starkly: 'We'd have a far healthier democracy if officials were able to take a more honest and open public stance. Clearly, we're not in the situation of the German civil service in the Thirties but if we accept what we now accept we won't know where to stop.'

13 March 1991: Melanie Phillips

A House built on shifty sand

Off to the Palace of Vanities at Westminster to discover whether it is possible to be a politician and not be a creep. Do MPs *have* to tell lies all the time? Do they *have* to betray their principles in order to get anything done at all? Do they *have* to double-cross colleagues in the pursuit of personal gain? Or is this shabby picture of preening ambition and deceit all got up by the media?

Confront politicians with the public's opinion that they are almost as awful as journalists in being shifty, untrustworthy, mendacious, sharp-practiced, ruthless and generally a disgrace to a civilised society and they all smile sadly and nod their heads. Ask them whether they are any of these things themselves and they almost all assure you that they personally are pillars of integrity, that they would never tell a lie or betray a colleague or mislead the public.

The Tories tend to be far more pragmatic than their Labour colleagues, who agonise more frequently over conflicts between principle and compromise. Yet Mrs Thatcher's Cabinet retained dissident ministers who had to be sacked rather than resign. One of these, Sir Ian Gilmour, who was ousted in 1981, explained why he had remained on the payroll of a government whose policies he found abhorrent: 'I thought the whole thing would get much better once it came into conflict with the facts but after a bit one had abandoned that hope. Looking back, I certainly should have resigned. I don't feel guilty about not having done so; I just think it was rather incompetent. You are in a stronger position if you resign rather than if you are sacked. I can't remember what brought me into politics, although I seemed to have some good ideas at the time.'

The great diehards of principle are generally to be found in the Labour Party. One thinks of Eric Heffer, whose refusal to compromise has sustained him in a kind of self-immolated moral grandeur on the back benches. 'I don't know whether you can do more on the back benches, all I know is that you can live with yourself,' he said. 'As Shakespeare said, to yourself be true, and if you can't be true to yourself you can't be true to anyone else.'

Or there's Peter Shore, who refused to shut up over multilateral disarmament or opposition to the EEC and who has paid the price for his consistent opposition to party orthodoxy by being marginalised on the back benches and harried by his constituency party.

Or there's Frank Field, making light of his sacking as Opposition social security spokesman over refusing to abstain in the vote on the GCHQ union ban and who has been physically sick before standing up to enemies in his Birkenhead constituency party who are determined to get rid of him.

But there are Tory dissidents too. Both Emma Nicholson and Richard Shepherd have felt the chill winds of disapproval for speaking their minds. Ms Nicholson, in particular, has taken a lot of stick for speaking out strongly against the poll tax and in favour of Mrs Thatcher standing down. Since becoming an MP, she said, she had found herself questioning her moral boundaries all the time and having to take responsibility for her decisions – like voting through the poll tax and admitting now that she made a mistake.

'It was difficult because it was pointing the finger at my own team, and in our divided political culture you're either on one side or the other. The poll tax became all bound up with the might and majesty of the PM. It made it infinitely more difficult for me because it meant I was setting my judgement against hers. It's commonly perceived as a virtue to stick to someone through thick and thin. But the Charge of the Light Brigade always seemed to me to be a mistake. I had no feeling of disloyalty because I'd realised some months earlier that my principles and the needs of my constituents meshed.'

Neither Ms Nicholson nor Richard Shepherd have yet been offered office. Both would like it, although Mr Shepherd talks with distaste of the 'frenzy of patronage' at Westminster and conceded that this posed a problem he had never properly thought through. He could never have bowed to collective ministerial responsibility over the Official Secrets Act, for example: 'When they strike something deep down in your sense of balance, undermine your sense of what is good or right, then there is no way they would drag me into a division lobby to support them.'

It's the compromisers in politics who find it difficult to talk publicly about the deals they've made with the devil.

The classic Labour Party justification is that even the worst Labour government is better than the best Tory government. One member of the Shadow Cabinet, who asked to remain nameless, confessed to serious doubts about his party's economic policy. He was worried that the party was now too close to the City and if Labour came to power public services would suffer while those who controlled the assets would prevail. 'I can argue in the Shadow Cabinet but I can't speak out publicly. I'm not sure what Neil Kinnock thinks because he says different things to different people, so there's enough for me to hang on to. People have said to me, "Why aren't you speaking up?", so I constantly have to decide: do I respond to that by speaking up and doing damage to the Labour Party and its chances of winning the next election or by living to fight another day on the issues that are important? To some degree in opposition you are play-acting.'

But wasn't he helping create public cynicism? 'I do worry about that. Part of the answer is that you get the politics you deserve. We've got ourselves into a situation where the smallest scintilla of a difference of opinion is a defeat. And that distorts public debate. You have to be pretty morally brave not just to take that on but to say, "I can attract all the attacks on my party for being disunited but my judgement is that we can take all that and emerge the stronger."'

This politician had attacked the Tories over their hostility under Mrs Thatcher to the EC, even though he is a long-standing anti-marketeer. 'You may think this is dishonest but I don't; I was able to do and say things I believed in by attacking the Tories for being divided. I was therefore able to be true to my own position by simply not mentioning it. If I had been asked I would have been uninformative, but I wasn't.'

Roy Hattersley, Labour's deputy leader, has elevated pragmatism into a moral force. It was Mr Hattersley, after all, who was once reported as saying: 'Pragmatism is not a squalid compromise; it is an expression of high ideals.' But he now winces at this quote and says: 'It was probably an attempt to be clever without much meaning.' For Mr Hattersley now believes less in compromise than he once did, as he says in his 1987 book *Choose Freedom*, and all because of Mrs Thatcher. 'I think winning elections nowadays requires a very clear ideological profile. If you tried to win elections in the way Wilson won by pragmatism you'd have great difficulty.'

But hang on: Mrs T. has been replaced by a man who is the epitome of pragmatism – no one knows what he stands for. So it would seem that Mr Hattersley, having made the pragmatic decision to junk pragmatism for ideology, may now have to be even more pragmatic and bring it back again. This would probably mean writing yet another book.

Mr Hattersley now bitterly regrets not having resigned from government when Labour passed the Immigration Act, which broke its promise to the East African Asians. This, he says, was a great betrayal. However, speaking out against party policy on unilateral disarmament earned him no Brownie points. 'I now realise it would have been much better for me personally if I'd announced my conversion every time the party changed its policy. I used to have terrible rows on the radio with Robin Day because one was breaking the convention that one did not speak out while keeping office.'

Why is it, though, that the first law of politics appears to be to pretend that black is white? 'The gravest danger for the politician is that if he fudges things for the general public he will fudge his own mind,' said Norman Tebbit. 'You have to be able to go back home and if you wake up at three o'clock in the morning and look at the ceiling you have to be quite clear that even if you let people mislead themselves over something you haven't misled yourself over it. At times you are bound to say things that are untrue. If you are asked if you agree with government policy as a minister you say yes, of course you do, even if you've opposed it tooth and nail.'

Politics is a rough world where loyalty and friendship and honesty get trampled in the rush for self-advancement. It disgusts Labour's Bryan Gould: 'Before I got to the senior reaches of the party people would say to me, "Politics is such a dirty business," and I would say, "What are you talking about?" But within the last few years I've seen what they meant. People are machine-politicians; it's all about wheeling and dealing and back-stabbing, and it sounds rather prissy but I very strongly disapprove and so far as I can I try not to do that.'

But there's one junior minister who, although wishing to be unnamed, doesn't just admit it's a dirty business but exults in it: 'I suppose I am somewhat reckless and I enjoy politics for the spills and the kicks. I quite like the deception and hypocrisies and panics: it is voyeurism, the degradation of it, an art form in itself.

'One gets cynical and there's an internal thing in everyone. It's Darwinian, I suppose. People who don't keep up with the herd get killed. Personal friendships here don't matter a toss. You say, "Frightfully bad luck, old boy, I do sympathise and we must try to do something; I'll have a word with the Chief Whip." But you don't really unless you think he may (a) come back later or (b) he has something he can let you have. The satisfaction lies in winning, in kicking people when they are down. Running a constituency is a bit like being a District Commissioner: you can't have all the tribes coming against you, you've got to have some on your side by encouraging them to pick upon each other. Most of the time I treat it all as a game, although many pretend to be much more serious. But you'd be driven mad if you didn't do it for the sport. It's a hellish life.'

13 March 1991: Melanie Phillips

Sour sweeteners

Lord Young is a devastated man. Hypocrites, he believes, have unjustly robbed him of his good name. He has seen his reputation laid waste by the report of the Select Committee on Trade and Industry, which took the former Trade Secretary apart over the Rover sell-off to British Aerospace. It said Parliament had been seriously misled, the gravest of all political crimes; the Department of Trade and Industry should have told both the committee and European Commission the full details of the deal, including the financial sweeteners it threw in to persuade BAe to buy Rover. When these were eventually disclosed, Sir Leon Brittan, Vice-President of the European Commission, told BAe to pay back more than £40 million as the payments had broken European law because they were state aid that should have been disclosed.

To Tory MPs, Lord Young is a bounder who has broken the rules of the club. 'Our system depends on our knowing that ministers are not lying to us except where lives are at stake in a war,' said Richard Shepherd. 'Lord Young overthrew constitutional principles. And he went on television and said he would do it all again!'

Norman Tebbit, himself a former Trade Secretary, stoutly defended his former Central Office adversary: 'Lord Young was absolutely right in what he did.' It was a dilemma that was occurring more and more. To Mr Tebbit, given the choice between saving British jobs and breaking European law, there was no contest. 'What do you do as a minister?' he said 'Let's take a shipyard where they could get an order for a series of ships to keep several thousands of men in work but could only do so by using the regulations of the European Community to the limits of their flexibility. Do you expose the fact that these limits have been gone to, and maybe in the judgement of some people gone beyond, and see the French take the order? Or do you stand there, Simon-pure, saying "I must tell Parliament exactly how far we've gone"? Rather than risk frightening the folk from Brussels and cause an argument you would be confident of winning in the longer run but which causes the order to be lost, you may decide that Parliament doesn't have to have every last detail.'

Wasn't this misleading Parliament? 'I don't think there's any doubt in my mind that anybody who holds ministerial office has given replies which might leave the questioner to come to a wrong conclusion. Parliament must not be told a direct untruth but it's quite possible to allow them to mislead themselves.'

In his chairman's office at Cable and Wireless, Lord Young indicated this support was about as welcome as a hole in the head. Gone was his normal ebullience; he was shaken and upset. Norman Tebbit had missed the point, he said, and the Select Committee just hadn't understood: as far as he was concerned, he had done nothing illegal or dishonest. He had not knowingly broken European law because it was not clear that the sweeteners were state aid and thus had to be referred to the European Commission. The European Court had still to rule on this very point and he had been advised by his DTI officials that it was entirely a matter of individual interpretation and definition.

He had been under enormous pressure. It was July 1988: BAe was playing difficult and Lord Young, as the Select Committee agreed, was in a poor negotiating position. Referring the sweeteners to Brussels would have delayed a decision until the autumn. He considered it essential to get the deal agreed before the car number-plate change in August which hugely boosts motor sales; Rover had told him that if it wasn't settled by the end of the month it wouldn't survive. 'There was no way I was going to see 200,000 jobs disappear,' he said. He contacted Peter Sutherland, then the European Commissioner responsible for competition. 'I said I didn't believe this to be state aid and this is what I was doing. He said, "I don't want to hear this but I understand."

'I started out as a solicitor. There is no way I would have done this if I thought these were illegal payments. If they had told me this was state aid I would have had to refer it to the Commission. I would have been in real trouble. When my officials told me it was a matter of definition I breathed a deep sigh of relief. It was classed as an illegal payment by Leon Brittan but he was pushed because otherwise he would have been heavily criticised by the French and Germans.

'We disclosed everything to the House. I told them the payments would be deferred pending the resolution of tax difficulties. We cleared everything in the estimate. We disclosed everything in every particular to the Public Accounts Committee.' But the Select Committee had criticised these disclosures as 'disingenuous' and accused the DTI of seriously misleading it by failing to tell it the full terms of the deal. 'There was no way I could disclose to the House the minutiae of a very complex deal. They were the small details, irrelevant.' Moreover, he added, the Select Committee had criticised the DTI for misleading it after he had left office. The Trade Secretary for that period had been Nicholas Ridley; why hadn't Mr Ridley been accused of misleading the House?

'I was subjected to a number of leaks from the Select Committee for a year, all of them wrong, in your paper and others, before the report was published. But I suppose I am fair game. The report was the worst day of my life apart from the day my brother died. It was a moral dilemma but I was able to satisfy myself I had a way through. That's why I said I would do the same thing again. I was accused of having the morals of a barrow-boy. What's wrong with barrow-boys?

'My reputation is now gone. I suppose it serves me right

for going into public life. Everyone in the business world understands what I did; no one in politics understands.'

7 March 1991: Leader

The secret high street

Who says the Nanny State is dead? There yet remains one area of administration where ministers insist that government rules OK. Eleven years of radical change have not moved them one inch on the public right to know. The same arguments that were trotted out a decade ago are still being used today: Joe Public wouldn't understand too much highly technical information; or he would misinterpret it; or providing the full facts would be too expensive and time-consuming. The *Guardian* has campaigned long and hard for a freedom of information act. But is it worth applying such principles to routine administrative business? Absolutely. Even at a mundane level, as the Consumers' Association notes today in its latest *Which?,* this is important. And, beyond, lives are being put at risk.

At the mundane level, take the public services which still enjoy a monopoly. Will British Gas tell you how often they fall short of fitting a gas cooker within five days of receiving an order? They will not, even though the five-day limit was set by the company. Does British Rail disclose compensation details about the passengers it has let down? It does not. Do you know how long you will have to wait, on average, at a Post Office counter? The Post Office does, but refuses to disclose its queue monitoring reports to the public on the grounds of 'commercial confidentiality'. Similarly, like British Gas and British Rail, the Post Office declines to provide the Consumers' Association with a breakdown of the complaints it receives. They 'would not be meaningful.'

There are more serious issues, however. Food and transport, as the report notes, are just two areas where lives have been lost because government and industry shelter behind official secrecy. Official reports, which were either never published or only given the most limited circulation, have pointed to the potential dangers of three recent disasters before they occurred: the sinking of the *Marchioness* in 1989, the Clapham Junction railway crash of 1988, and the Bradford football stadium fire of 1985. Two years after the Zeebrugge ferry disaster, the Department of Transport produced new stability standards. Several existing ferries fell short. Were these ships named? Unbelievably, they weren't at the start. The names were withheld on grounds of 'commercial confidentiality' until pressure groups, MPs and the media made a fuss.

There are similar stories in the food world. Health warnings about listeria were delayed; none of the abattoirs which failed to meet EC hygiene standards were named by Ministry of Agriculture officials; and although the safety studies on food additives are no longer secret, access to them is still strictly limited.

A freedom of information act would ensure that officials could not automatically plonk a hermetically-sealed lid on their secrets. There would be a public interest test on commercial confidentiality. Consumers would be allowed to decide for themselves. The minister, like Nanny, does not always know best.

20 March 1991: Peter Hetherington in Scotland

Can't pay, won't pay, and don't exist

Peeping behind the security grill on the liquor counter in

Gindha's grocery store, where the outer shutters remain permanently closed, the trader smiles broadly when the poll tax is mentioned. His customers, he says, have a simple priority – survival. They struggle and borrow to buy food, pay the rent and electricity, if they're lucky, and the tax just doesn't figure in any family budget – especially when it's likely to be scrapped. 'Many of them just don't officially exist any more. Gone to ground. You can't really blame them.'

Wheeling their young daughter, Alex and Norma snigger when the issue is raised. The poll tax now provokes dismissive laughter as well as ridicule. 'No one can afford it. They've got other priorities – food, heating, clothes for the kids. Some were registered – but no longer – while others didn't bother.' Alex has decided to become a non-person, too, like thousands of other Scots. And 60,000 are said to be dodging both the electoral and poll tax registers, according to one recent study.

Throughout Ferguslie Park, barely half a mile from the centre of Paisley yet a world away from a bustling Clydeside, the story is much the same. It is typical of the large housing estates ringing Britain's towns and cities – 2,400 low-rise houses and flats, built mainly in the 1930s, where around 40 per cent of the adults are jobless, 80 per cent of children receive free school meals and 75 per cent of households qualify for housing benefit.

'Poverty is endemic,' noted a study by the Scottish Office two years ago, shortly before the poll tax was introduced north of the border, a year ahead of England. 'The people . . . live in a depressed environment isolated from the rest of Paisley . . . Ferguslie Park is renowned throughout the west of Scotland not so much for what it is but for what people think it is.'

If the growing non-payment rebellion was confined to estates like Ferguslie, Scottish ministers, architects of the tax (they persuaded sceptical English colleagues to back abolition of the rates six years ago) could at least argue that most 'responsible' adults were keeping within the law. But civil disobedience, if anything, is intensifying. Scottish councils are now owed approaching £600 millions for the first two years of the tax; summary warrants have been taken out against 1.25 million people, a third of Scottish adults; nearly 730,000 cases are now with sheriffs officers (bailiffs).

A system that initially cost £30 millions to implement, with new computers, software and at least 2,000 extra staff, is at the point of breaking down. Poorer tax payers are caught in a deepening spiral of debt, which is seriously depleting council finances. As the charge rises in Strathclyde Region, which incorporates Paisley, partly to cover high non-payment for 1989–90 (14 per cent) and 1990–91 (probably 25 per cent at the last count), more people default, thus forcing even bigger increases. Others are holding back in the thought that the tax will soon be abolished or in protest at the growing non-payment rebellion – an attitude of 'Why should we pay this big increase when others are getting away with it?', according to John Mullin, chairman of Strathclyde finance committee.

Welfare rights workers say residents in Ferguslie Park, under pressure from sheriffs officers, made 'impossible arrangements' for repaying debt, sometimes as much as £20 weekly. With help from counsellors, some managed to reduce this to £2 – although a chaotic collection and administration system, creaking further as non-payment increases, ensures that others have been overlooked by officialdom.

Two young mothers are typical. Janice has not paid and has heard nothing from the council. 'That goes for many. Anyway, they wouldn't dare send the sheriffs officers into here to do a warrant sale.' That's the peculiarly Scottish system of debt recovery under which a defaulter's luxuries can be sold in the home. Janice smiles: 'They wouldn't get a very friendly reception here.' Maria has made a small contribution, after being threatened with a fine, 'but I've heard nothing else from them.'

In Paisley, the new combined regional and district poll tax of £431 (27 per cent up on last year) includes an additional £42 to cover default. Although the region has already cut £75 millions from its budget, John Mullin, himself a Paisley councillor, says that if payment does not improve further multi-million-pound economies are likely as the year progresses.

Another growing concern is the fast-depleting register – posing, Mullin believes, a serious threat to democracy itself. Studies by the Applied Population Research Unit at Glasgow University confirm his worst fears: 60,000 voters have disappeared from poll tax and electoral registers since the tax was introduced in Scotland.

Dr Ronan Paddison, senior lecturer in political geography, says register-dodging is highest on Glasgow's large, peripheral housing estates and in places like Ferguslie Park. But in several inner city seats – sometimes key marginals – researchers calculate that the defending MP could go into the next election at a distinct disadvantage. For instance, in Glasgow Hillhead (Lab majority 3,251) 1,600 electors seem to have disappeared, while in Edinburgh South (Lab majority 1,859) 2,430 have gone. Ayr, the most marginal of all (Tory majority 182) has 'lost' 665. Paddison says such 'very substantial' drops are much higher than he expected.

While Paisley, in Labour's heartland, is unlikely to be rendered marginal by dodging, local councils fear that electors, once 'lost' to the register, will be quite happy to remain non-persons. Their other concern is that a new culture of tax evasion, once born, will prove impossible to eradicate in an area where collection was once regarded as super-efficient. Under the old rating system, after all, 99 per cent of households paid up.

12 November 1990: Peter Lennon

The indiscreet evangelist

In the Church of All Saints, Wrington, Sussex, on All Saints' Day the congregation of 231 was jubilant with joy. Bishop George was amongst them for the first time, telling them that Faith was precisely a matter of dealing with uncertainty; that the Church was always at its best when challenged. The Anglican Church had not had a martyr for a long time – not that he was eager for the role (there was a delighted sound like a deep purr from the predominately middle-aged congregation). He, Bath and Wells, was mindful of the fate of another Bath and Wells who went on to Canterbury only to have his head chopped off (an eruption of laughter which visibly loosened that trance-like posture of piety which afflicts the prayerbook-clutching classes in the presence of their bishop).

The congregation then filed out pew by pew to queue for communion from the hands of the Archbishop of Canterbury elect. Only one sinner remained breached in the pews for all to pretend not to see: an interloping reporter.

'We thought you were his chauffeur,' a parish lady said to me, sweetly offering coffee and biscuits while the bishop at the door shook the hand of every departing parishioner.

In the sunny churchyard the demeanour of the liberated faithful was that of those who have taken a walk in the high hills and are still breathing deeply after a wholesome experience; in this case it was that of sharing the company of their bishop for probably the last time as George Carey heads towards the heights of Canterbury and world renown.

It was a moment when Christian charity could not be denied; so when it was discovered that the Lazarus reporter at the gate had no transport back to his temporary base in Wells, 20 miles away, the vicar declared impetuously that the bishop would be glad to offer a lift.

There was an initial moment of constraint. Since the press conference, following the announcement in July, Bath and Wells has not been speaking to journalists; indeed, his diary had been cleared of most public, including pulpit, appearances, presumably to reduce the possibility of a public utterance reflecting on the incumbent Canterbury. Or perhaps to avoid prematurely giving hostages to the professionals of Church of England politics, lay and clerical, whose rotund oratorical tropes often mask a profane machiavellianism.

There were also the additional hazards of finding oneself locked in a car with a reputedly unrepentant evangelist; one in addition who was supposed to have had what sounded like a spooky experience of 'renewal' at a Toronto charismatic knees-up. Then, being closeted with an allegedly 'Thatcher appointee' is not everyone's idea of a restful Sabbath.

But it came to pass that with Bath and Wells in the back, myself and his chauffeur in front, we fell into animated discourse. By then I knew some things about Bath and Wells that his Wrington congregation probably didn't.

But for a meddlesome brother he might not even be a Christian at all today. The brother Bob, who now runs a language school in Helsinki, told me what happened. Bob, aged 11, having had a religious experience, demanded that the family, including 15-year-old George, should start going to church. This decent East End family winced at the suggestion. What would the Becontree neighbours think!

But the infant evangelist persisted and exacted a promise from his parents that when they next moved house they would assume a new identity as churchgoers. Impatient Christian destiny had them in a new house within a year. It was only a mile down the road in Dagenham but far enough to be out of range of Becontree rhyming slangsters.

Bath and Wells had also, it was reported, come out publicly against the poll tax. 'He is not an open-minded gentleman from the East End for nothing,' the Bishop of Durham had explained to me. So the chances of his being a human being were pretty good.

George Carey left school at 15. His first job was to help ensure the electricity supply for Lambeth. He then did his military service.

As we sped through sunlit Somerset, a prosperous fortress against infection and the hand of war if ever there was one, George Carey recalled with affection the country where he spent most of his military service: Iraq. He told how he had supped with the Bedouin and of his admiration for Arab culture. 'I tried to learn Arabic and regret now not having kept it up,' he said. 'Arabic will no doubt become one of the most important languages in the world.'

He spoke with concern about potential conflict in the Middle East and of his impression that President Bush seemed to be preparing people's minds for war. 'In such circumstances very often an American President is left with very few options,' he said anxiously. They had debated this problem recently in the Church, he said. His stance was that every option of sanctions and diplomacy should be attempted before taking a step which would lead to terrible human suffering. He was concerned too about the unravelling of the Arabic question that such a conflict might bring. He felt that the relationship between Israel and the United States 'will never be the same after'.

His military service in the Gulf was uneventful but for the final week when he had to deal with an emergency landing. The bishop leaned forward from the back of the car and from between gapped teeth said in my ear: 'Dee-dee-dee-da-da-da-dee-dee-dee.'

Was he speaking in tongues?

'The plane came in on one engine,' he explained. 'SOS dee-dee-dee, da-da-da, dee-dee-dee.' George Carey was a wireless operator and guided the plane down by morse code.

The time in Iraq had a direct bearing on his ministry. There was no chaplain out there. He found himself taking over that role. 'Not giving communion,' but leading Bible readings. It was then he had his real notions of ordination. He was 19.

He enjoyed his time in the RAF, and left with the rank of senior aircraftman to resume his education at King's College and the London College of Divinity. He felt military service was a good thing: 'Everybody would benefit from it,' he said.

Did he have a religious experience at a charismatic meeting in Toronto? 'It wasn't a charismatic meeting,' he said. 'In fact it was a rather dreamy little evensong.' They were visiting his sister-in-law at the time. (His wife is a nurse; he has two sons and two daughters.)

What was it exactly, this experience? He explained it was nothing dramatic, rather a feeling of intensification, a deepening of his sense of communion with Christ. He arrived at his experiences of spirituality, he said, by 'a process of thinking and reading'. All of these experiences, his first day in church at Dagenham, Bible reading in Iraq, a sense of renewal in Toronto, were like the experience of a sailor crossing the ocean who from time to time came across a lighthouse.

George Carey is not yet the polished diplomat that one associates with Lambeth. He has only been a bishop for two and a half years. He has a way of talking as if he is quite unaware of his high office. His style is of eager, even urgent enquiry.

'Perhaps I am being indiscreet,' he said, prefacing remarks about how worried he was about the low level of the press today. 'It is almost as if they make up stories deliberately to create mischief,' he said with an air of wonder. 'Certainly on the level of the gutter press.' But he also had in mind an item in a quality Sunday which had reported that while he was principal of Trinity College, Bristol, he had obliged a member of the staff to leave because he was homosexual. 'It made me out to be homophobic,' he said. 'I never dismissed anyone. There were no grounds for that story. No grounds whatsoever.'

He was eager to know what people thought of a book he was reading. *Lies of Silence* by Brian Moore deals with the dilemma of a man obliged to drive a bomb to a Belfast hotel to blow up a cleric while his wife is kept hostage. He seemed enthralled by this moral dilemma and could not wait to discover how it was resolved.

Although his background of self-made man and firm supporter of 'traditional Christianity' must have made it easy for the Prime Minister to accept his nomination, no one who knows him believes that George Carey could possibly be characterised a Thatcherite, at least where that secular creed stands for callousness, greed or self-serving servility.

The speed with which his name emerged from the secretive Crown Appointments Commission sessions was much more a sign of an exceptional unanimity in the Church. The fact that older men – Habgood, Sheppard, Taylor – were passed over is also believed to reflect a will to provide the Church with the continuity that a younger man could offer. Carey will be 55 tomorrow.

An extraordinary range of tendencies in the Church claim him as their own – Catholics, evangelists, charismatics, even the Central Line group (not a brotherhood sworn to uphold a rigid orthodoxy, but a loose federation of Anglican vicars whose churches are adjacent to the Tube's Central Line).

In a remarkable essay contributed to the magazine

Theology two years ago George Carey laid out his position on the three main tendencies in the Church. He favoured a 'revived and renewed catholicism for our times'; he described statements about the death of Catholicism in the church as 'grossly premature'. But inflexible traditionalists were given notice that he could not find 'any real ground for the contention that the enemy of faith is liberalism'. This is why a maverick liberal such as David Jenkins has no reservations about the new appointment: 'If he advances the evangelical cause it will be in a very fair, sober, and sane way,' the Bishop of Durham said. 'He is the sort of man who does not allow one argument to take him over.'

The Rev. Anthony Higton – of the rather rebarbative and chauvinistic Action for Biblical Witness to Our Nation – places the new archbishop 'very definitely in the charismatic movements: healing, prophecy, speaking in tongues'. Higton says Carey's conversion to this strand came in the early 1970s. When vicar of St Nicholas, Durham, Carey had the old rafters painted magenta and green, whipped out the pews and led charismatic guitar sessions. (This is believed to be 'the decade of evangelism' with fundamentalism on the upsurge in Britain as much as Iran.)

But in that *Theology* essay Carey criticised a certain kind of evangelism. 'I owe my very soul to evangelism,' he admitted, but he warned against the kind which is 'too constricting intellectually, too narrow academically and too stifling spiritually'.

Although he has engaged in open debate in his sermons and in his writings – *The Church in the Market Place*; *The God Robbers* – Carey cannot be a very experienced church politician. He was not one of the 24 bishops with access to the House of Lords.

George Carey will be the youngest Archbishop of Canterbury since E. W. Benson in 1883. He will have to preside over two of the most divisive issues in the church's history: the ordination of women and homosexual clergy.

Women's ordination is the most inflammable. Lined up against him are Ecclesia, Church In Danger and Cost Of Conscience. Carey once declared that clergy who cannot accept the eventual ordination of women should 'consider their position'. The Rev. Geoffrey Kirk (Marylebone St Mark) of Cost of Conscience chose to take this as virtually notice of dismissal. 'I am staying on,' Mr Kirk said, 'and that's not a promise, it's a threat.'

The issue of homosexuality also goes deep because it not only involves sex but also disputatious interpretation of the scriptures. Generally speaking, evangelists tend to steer clear of sex and few of their theologians are prepared to say anything from that standpoint. But far from evading this problem Carey is known to be consulting 'widely and in depth' on this issue. He is expected to treat it as a 'human and not a quasi criminal matter'.

In theory George Carey could be at the head of the Church of England for the next 15 years, until he is 70. There will be no easy solutions. He is not a Pope and cannot act from a Curial position. Anglican bishops often look wistfully at the Roman Catholic Church in which what was forbidden one day can become compulsory the next. The archbishop is subject to the Synod, a quasi Westminster model, which many clergy find 'a pain' if they want to get something done. There is a certain restlessness at the fact that bishops cannot even rule on doctrine without interference from lay people.

Although he reads the Bible in Greek for recreation, George Carey is in many ways a plain man. But the debris which plain men with a spiritual mission leave in their wake can often be far from plain. With such contentious issues to settle it will be interesting to see how far George Carey may succumb to the lies of silence which inevitably become the defensive tools of all leading politicians, ecclesiastics included.

10 April 1991: Melanie Phillips

'Twixt Devil and the deep blue sees

Is God desperate to keep his Anglican show on the road? Robert Runcie was and much thanks he got for that when he was Archbishop of Canterbury. He papered over cracks, tried to limit internecine strife, sought to make religion relevant. He thus embodied the central dilemma facing the Church of England. How far should the church compromise, trim, play politics with its principles, for the supposed greater good of church unity or attractiveness to the public?

Surely the religious agenda, founded on absolutes of belief, is not negotiable? On the other hand, hasn't Anglicanism always redefined itself in the light of contemporary cultural pressures, or is that merely to sanitise expediency? Dr Runcie took the pragmatic line, and for that he was denounced. Bland! they sneered. Weak! Vacillating! Ambiguous! Incomprehensible! Selling the divine pass! He thus achieved church unity of a sort: he managed to unite the low-church evangelicals with the high church Anglo-Catholics in loathing of him.

Now the Church of England has a new Archbishop of Canterbury, George Carey, to be enthroned next week. Bland he is not. Ambiguous he is not. Since being appointed archbishop last July, he has stated that: the bishops had agreed not to ordain practising homosexuals (a claim immediately contradicted by the General Synod's House of Bishops); that homosexual practices were a scandal; that the idea that only a male could represent Christ at the altar was a most serious heresy, a solecism (he subsequently apologised and retracted); and that the Church of England resembled 'an elderly lady muttering ancient platitudes through toothless gums'.

So before he has even passed Go he has managed seriously to offend all those who support homosexual priests; all those who oppose the ordination of women; all those who have tried to keep the show on the road until now; and all those who believe that an Archbishop of Canterbury should know the meaning of the word heresy.

Consternation! Church bureaucrats are aghast. They've got an unpolitical archbishop on their hands, a man who doesn't understand the enormous power – more than that, the very *meaning*, heaven help us – of words. The bishops and the clergy are a-twitter. The new chap has already managed to achieve his version of church unity; he has managed to unite the Anglo-Catholics and the liberals, this time, against *him*. 'What we need,' sighs one bishop, 'is Cardinal Hume: someone who looks holy but is actually a supreme politician.'

The great row that has engulfed the church is about its alleged unwillingness or inability to speak plainly the word of God. Here is Dr Carey from the evangelical tradition, the plain speaker who believes in the simple truths of Scripture, who won't fudge or mudge, trim or compromise.

But the Church of England isn't a simple body. It's as riven with factions as the Thatcher Cabinet, or a university faculty, or a Fleet Street newspaper. Unlike Cardinal Hume's Catholic Church, it agonises in public. And it needs a political brain to hold it all together, to unpick reality from fantasy, to understand that each side in its raging controversies lays claim to mainstream Christian tradition. As a bishop remarked, 'Do you want to do good, or feel good?' Do they want to uphold their pure ideals only to watch the factions destructively reduce the church to a federation of sects?

And fantastic these factions are; venomous as the Birkenhead constituency Labour Party on a bad day. Thus evangelicals and some liberals are in favour of ordaining women priests (except that some evangelicals have a serious problem with accepting the authority of women bishops, so that's an ambiguity for a start). This sets them both at the throats of the Anglo-Catholics who tend to be opposed to women's ordination but to be in favour of homosexual priests which the evangelicals are against. Not surprising, say the evangelicals nastily, since so many Anglo-Catholics are themselves homosexual. Homophobes! hiss the Anglo-Catholics. Misogynists! snipe the evangelicals.

On gay priests, the Anglo-Catholics line up with the liberals. Well, all right, with some liberals. The gay lobby claims many of those in the church who denounce gay priests are either gay priests themselves or are spineless liberals who won't stand up to be counted. And no one at all has a kind word for the Bishop of Durham – Inept! they mutter. Publicity seeker! Heretic – though, bafflingly, many critics say there's nothing he says which they find out of order or even that they disagree with; it's just the way David *says* things . . . in sound bites (this through gritted teeth: if it wasn't the church, one might call it jealousy).

The essence of the dilemma is the interpretation of the word interpretation. There are now those who claim that the church has lost its faith in God and replaced it with worship at another shrine: the golden calf of the human intellect. Gnosticism! says Stuart Wilson, vicar of Holy Trinity church in Hoxton, who would declare UDI from his bishop if he ever ordained women. Those who think they know better than the words of the Bible are modern gnostics, people who elevate knowledge above everything else. 'What gets lost is the revelation, the belief of countless Christian people, because once you have put your intellect above all else, you say it doesn't matter what people have believed for 2,000 years: they are wrong. It's relativism. The gnostic doesn't always look for truth: he looks for satisfaction of his intellectual abilities.'

It brings to mind the Bishop of Southwark's complaint to the doubt-ridden vicar Lionel in David Hare's play *Racing Demon* that his parishioners have no idea what he believes: 'Your answer to everything is to say, "Well, it's complex . . ." '

The Archbishop of York wasn't having any of that. Dr John Habgood is the embodiment of the learned, thinking, erudite church. 'All knowledge is ambiguous,' he says. 'We are all in the business of interpreting ambiguous texts.' In other words, to have knowledge *is* to question, to doubt; and if you don't have knowledge, you don't know that this is the way the church has always been: thinking, doubting, adapting.

He jumps from his chair and retrieves a book from the shelves that stretch from floor to ceiling in his study at Bishopthorpe Palace. 'Compromise? It's a debate as old as Christianity.' He turns up the page in Richard Niebuhr's *Christ and Culture*. 'Look, here, five different ways in which Christianity can relate to contemporary culture: it could be against it, it could be embedded in it, transform it . . . You see, it's all here. The trouble is, no one reads books any more. They just don't know people have always thought about this.'

Others agree that those who cavil at compromise as a betrayal of faith display a profound ignorance of the church and its history. One rector says the church was founded upon ambiguity at the Reformation. 'Dr Runcie had a sense of the complexity of things when people think they want to hear, "Nuke the Argies", "Smash the buggers", "Up with the women".

'Archbishops *have* to be enthroned on the fence; that's their proper position in life because our institution is a coalition of various truths in dialogue with each other; and if you start trying to model the Church of England on one load of convictions you're going to unchurch the other lot. A principal responsibility of a bishop is unity, keeping the show on the road.' Upholding truth against error? 'Certainly. That too.'

Off to Hawkwell in Essex to visit the rector, Tony Higton, evangelical scourge of gay priests, the Bishop of Durham and the ecumenical Commonwealth Day of Observance service in Westminster Abbey. 'That extremist,' shudders one church source. Unsurprisingly, Mr Higton doesn't quite see it that way. He thinks he's upholding the true principles of Christian belief which are being betrayed by the liberal intellectuals of the church hierarchy.

Mr Higton is the *enfant terrible* of the General Synod, putting forward motions to outlaw priests who are gay or who don't believe in the virgin birth or the doctrine of the empty tomb. He claims 77,000 people have signed his petition against the Commonwealth service where, he says, the fact that the church allows different faiths to pray to their own gods within the abbey, denies its own belief in the uniqueness of Christ.

'If the church has got rules over important things,' he says, 'it either keeps them pretty definitely or it changes them, but at the moment we seem to be allowing people to throw the rule-book away with no more than a murmur of disapproval. The vast majority of Scripture is self-evidently clear, and those who say it is not are saying it because they don't want it to be clear. The issue is whether you accept the Bible or not. There has never been someone as seriously in error as Durham, who hasn't been required to make a statement of orthodoxy. On a Sunday he affirms belief in the virgin birth and on a Monday he denies it. The man in the street believes this is dishonest, and I agree with him. In trying the middle way the church doesn't take note of history or statistics. Where the church teaches the Bible and believes in prayer, it is growing and attracting people. The churches teaching the liberal line are dwindling.'

But the Archbishop of York says: 'In life there is nothing that cannot be questioned. There are certain forms of the quest for certainty which are immature or even neurotic, and you won't actually grow up unless you recognise what is certain and what is not. Christian and Muslim fundamentalists are similar in social profile and style, and this suggests that we are dealing with a sociological phenomenon and not a theological one. People want the Bible to be treated like the Koran.'

So where does conscience allow the clerical bottom line to be drawn? One bishop confides: 'I've got a doctrine of positive ambiguity. I don't feel lukewarm or woolly or that I'm sitting on the fence. Yesterday I preached at two confirmations. At the one in the morning I was using incense and was dressed in a chasuble and mitre, and I was preaching the language they use. In the evening I was at an evangelist church wearing choir dress: I preached the same sermon but at a table not an altar, and I read the Gospel myself. These priests were from different tribes. And the bishop's job has been to give space to all these tribes. I am not too concerned with what I wear because I understand different clothes carry different symbolism. In the morning it was all focusing on Christ at the altar; in the evening it was focusing on the exposition of the Word, and what I was wearing focused on that. Both these things were right. Christians believe that God looks like Jesus and that's the important thing, not the virgin birth or this bit or that bit.' Not so much Holy Communion as holy chameleon.

But where does all this mature ambiguity leave gay priests? In a ghastly kind of limbo, that's where. The church's position, expressed through the Synod, is that while homosexuality is not in itself sinful, being a given condition, homosexual genital acts are. Tony Higton believes this means that gay priests must therefore either remain celibate or resign, and that the bishops are dilatory in enforcing discipline against them.

Liberal bishops are horrified by his approach and call him homophobic, a charge which Mr Higton strenuously denies. But even liberal bishops are in a terrible twist over the issue because they can only covertly support their gay priests. To do otherwise, they are certain, would grievously offend their congregations.

One bishop says: 'If I interview someone for a job and he says he's homosexual, I say "How do you handle this?" He might say he's celibate, or he has to have physical relationships from time to time but that's a matter for his spiritual director and he repents of them. Another might say he's got a long-standing relationship. This is far less dangerous to the ministry, but from the point of view of the church, because he's not at all repentant, he has to be condemned while the first who repents is not. But from my point of view, the first one is a real danger and the second isn't; but I know I couldn't give either of them public protection. If I were wise I wouldn't employ either of them, but I do have a number of gay clergy. A clergyman's private life is news if it goes wrong, so I need to know to give him protection. Is homosexuality doctrinally wrong? I don't know. I do find a dilemma. If I'm absolutely honest I don't find homosexuality easy to relate to in my guts.

'My dilemma is that the one who has a discreet permanent relationship, if he is exposed it damages the ministry and the unity of the church; but I might be dealing with a devout and pastorally sensitive Christian priest. We'd be a lot poorer without some of these guys. Hypocrisy? It's the way the bishops have always worked.'

More than any other issue, the church is caught on gay priests because it just can't square the circle. It believes that homosexual practices are wrong; yet it also believes that outlawing gay priests would mean a witch-hunt. So it permits covertly what it condemns publicly; it says to its gay priests, 'We'll ignore you, or maybe we'll give you discreet support, unless you go public which will mean a scandal, in which case we will disown you.' Thus it traps them into a life of dishonesty and deceit. How can this possibly square in all conscience with Christian ideals of truthfulness and human dignity?

Dr Habgood cannot agree that it is a deception for a priest not to say he is homosexual. But one gay curate says his whole life is an agonising deception. His bishop ordained him on condition that he kept his homosexuality secret from everyone: from his rector and from his parishioners.

'There is a whole side of me that has to be concealed from the parish in its entirety. Obviously one wants to discuss with one's rector how things are going on a personal level, but one can't. For a bishop to say that it's the clergyman's own business whether or not he is gay is the most massive pastoral cop-out. It's saying, "I am not interested in you personally; I am not interested in your loneliness, and the fact that your same-sex partner has been killed, or whatever." Effectively it means I have to seek my support network outside the parish. You find you have increasingly to work in abstractions. In a pastoral encounter there is no way I can call upon my experience as a gay person and what that means to me, in the light of the faith I am representing, in the same way that a married priest can call upon his experience. I find the more candid people round the parish will make comparison with my predecessor who was married. They will say things like, "You're not as warm as he was, not as approachable." My capacity for living a fulfilled life is fairly massively restricted. You really are very trapped because it comes at you from all sides, the interdependence of your personal and professional life. Having to keep something secret is hideous and ultimately unChristian.'

But what of the still deeper charge against the church,

that it has lost its faith and its way and stands for nothing any more? Dr Edward Norman, formerly Dean of Peterhouse, Cambridge, and now Dean of Chapel at Christ Church College, Canterbury, claims the church is losing its spirituality. For him, gay or women priests are issues of discipline rather than doctrine, and thus relatively minor. The big one is that the church no longer talks about God. The main things that preoccupy the clergy, he says, are the secular issues of the age dictated by pressure groups like Shelter or Oxfam. 'But religion addresses itself to things that don't alter: inherent loneliness, frustrated ambition, marriages that fail, things that are with us always. Often the church's advice could be given by a social psychologist on *Newsnight*.

'Divorce is a sin in the canon law of the church, but there are a number of divorced vicars, and the church has given advice to the Government on reforming the divorce laws. Deals are done in the Lambeth Conference over polygamy and terrorism. One shouldn't be worried about numbers, one should be worried about truth.'

When charged with never talking about God on the telly, the Archbishop of York evinces mild irritation. 'We've been talking about God for the past hour and a half,' he says. Had we? We'd been talking about compromise, religion and culture, the dilemma of gay priests. 'Very often the profoundest truths of life are expressed in prayer and poetry, and in the kind of utterances that run off into silence,' he continues.

'As Eliot says, language breaks in your hand. Chasing after the inexpressible, which is nevertheless rocklike, is the essence of the spiritual search. That is what is meant by having faith in God. Sometimes you have to talk about God in ways which come at a slant because you are trying to find points of communication with people. The Bible comes out of a tumultuous conflict of history, people led on in faith who made terrible mistakes, who were by no means consistent. It's a hugely creative and pretty muddled process. That's very different from the view that God simply decided a set of instructions for human living, and all you've got to do is turn up the right text to get the right answer.

'And now,' says the Archbishop of York, looking at his watch, 'I really do have to go. I must go and preach a sermon. About God.'

He smiled at his own joke.

23 March 1991: Jocelyn Targett

The Lincoln handicap

Four years ago at Lincoln Cathedral in the middle of the fortnightly Chapter meeting, the dean, the Very Reverend the Honourable Oliver Twisleton-Wykeham-Fiennes, dropped his pen. He went to pick it up, but found that his arm wouldn't move.

'Excuse me, Mr Archdeacon,' he said, interrupting the canon on his right, 'I appear to be having some kind of stroke.'

Indeed he was, thankfully a mild and largely painless kind which enabled him to spend a pleasant month or so tucked up in a hospital armchair with a blanket over his lap. Gone was the daily contact with his colleagues in the cathedral and gone too, if not forgotten, were the set-to's, to-do's and no-can-do's, the wearisome political manoeuvring in the chapter which had little to do with God and which, after nigh on 20 years at Lincoln, had done for Dean Fiennes's ambitions, and very nearly his heart as well.

The dean, a man appointed for the grandness of his vision, is the most prestigious man in Lincoln after the bishop. But for all the pomp of his position, he has few clear powers. He is effectively the chairman of chapter meetings, where the day-to-day work of the cathedral is planned and agreed, and where pettiness, pressure and stress are always on the agenda. The dean cannot instruct his canons to do what they don't want to, and if he disagrees with them, they, by a majority of four to one, can out-vote him. It's a job where the antagonisms and obstructions are as regular as matins, life an any-other-business of dispiriting tussles.

Predictably enough, Dean Fiennes's troubles began again as soon as he went back to work. He thought it would be nice to lay down some carpeting under the Sempringham Pots in the retro-choir, cosiness for those seeking Godliness. The chapter wouldn't agree – but the dean got the works department to do it anyway. The Venerable Christopher Laurence, archdeacon, encapsulated the mood of his fellow canons when they found the results of the dean's unilateral act of shagpile DIY luxuriating beneath the big pots: 'Chapter has not taken it well. We shall have it pulled out as soon as we can.'

It was all too much for the poor dean. After another mild heart attack he decided to throw in the towel. 'Early retirement' is what he called it: 'Ousted!' said the archdeacon, with inappropriate glee.

At the farewell party, the dean's verger, Roy, shaved off his moustache, put on a navy silk-satin gown and, sitting on the knee of one of the canons, sang 'Diamonds Are a Girl's Best Friend'.

A new dean was appointed with unusual haste and, like eight centuries of Lincoln deans before him, a brief to sort the place out. Dean Fiennes moved to a little village south of Grantham. 'By the end,' noted the subdean, Canon Rex Davis, without cruelty, 'he was coming to the chapter to get permission to go to the loo.'

Lincoln's new dean, formerly Provost of Bradford, came with a formidable reputation for being pettier than thou. He once sacked the Brown Owl of Bradford's Brownies, 17 years in the job, for reading a book during his sermons.

He dismissed Dean Fiennes's work at Lincoln as 'gimmicky – rushing around the cathedral on motor bikes and bringing in jazz bands: none to do with God, in my mind.' And he described his predecessor's burdensomely baroque name as, 'Great – if you want that sort of handle' (he doesn't, and hasn't got it: his name is Brandon Jackson).

Dean Jackson emphasises that he is a working-class city kid and a northerner to boot, a first-generation graduate not like the aristocratic, Old Etonian Fiennes, second son of a baron.

When he moved to Lincoln in the spring of 1989, Dr Jackson chose not to live in the old deanery. 'Oliver was brought up in a castle, so he was accustomed to living in a great big baronial mansion with enormous rooms. I don't want to have anything posh and slick.' He is a young 56, leggy like a wolf, with been-to-bed hair, and like all evangelicals, he's keen on the drama of his conversion: Dean Jackson realised he must be a Christian when he stopped cheating at school.

When first approached for the Lincoln job, Jackson wrote to Robin Catford, the Prime Minister's appointment secretary, turning it down. Being Low Church, he couldn't in all honesty countenance the flounce and fluster of cathedral liturgy. But he promised to pray hard for God's guidance in this as in all matters, and would ask his wife, Mary, to pray as well.

Catford responded by informing Jackson that Lincoln was the Prime Minister's home diocese and that Mrs Thatcher herself had taken a personal interest in his appointment. Such information, Catford supposed, might be interpreted by the Jackson family as a message from the Lord.

The Prime Minister, Jackson learned, had heard all about the dean-baiting and back-biting at Lincoln Cathedral from friends who still lived in the vicinity, particularly (in Dean Jackson's own plainspun recollection) 'two very influential biddies': Professor Kathleen Major, once the principal of St Hilda's College, Oxford, and Margaret Wickstead whose father, 40 or 50 years ago, gave Thatcher the Latin schooling she needed so that she too could go up to Oxford.

After that, Brandon Jackson quickly wrote again, telling Catford that he'd received God's calling to Lincoln and that he'd be only too pleased to be the new dean. 'There'll be blood on the carpet before he's finished,' the Prime Minister is said to have muttered with dark mischief, mindful perhaps of Jackson's run-in with Brown Owl.

Word of Margaret Thatcher's approval of Jackson sent a shudder of unease through the chapter house. Canon Davis, the subdean, who sweetly boasts of his skill as a manipulator of people, thought it worth paying Jackson a visit before he'd left Bradford, just to let him in on how chapter decisions were made at Lincoln, and to emphasise that the dean is merely *primus inter pares*.

So, after evensong, over bread and cheese in the provost's kitchen, Canon Davis kindly informed his new dean that, actually, he would soon find out that he had less power in the running of the cathedral than the four canons. They were used to getting their own way and were bedevilling when they didn't. Ask Dean Fiennes.

Dean Jackson had been warned about Canon Davis. His Lincolnshire informants had spelled out that Canon Davis was wily, sharp-witted and dangerous and he'd been told that Davis only got the job of subdean after making a gentleman's agreement to leave inside five years; that was in 1977. Davis's name had also cropped up in conversation at Downing Street.

The dean quickly formed the opinion that if he could out-smart Davis he would be able to contain the rest of the chapter. He recalled all he'd heard about the subdean, and he looked up the entry he'd made in his diary the night he'd met him in Bradford. It confirmed that the picture he'd been given of his adversary fitted with his own impressions. He knew that Mrs Thatcher expected changes . . . and he decided, before he'd even held a chapter meeting, that Canon Davis was going to be one of his biggest problems.

Two days after that first chapter meeting, a blustery affair to which we shall return, the subdean popped round to see Dean Jackson at his temporary home, 23 Minster Yard, a pretty but modest Georgian cottage in the shadow of Lincoln Cathedral's grim Norman west end. It was tea-time, but Canon Davis ascertained that he was not going to be served tea by his new dean. This upset him: since he's not English himself (he's Australian), he considered the tealessness very unEnglish.

'Now, Brandon,' said Canon Davis, with that slow, suspicious impersonation of chumminess some clergymen affect, 'are we going to hit it off or what?'

Dean Jackson reminded Canon Davis of how they had got along at the time of the dean's installation a week or two earlier: Jackson, in line with his evangelical leanings, had requested that it be a low key affair – but the canons, disregarding his wishes, went and phoned Lincoln's parish churches and rounded up their thuribles, the swinging incense shakers, so that all of huge Lincoln Cathedral was cloying with the heavy-duty floweriness of Anglo-Catholicism. This contrariness, said Dean Jackson, was at best mischievous and at worst, wicked. (Canon Davis, somewhat taken aback, told the dean that the chapter were innocently trying to revert to twelfth-century processional custom.)

Dean Jackson then filled Canon Davis in on the substance of his various conversations with 10 Downing Street, said he knew he was a 'wrong 'un', and made hearsay accusations about his secular life. He told his subdean that he knew he'd only got his job on condition that he'd leave by 1982, and he said he'd looked up the correspondence between Dean Fiennes and the then Bishop of Lincoln which suggested they were anxious for Davis to move on to a new job somewhere else. Canon

Davis retorted that he'd consulted his solicitor about that and had been assured that the gentleman's agreement was not legally binding. ('Unless you're a gentleman!' chimed the dean.)

The Reverend Canon Davis informed Dean Jackson that he'd been brought up in the slums of Sydney, and that he was a born street fighter. The dean informed the canon that he'd been a schoolboy champion boxer, and asserted that a good boxer would always beat a good fighter. He then said that he thought he and Canon Davis should pray together.

Both men clasped their hands. Canon Davis bowed his head and closed his eyes. Dean Jackson, as is his manner, raised his face to the ceiling. The dean spoke an evangelical prayer about casting out the Devil and then asked Canon Davis to leave. Canon Davis said hold on; he hadn't prayed yet.

The two men assumed praying positions once more, the dean's eyes up, the subdean's down. If, by now, Dean Jackson had thrown down the gauntlet, Canon Davis was about to pick it up: instead of a prayer, he feigned a trance and, as if the spirit was using his body as the channel for a divine proclamation, he started speaking in tongues, making solemn, outrageous fun of the dean's charismatic evangelism. He spoke nonsense, but it meant war.

This was in June 1989. The previous year, Canon Davis had taken Lincoln's copy of the Magna Carta off to his homeland, Australia, on a six-month fund raising trip. He also took his wife, Caroline, his 25-year-old daughter, Sarah, her friend Rachel Johnson, and his colleague, Mrs Jo Brogden, the managing director of the cathedral shops.

In Australia, he appointed a cousin to co-ordinate PR and another relative to organise volunteer help. Unfortunately, the Davis family, friends and Magna Carta failed to raise many Australian dollars for Lincoln's needy coffers. In fact, their fund raising sojourn set the Cathedral back £56,075.

It was Magna Carta's first time in Australia, although it had been abroad on similar missions many times before. Travelling with it had been one of Dean Fiennes's passions. He'd taken it to America on several occasions, the first in 1976 to commemorate American independence as part of a display organised by the Standard Chartered Bank. This four-week stopover netted Lincoln donations of over $1 million, thanks largely to the skill of the bank's promoter, an earnest, almost invisible young man with an arid idiom – the 34-year-old John Major.

Lincoln was a famous name in America even before John Major and the Magna Carta – it's the capital of Nebraska, a president, and a long shiny limousine. In Australia, as Canon Davis found to the cathedral's cost, no one had ever heard of Lincoln. Set up in its own dressy pavilion alongside the Vatican's at the 1988 World Expo in Brisbane, an exhibition visited by nearly a million Australians, Lincoln's Magna Carta attracted donations equivalent to £938. When the six months were up, this was paid into Sarah Davis's personal bank account in order, said Canon Davis, to avoid it getting swallowed up by the World Expo authority's expenses. She then passed it over to the cathedral when she got back to Britain.

Before he'd left Bradford, Brandon Jackson had been tipped off about the Brisbane debacle; indeed, his contacts had led him to regard the loss of money as suspicious. He was drawn to the conclusion that his adversary's handling of World Expo '88 was either inept or corrupt. Either way, Davis stood to lose when the financial details of the Australian mission came to light.

At his first Chapter meeting in Lincoln, in June 1989, Dean Jackson demanded, with Thatcherian brusqueness, to see the accounts of the trip. Canon Davis, taken off guard, prevaricated – they were unavailable, he hadn't seen them yet himself.

Actually, although they had yet to arrive in Lincoln from Australia, he knew they must be pretty disappointing (though not incriminating), and that as treasurer of the cathedral funds as well as the Brisbane venture, they reflected poorly on his judgement. For the time being, stalling was sufficient to hold off Dean Jackson's barrage of enquiries – but the absence of any details made the dean more suspicious than ever. He simply couldn't believe that the treasurer was telling the truth when he said he was ignorant of the finances of such an extravagant venture.

By chance, Dean Jackson had overheard his colleagues in the canons' vestry joking about keeping him busy away in the diocese, leaving Lincoln in their hands. The dean soon discovered that the preaching schedule, drawn up in committee by the canons, required him, more often than not, to give his sermons in Lincoln's little parish churches, not in its cathedral.

When, shortly after his installation, he was invited by chapter to spend a fortnight in Canada with his wife and Magna Carta he grew extremely uneasy: it must be a plot. What might they be planning to get up to once his back was turned? He even thought chapter might be trying to buy him off with a fancy foreign trip, and feared that if he went off and enjoyed himself he might live to regret it. So he sent old Oliver Fiennes in his place. Oliver, now in the happiest of health, was only too pleased to be on the stump once more and, in two weeks, he'd earned £600 for the cathedral.

Fiennes's Canadian money prompted Dean Jackson to regard the paltry Australian sum as still more astonishing. He demanded to see papers relating to the business of the Magna Carta Trust. When he was refused these he contacted Magna Carta's accountants and instructed them to forward him details of the World Expo expedition just as soon as they were available. His copy, issued illegally as it happens (Dean Jackson was not a trustee of Magna Carta Australia and so had no right to see its accounts) arrived two months before Canon Davis's legitimate one. It was a juicy, or painful, document, depending on who was reading it.

One Sunday, in October 1989, the dean was giving a rare sermon in the cathedral. He generalised about working with obstreperous colleagues and wrestled with the difficulty of forgiveness. The editor of the *Church Times*, John Whale, happened to be in the congregation and he approached Dean Jackson after the service. He introduced himself and said he had once had a comparable problem. Dean Jackson, surprising Whale with his intimacy, gushed out all his troubles.

Whale assigned a freelance journalist to the case. The dean was most helpful, putting the journalist up, furnishing him with phone numbers and the confidential accounts, as well as garrulous company and fine cognac in the evenings. John Whale ran the story in the issue of 19 January 1990: 'How the Lincoln chapter "burnt its fingers" in Brisbane'. He considered it worthy only of the page nine lead.

After its publication, the four canons called an emergency chapter meeting to discuss what they considered unchurchmanly conduct by the dean. Jackson, they said, had betrayed them and acted outlandishly in leaking a report to the newspapers which he'd no right to in the first place. They considered the article grossly one-sided and announced their intention to complain about it to the Press Council.

By way of answer the dean raised another grievance: word of chapter's plans to send Magna Carta off to New Zealand had reached him. They weren't 'plans', argued Canon Davis nonplussed once again by the dean's debating tactics, they were merely tentative enquiries. Not any more they weren't, said Dean Jackson: he'd contacted the New Zealand authorities himself and told them Lincoln wasn't interested. Magna Carta's jetset, peripatetic lifestyle was over. From now on it was grounded.

In a rancorous discussion, unbecoming but not unprecedented in Lincoln's thirteenth-century chapter house, they still managed to find agreement on one issue: that the canons mistrusted the dean and the dean the canons, and that no one, save perhaps the bishop, could sort it out. That was passed unanimously.

When he was called upon by dean and chapter, Bishop Bob Hardy pronounced himself pleased to be of some pastoral assistance. Until then, he had largely kept out of the way of the infighting, preserving, in public at least, the grace and honour of his position. Privately, however, he had given encouragement and reassurance to his next-door neighbour, the dean, in his overall aims.

In early February, Bishop Hardy wrote asking Canon Davis to supply a number of documents relating to the finances of the Magna Carta Trust, the exact ones in fact that Dean Jackson had been after. Canon Davis informed his bishop that he would not be replying to the request and would be referring the matter to his solicitor.

Pastorally, Bishop Hardy had come a cropper. So he decided to conduct a formal Visitation, a general enquiry into the workings of a cathedral that bishops, every few decades, are free to undertake. He engaged a number of professionals to assist him, notably the accountancy firm Coopers & Lybrand Deloitte, and borrowed recording equipment from the Lincolnshire Constabulary. The Visitation, intended, among other things, to determine once and for all what had become of the £56,075, cost the Church of England £20,000.

Almost immediately, it was delayed. Its legal adviser, an experienced man in the county court and an eminent layman in the cathedral, was suffering extreme stress – a response, some said, to having to deal with this unlikely and distasteful case.

Life in the chapter went on more or less as normal, which is to say riven with squabbles and quarrels. Canon Davis irritated the dean by referring to the cathedral nave as front of house. 'He is not an Englishman,' flapped Dean

Jackson, with working-class brio, 'and he doesn't think like an Englishman. Forever name dropping all the time . . . Peter Palumbo!'

In the spring, the dean got even angrier about the chapter's decision to let one of its properties to what he thought was the wrong sort of people, and later he caused a ripple of amusement beyond the cathedral when he revealed that he thought the Lincoln Imp, a cheeky demon carved into a pillar near the angel choir, had long exercised a satanic influence over the diocese. He said the cathedral would do better without the gargoyle and strongly opposed a proposal that the cathedral shops should stock plastic replicas of it.

Later in the summer of 1990, an exhibition of art was staged in the cathedral, the product of more than a year's planning by Canon Davis and Lincoln's Usher Art Gallery. One of the larger exhibits, sited in the north choir aisle, was a life-size statue of a man, standing upright on a big plinth, his arms by his sides, stark-staring naked and coloured gold.

The exhibition and, in particular, the statue caught the attention of the national press. In one paper, a Catholic nun was moved to write, 'The Golden Man stands poised, serene, one hand at rest, one hand tense, every golden inch of him intent on God. He waits for his divine summons, but he waits naked. And his neat little genitals are as golden, as beautiful as every other part of him.' Dean Jackson didn't agree, and was much affronted by the Golden Man's exhibitionism. He asked chapter to move him to a less conspicuous spot, reporting that the vergers had felt obliged to put a surplice on 'it' so the tourists and parishioners wouldn't be too offended.

Remarkably, chapter concurred with the dean, and the Golden Man was moved. The artist positioned it in the south transept, on the precise stone where Dean Jackson stands to pray, flanked by his canons, before a service. For the next few days, the dean at prayer stood gazing upwards into the mighty crotch of the golden impostor. When he ordered it to be moved again, convinced that the canons were trying to provoke him into over-reaction, the artist withdrew his work from the cathedral altogether. 'It might be all right tucked away in a London gallery,' said the Dean in his triumph, 'but the people of Lincoln are from a very different culture altogether, and it is not my job to expose them to anything that is contrary to Christian faith and practice.'

Down in London the critics were much entertained by Dean Jackson's odd unworldliness and the Golden Man resurfaced at the Tate, where it stood in the main entrance for a year.

This was not Dean Jackson's only dabbling with art appreciation. In the Fifties, the Russell Chantry at the east end of the cathedral had been painted with biblical scenes of a bright, bare-chested Messiah being crowded by a number of happy disciples. The mural, explained Dean Jackson, is by Duncan Grant, an infamous homosexual and, since the model for Christ was one of Grant's lovers, he considered it obscene and inappropriate in a cathedral. So he has kept the little chantry permanently locked. It's not, he said, that he's got a problem with nudity – he plays squash, he says, and often can't help seeing 'the human form undressed' – 'It's just . . . we couldn't possibly afford the heating. And there's rather a nasty step on the other side of the door.'

On 29 September 1990, Bishop Hardy finally emerged with his Admonition, the result of the Visitation. A book-length document, it runs to as many words as it cost in pounds to produce.

It failed to please anyone. Canon Davis was disappointed: the Admonition cleared him of the allegation that he had benefited personally from the lost Magna Carta money, but he feels it did so only grudgingly. Moreover, he found his attitude to the dean roundly criticised, and thought his abilities as Magna Carta's treasurer down under had been belittled. The other canons were disappointed too: they felt their goodwill and integrity had been impugned. Even Dean Jackson, censured for his tactlessness and indiscretion and particularly for leaking the Magna Carta accounts to the press, was disappointed. More than that, he felt betrayed by Bishop Hardy, who, he said, had supported his crusade against the chapter from the first. He considered that the bishop pulled his punches for fear of legal action by the chapter, and so missed an opportunity to get rid of Davis for good. 'I knew I was going to get a bollocking,' said the dean, unrepentantly.

Since then, Bishop Hardy has retreated from the limelight, and is still observing his instruction to remain silent to a hungry media. His Admonition got the dean and chapter nowhere. It put on record what the chapter already knew to be true – that in taking Magna Carta to Australia the canons over-stretched themselves, but not disastrously. Alas, the effect of the Admonition was also to entrench the personal hostility between the dean and the subdean.

The bishop had told the canons what they wanted to hear – that they should work hard at reconciliation with the dean. And three paragraphs later he suggested that the canons resign. Which was what the dean wanted to hear.

Within three months of the Admonition, Sarah Davis, Canon Davis's daughter who'd helped on the World Expo trip, died of cancer after a brief, cruel illness. The subdean and his wife were laid down with grief but, even before her funeral, the police were asking them for back copies of her current account statements so they could check that the Australian money she'd banked in Brisbane was equivalent to the sum she handed over in Lincoln. They were acting, they said, on an anonymous tip-off. Dean Jackson denies being their informant, but the Chapter Minutes refer to a formal statement by Jackson to the police on 13

November – a month after Sarah Davis became seriously ill.

Ten days after that interview, Dean Jackson sent a round-robin to the gentlemen of the chapter, copies to the bishop and the chapter clerk, imploring his four canons to give in and resign.

'We must resolve this one way or another and that right soon,' he wrote in character.

'The only solution is a parting of the ways. I would love most of all to see you, all older than me, find fulfilment, happiness and positive ministry in your final years before retirement. But what can you do and where can you go?'

He then dealt with each canon in turn, beginning with the 65-year-old precentor, Canon David Rutter, 25 years at Lincoln and a stubborn voice of tradition who none the less was in favour of girl choristers.

The Dean wrote: *'There is only one place where you, David, ought to go, if I may say so gently and politely, and that is into residential care where you will be properly looked after. You are a sick man and you are not capable of carrying out the duties of precentor and the cathedral is suffering as a result.'*

Canon Rutter is indeed ill, being diabetic and registered partially blind. 'As blind as he wants to be!' said Dean Jackson; 'He's blind when it's time for evensong, but he can see plenty well enough to trot off for lunch in the White Hart!' Actually, Canon Rutter, who is on sick leave and doesn't give services, had to be driven to the pub, although it's only a quarter of a mile down the road.

'The state of Atherstone Place and now what is happening to Cantilupe,' the dean's letter continues, referring to Rutter's houses, *'is the clearest evidence that you cannot look after yourself. Only a place with professionally trained staff would be appropriate.'*

For his second canon, Canon John Nurser, the 61-year-old Chancellor, of whom the dean speaks most disrespectfully in conversation, Jackson recommended a small parish on the outskirts of the diocese – Colsterworth, actually Oliver Fiennes's village: 'It would be splendid for you to go and be his vicar!' he wrote. 'It's not far from Nottingham, it's on the A1 . . . '

He suggested the third, 61-year-old Canon Christopher Laurence, should surrender his chapter seat so that he might have more time to perform his archidiaconical duties. Then he came to Canon Rex Davis.

Dean Jackson wrote: *'Although there have been calls for your resignation, following the Admonition's findings based on Coopers & Lybrand Deloitte's analysis of Magna Carta Australia, you are clearly determined not to resign. There is no doubt that in any commercial company you would have been forced to resign. But the cathedral is not a commercial operation in that sense. So here you remain.*

'It is no secret that my appointment was not well received by you and that you came to Bradford to make that plain to me. It is also true that I have found it virtually impossible to work with you and feel that you have tied me down by manipulation of the statutes, the chapter, and personnel. Let's face it, we have both found a match for one another: you are not going to give way to me and I am no pushover for you. You are now in a very difficult position. Your wife lives in London, your daughter is gravely ill in London. The police are investigating you and you must feel holed in.

'You may think that if you keep your head down for long enough it may all pass over. It will not. The matter has got to be resolved. It could destroy you and, believe me, I do not want that. You need to get away and London is where you gravitate. You are a city rather than a provincial man. For all your years here I don't see you as a Lincolnshire type of priest or person at all. I don't know what you would do there but there must be scores of livings in London/Southwark dioceses where you could fit

in and do an excellent job and have all your City contacts at your fingertips instead of a day's journey away.'

The letter didn't solicit the response Dean Jackson required, which baffled him. Canon Davis did not do a Golden Man and disappear down to London, and none of the others have shown any sign of budging either. Dean Jackson was even more surprised when the letter came to the attention of the 40-strong general chapter (the senior clergymen in the diocese who do not work in the cathedral) as evidence of his unsuitability for management. It was full of good intentions, the dean said, an honest effort to see the cathedral through the crisis. The general chapter, at an extraordinary meeting called to consider the canons' position, approved Bishop Hardy's first solution, that the dean and chapter seek conciliation, and moved that the canons should not resign. The democratic vote had dashed the dean's hopes once more.

The five men are all now in regular group psychotherapy, where they bicker openly under the illusion that it is doing them good. Dean Jackson is more than ever convinced that Canon Davis is scheming and devious. He thinks conciliation will fail because the therapist does not believe in the reality of evil, which means, it seems, the reality of Canon Davis's evilness. For his part, Canon Davis, upset that he, a churchman of long standing and some repute, should be thought so badly of by a fellow Christian, has come to the conclusion that Dean Jackson is paranoid and suffers from a troubled personality. The canon has given a sermon about his problems of belief: 'I feel rather badly about God,' he told the congregation at morning service one Sunday last month; 'I assure you, in these last months, (my faith) has been in tatters.' He spoke of his 'faithlessness', his 'anger with God', his 'sense of abandonment'.

The wrangling continues, one week over a consignment of tea-towels, the next because the subdean ordered a dog-gate for his house at a cost of £48.06 to the chapter.

And Dean Jackson is still in the habit of passing on second hand gossip about Canon Davis.

Therapy isn't winning. Dean Jackson rather hopes his colleague and enemy will one day be hauled away in a Black Maria; Canon Davis fancifully wishes the dean would, like Canon Rutter, be taken to a place where he can be properly looked after.

They both have nearly a decade to run before they are forcibly retired, so the end to Lincoln Cathedral's embarrassment is not in sight. But the two men still work at it, kind of: every day at evensong, dean and subdean take their stalls in the cathedral and, side by side, divided by nothing but a wall of enmity, they send up their separate prayers in their separate styles to the same God.

Salesmanship

10 January 1991: Roger Cowe

Money down the tube

Crisis, what crisis? If Stanley Kalms and his followers in the press are to be believed, retail gloom is over.

'The new consumer technologies of the Nineties provide major opportunities for Dixons Group,' Mr Kalms announced yesterday. 'We expect the group to make excellent progress as consumer confidence recovers.'

The company's advance publicity in the *Sunday Times* trumpeted: 'Dixons will this week lift the gloom hanging over the High Street. . . . Dixons has been firing on all cylinders since its seasonal rush began at the start of November.'

Um, hang on a minute. Those half-year results ('better than expected') show sales down 11 per cent, profits down 15 per cent and earnings down by nearly a third. And that is by comparison with figures which were themselves down on the year before by 3 per cent, 24 per cent and 11 per cent, respectively. And that year was also down on the year before. In other words, the result is down for the third successive year and profits of £27 million for the latest half-year are barely more than half the peak of three years ago.

Having had their expectations massaged down, and therefore exceeded, analysts are now busy increasing their forecasts for the full year. They now believe Dixons will make as much as £70 million. Which is less than in any year since 1984/5 (before the takeover of Currys) and will leave earnings per share below where it was five years ago.

The group admitted yesterday that sales in the first half (from continuing stores) were down on the previous year by 2.5 per cent in Dixons stores, a massive 10 per cent in Currys high street stores, and 1.2 per cent in the US. Only Currys superstores increased sales.

If that is lifting the gloom, heaven help us all if darkness were to descend again.

The truth is that Dixons and Currys stores in the UK, and the Silo subsidiary in the US, have all made a loss on their basic business of selling cameras, computers, camcorders and the rest. The only reason the group is able to show a profit is because it still managed a profit on property and on selling service warranties.

Of course, that puts Dixons a step ahead of Burton and the others which have been forced to abandon their adventures in property and finance. But it is a miserable basis on which to trumpet recovery. Especially because extended warranties may be in the sort of position credit cards occupied a few years ago.

Then nobody worried too much about enormous APRs, and the credit card companies raked in the profits. But gradually, card holders have realised it is crazy to borrow from the banks at up to 30 per cent interest rates.

It is time buyers of consumer durables got the same message. Paying for an extended warranty on a washing machine or television is money down the tube, as it were.

Don't take my word for it, listen to Dixons: 'Operating profit includes profit of £5 million representing the release of excess provisions for extended warranty liabilities.' In English, that means claims against the service warranties have been even less than Dixons expected.

Mr Kalms is relaxed about the prospect of customers cottoning on to this wheeze. He says if the group doesn't make money on warranties, it will make it on service. But that assumes customers will sign up for Currys' service, rather than using the manufacturers' own (improving) service networks.

And if the service engineers know as little about the products as the sales staff, that is a rash assumption. On the basis of a limited sample of two recent visits, customers will know more about products than the sales staff merely by reading the labels. (Sample conversation: 'What's the difference between these two washing machines?' 'You get a free plastic soap dispenser with this one.')

But Mr Kalms, having helped put many an independent electrical shop out of business and snapped up Currys, is not in an entirely uncomfortable position. He is sitting on market shares of between 20 and 30 per cent in its main product categories (according to the Monopolies Commission, which stopped Comet group Kingfisher buying Dixons last year). Sadly for customers, Dixons has learned not to slash prices simply to get products out of the door, and is therefore making more money on what it can sell.

And eventually business is bound to buck up. Interest rates will come down. The housing market will pick up, helping sales of 'white goods'. Much-touted new electronic products will eventually arrive in sufficiently high numbers and low costs. The upheavals among white goods manufacturers might even help, as the new alliances improve both their manufacturing and distribution performance, and as European retailers get together to match their power.

But whatever Mr Kalms says about Santa's efforts over the last couple of months, 1991 is going to be grim for any retailer asking people to part with hundreds of pounds for something they don't really need.

4 April 1991: Ben Laurance

Supermarketry

For those who are fond of little shops – butchers, bakers, greengrocers and the like – the picture is uniformly depressing. Tesco's extraordinary advance, detailed in its financial results yesterday, only underline what we already knew: most people have a car, people with cars like shopping in big superstores with parking outside the door, and for grocery companies, big stores are highly profitable.

Over the last decade, small grocery outlets have on average increased their sales by less than 2 per cent a year. For butchers, the annual increase has been 2.3 per cent, and for greengrocers 5.3 per cent. Large grocery companies, meanwhile, have shown annual sales increases averaging nearly 12 per cent. In food retailing, bigger is better. Like it or not, Britons are choosing to spend an increasing proportion of their housekeeping with the Sainsburys, Tescos, and Safeways of the retailing world. Smaller companies – and particularly those who lack edge-of-town outlets – are being squeezed.

But what is likely to happen over the next ten years? The argument about saturation – the number of new superstores which can profitably be opened before they start competing too fiercely with one another – has been well rehearsed. And generally, it appears that while saturation is bound to happen one day, that day is a long way off. After all, despite the proliferation of superstores over the last decade, they still account for less than 30 per cent of all grocery floorspace in the country. There are hundreds of areas where the big companies would still dearly love to open a new outlet.

We should assume, therefore, that the dominance of the superstores will increase. Tesco alone plans to open 21 within the next 12 months. Each will average 40,000 square feet. Once bedded down, each will sell perhaps £700,000-worth of goods each week – goods that would otherwise have been bought in the High Street, from the local shops you hold so dear. The average of Asda's *existing* stores is already within a whisker of 40,000 square feet.

The increasing sophistication of the craft of retailing seen over the last decade has been extraordinary: not so long ago, the idea that the sale of a packet of frozen peas could be recorded simply by wafting it over a glass slit in a checkout seemed like something out of science fiction. Now it is commonplace. And the store's computer can and does achieve much more: it can place orders from the warehouse and it can nudge the warehouse's computer into placing a fresh order with the manufacturer.

But if, by the end of the decade, there is a superstore within reach of every town, where will that leave the remainder of the shops which have hitherto supplied our everyday needs?

Without doubt, the number of big standard town-centre supermarkets will shrink. So will the number of specialists like greengrocers, fishmongers, bakers and butchers.

But there are still plenty of people without cars, lots of people living on pensions and lots of people who are unemployed and/or struggling to get by on benefits. Tesco or Safeway may well provide them with a free bus to the store. But for those for whom eking out a limited income is a weekly challenge, that is less of an attraction than the sort of prices offered by the likes of a Kwik Save, a Lo Cost or an Aldi.

There is not much fun in shopping in one of these places. There is not meant to be. The range is limited: a typical Aldi outlet carries about 600 lines, Kwik Save 1,500-plus and a Tesco or Sainsbury superstore upwards of 15,000. There is very little of the 'added value' stuff like ready-made salads and deserts on which the bigger chains place such great emphasis. The attraction of these no-frills outlets (Andy Brown, food retailing expert at Morgan Stanley, accurately calls them the humourless discounters) is simply their prices: shopping for basics costs less. In Aldi, a loaf of bread is priced at 29 pence. Payment is by cash only. And as Smith New Court put it in a recent study, 'If the customer does have a car – tough luck.' There is no parking at most stores.

So we can foresee that the large grocers will take an increasing share of the top end – the weekly or monthly shopping trip end – of the market and the discounters will take more at the bottom end. But that still leaves a gap. There is and will continue to be room for corner shops which are prepared to stay open all hours. They will always be principally family businesses: after all, what sensible employee would work 16 hours a day unless he or she had a cut of the profits? And if those profits start to fall, the family concern is much nimbler in reacting to change: there is no need to refer to head office hundreds of miles away in order to turn over a couple of shelves to hiring video-tapes.

So, console yourself with the thought that corner shops should survive. And those who react against advertisements showing Dudley Moore enthusing about cheese can console themselves by kicking their way through the clutter of cardboard boxes in Kwik Save.

But the main point still stands: large, efficient supermarket operators will continue to claw away at the middle ground. They are becoming ever cleverer in their exploitation of technology to monitor what we buy and why we buy it. Andy Brown makes the plausible suggestion that Sainsbury or Tesco could within the next few years launch 'frequent shopper' schemes, mirroring what is done by airlines. It would be worth their while: a comfortably-off family with children spends several thousands of pounds a year with their main supermarket. The operators want more detailed information about their customers: a supermarket may make nothing selling tinned lychees, but will continue to stock them if their removal from the shelves were to drive a shopper with £60 to spend on a Saturday into the hands of a rival.

Which, strangely, could mean that the supermarket exploits technology in so sophisticated a way that it can react to the wants of its customers exactly as the local grocer did a couple of decades ago. It may sound creepy, but it will happen. Superstores and the companies which run them are the inevitable victors in the competition to take our money.

24 April 1991: Sarah Boseley

Rough diamonds

The millionaire with the best line in barrow-boy patter and some of the worst quality merchandise to be found in the average high street proudly told the elite pin-stripes of the Institute of Directors yesterday that they too could ride the recession – by selling 'total crap'.

Gerald Ratner claims his cut-price jewellery stores give people what they want, although he himself has apparently never wanted it. The only ornament he wears is a Rolex or Cartier watch, his suits are dark and immaculately tailored and his houses (Mayfair and Maidenhead) are expensively tasteful.

But to the public which keeps him in the style to which he has become accustomed, his advice is to never mind the quality, buy in quantity and have a bit of fun.

Cheap fun comes in the form of a pair of silver earrings

for 99p which, Mr Ratner said, had 'very little to do with quality'. Another winner was an imitation open book with curled-up corners and genuine antique dust. It was in 'the worst possible taste', Mr Ratner cheerfully declared – but 250,000 were sold last year.

He added: 'We also do cut-glass sherry decanters complete with six glasses on a silver-plated tray your butler can serve you drinks on, all for £4.95. People say how can you sell this for such a low price. I say because it is total crap. Our Ratners shops will never win any awards for design and they are not in the best possible taste. In fact, some people say they can't even see the jewellery for all the posters smothering the shop windows. But these shops, that everyone has a good laugh about, take more money per square foot than any other retailer in Europe, because we give the customers what they want.'

In defiance of current retailing blues, his British chain of 1,000 stores, which includes Zales and H. Samuel, yesterday announced increased pre-tax profits of £112 million.

Mr Ratner is a hard-working and ambitious man, who compares his business strategy to the street market traders he admires. He sells cheap goods cheaper than anyone else. His success is also based on the acquisition of other jewellery chains, and, hoping to diversify, he has bought Salisburys and failed to secure Dixons.

What he describes as his most difficult takeover, however, was his earliest. Ratners was founded by his father Leslie in 1949. Gerald joined from school and eventually became joint managing director with his father, which led to arguments and power struggles.

Seizing his chance when his father went to America, Gerald plunged down-market for the first time, with notices in the shops offering reductions on watches. Business, which had slumped, started to pick up.

When his father returned, Gerald told him the other

directors wanted him to run the company. He told the directors his father wanted him to take over.

A totally unpretentious man, 41-year-old Mr Ratner has the grace to say that he hopes one day one of his three daughters will play the same trick on him. He wants to retire quite young.

21 February 1991: Judy Rumbold

Looking down the plughole

Alan Cluer is a casting agent. He invites famous people to wrap their glamorous gobs around lacklustre chocolate bars for up to £100,000 a throw. He's a busy man. 'Sorry, I can't talk at the moment. I'm in the middle of a huge deal and we're faxing the crap out of each other.'

Cluer is one of those fierce, thrusting types; you get the impression that hiring God and the Pope to indulge in a bit of vacuous chat about coffee beans wouldn't be beyond him. If the price was right. 'I always operate on the basis that these deals are do-able.'

It must irritate the hell out of him that near-deities like the Michaels Caine and Palin, Sean Connery, Alec Guinness and Clive James habitually turn down advertising offers.

'At first I thought it looked a little greedy,' says Clive James, 'but then I decided that if you set yourself up as an intelligent, independent thinker, it's hard to stand there and say a washing machine is the best model on the market, or that this is the best refrigerator so you should buy it. Because it would imply that you've tried all the others.'

Very commendable, Clive. No such scruples for the rest.

Look at all those preacherly alternative comedians gone mainstream ga-ga over Pot Noodle and nasty, capitalist institutions like banks and building societies. When did it suddenly become all right to put your patch of moral high ground up for sale? Perhaps Laurence Olivier set conscience-salving new standards when he promoted Kodak in the US during the Seventies. But Nick Welch, a creative director at J. Walter Thompson, thinks the watershed came later. 'It was the Thatcher effect. People started to be less iffy about money.'

Winston Fletcher, president of the Institute of Practitioners in Advertising, agrees: 'Cynicism is out in the open. We know they get a load of money, so the best we can do is make them earn it.'

The load of money bit is certainly true. Between £50,000 and £80,000 will buy you a nearly-famous celebrity to endorse something miserably workaday like fish fingers or kitchen towels. But for shiny, top-of-the-range models – highly efficient in the field of banks, soft drinks and electronic gadgetry – large companies are prepared to fork out a good deal more for 30 seconds' worth of wobbly promotion. Seven million dollars bought Michael Jackson's five-year contract with Pepsi: John Cleese, promiscuous endorser and advertisers' darling, commands fees upwards of £150,000 and Maureen Lipman gets around £200,000 a year from British Telecom.

'A carefully cast star can save a company up to £1 million on its spending budget, because the result receives more attention than lots of smaller, cheaper ads,' says Chris Powell, chief executive of BMP DDB Needham. For instance, when Daley Thompson was hired to promote Lucozade, it went from being perceived as a sticky Day-Glo drink to something far more alluring. Now it was a sticky, Day-Glo *sexy* drink. 'If £4 million works like £8 million, it's money well spent,' says Dave Trott of Bainsfair, Sharkey, Trott. 'I mean, £5 for a glass of water in the City is expensive, but in the Sahara it's a bargain.'

Countless sets of dried-up sales figures have paddled in consumerist oases as a result of shrewd celebrity advertising. But sometimes no amount of money can buy a successful campaign. Inspired by *Local Hero*, Foster's advertising agency BMP DDB Needham hired both its director, Bill Forsyth, and its star, Burt Lancaster, to re-create the film's expensively rural mood.

Lancaster was paid £500,000 for 10 days' shooting in Scotland, and Forsyth got £10,000 a day. Still the mini-epic lacked the pulling power of the previous campaign starring Paul Hogan. Perhaps it was a case of wrong place, wrong bloke, weak storyline. One ad-man wasn't prepared to spend time luxuriating in doubt. 'It was,' he says, 'a sack of shit.'

'Personalities have to be used intelligently,' says Grant Duncan, account director at Collett, Dickenson Pearce. 'The way not to use them is in the absence of an idea to give a product some kind of impact. The important thing is to ensure there's a direct relationship between what you're selling and the person you're using, or that the relationship is an intriguing one.'

Often the relationship is not only unintriguing, it is downright implausible. Does Dudley Moore shop at Tesco? Does he hell. Is Jerry Hall a Bovril drinker? I don't think so. 'It's extremely tedious when it's star-fucking for the sake of it,' says the writer and director Tom Bussmann.

Even though the agency behind Joan Collins promoting Bristol & West said awareness of the Society increased by more than 30 per cent, no one thought for a microsecond that she actually had a snivelling little savings account with them. We know it's bullshit, they know it's bullshit. 'But at least it's glamorous bullshit,' concluded an ex-advertising executive.

Given this climate of mass cynicism, the trend for trashing your product off-screen hardly seems to matter. 'I don't like aftershave,' said Paul Gascoigne at a press conference to launch himself as the oikish new endorser of Brut. 'I never wear it.' Nor does Linda Bellingham, the cosily believable Oxo mum, much care about real-life loyalty to her brand. 'I don't eat meat,' she told Terry Wogan. And didn't Griff Rhys-Jones say publicly, in not so many words, that Holsten Pils possessed a bouquet reminiscent of fermented gnats' urine?

It doesn't affect our enjoyment of the ads, because we were never stupid enough to believe the 'I'm famous, I use this, so should you' type of endorsement in the first place, says Tim Delaney, of Leagas Delaney. 'What is certain is that consumers are much more sceptical, but equally they are extremely aware of the games being played and methods being used,' says Frank Lowe at Lowe, Howard Spink. 'They collude in the games, and much advertising deliberately involves the public. When they are involved, they are much more interested.'

Moreover, when we are interested, we are more likely to remember, through the dense fug of clever lines and funny faces, both the celebrity *and* the product. Maureen Lipman and British Telecom are now almost inseparable in the public consciousness. In a *Marketing* magazine survey last year, 87 per cent of 35–44 year olds made the right connection between personality and product. The same survey showed that recall of a personality's brand actually increases long after the marketers ditch the association. Paul Hogan was associated with Fosters by 48 per cent of consumers when he was doing their ads. But as soon as he stopped recognition rate went up to 63 per cent.

Dave Trott recalls a time when things were much simpler. Surely catchphrases and slogans are easier to remember than which famous face endorses which similarly packaged, highly forgettable coffee, lager or bedtime drink. 'Most ads are too clever for their own good. I know something works when I hear people on the streets reciting things like "Hello, Tosh Got a Toshiba", "Ariston and On and On", and "Brr Brr Busy line".' When an advertising agency is faced with the challenge of promoting a new deodorant, a famous armpit is infinitely sexier and more entertaining than an ordinary one. But are there enough armpits to go round? 'They're being soaked up all over the place,' says Alan Cluer, with a hint of desperation. Although, he says, there's always politicians: 'They like the humanising effect of advertising.'

'Yes,' says Nick Welch, 'there's always someone. Look at Fred Housego. He drives a taxi. He won Mastermind. He's a celebrity.'

But Cluer likes to think his methods of financial persuasion can stretch to something a little more glamorous. No star is too intimidatingly grand for him. He says he has reason to believe the queen is unavailable, but no matter, he'll find someone else. 'And anyway, to tell you the truth, royalty is a bit small-scale for me.'

Justice on trial

12 July 1990: Hugo Young

Judges' convictions

My first encounter with the impenetrability of the judicial mind occurred during a *cause célèbre* of the 1960s. Dennis Stafford and Michael Luvaglio were convicted of murdering a man in South Hetton, Co. Durham, but the case raised major problems of proof and identity, and appeals were pursued in and out of court for several years. There remained enough lurking doubts about the convictions to excite the interest of any open-minded investigator.

Shortly after writing an article to this effect in the *Sunday Times*, I ran into one of the judges who'd been involved in the case. What stayed indelibly with me from our conversation was not his predictable belief that the law had taken its proper course but his brass-bound certainty, delivered over the sherry from some Olympian plane to which a mere journalist could never hope to aspire, that Stafford and Luvaglio had without a shadow of a doubt done the deed for which they were convicted.

The possibility that the system has erred is the lifeblood

of any barrister who finds himself in front of the Court of Appeal. Yet when that barrister becomes a judge, the same proposition inexplicably seems to tend towards one which he feels obliged to repudiate unto his final breath.

This is the motif that defiles every stage of the saga that reached its penultimate moment yesterday with the Home Secretary's announcement on the Maguire case. The Maguires and their associates, released in the mid-1980s after serving up to nine years in prison, will now be officially told they were innocent of the crimes for which they were jailed. This follows the release, after similar proof of defective trials, of the Guildford Four. Sooner or later, the Birmingham Six seem sure to be supplied with evidence supporting the same plea. The system, which unnumbered judges and ministers have stretched every brain and bone to insist produced results no honest man could challenge, has finally been shown, in this succession of Irish-related cases, to be prone to scandalous error.

No less a man than Lord Denning actually foresaw this. In 1980, he heard an appeal in connection with the Birmingham Six. The question was whether they should be allowed to go forward to full appeal on the basis of new evidence. Denning thought the prospect too terrible to contemplate.

'If the six men fail,' he ruled, 'it will mean that much time and money will have been expended by many people for no good purpose. If the six men win, it will mean that the police were guilty of perjury, that they were guilty of violence and threats, that the confessions were involuntary . . . and that the convictions were erroneous. That would mean the Home Secretary would either have to recommend they be pardoned or he would have to remit the case to the Court of Appeal. This is such an appalling vista that every sensible person in the land would say: It cannot be right these actions should go any further.'

The common response to this remarkable statement has been to say how disgraceful it was. Lord Denning has since said that he regrets it. But as each item among his presentiments of doom has come to pass – the perjury, the corrupt evidence, the bad convictions, the remissions and the quashings – the more relevant response is to note how shrewd he was. Sensible persons have indeed lost confidence in the system, and since the system is so imperfect it is a good thing that they have.

Heading the objects of reappraisal ought to be the judges. Not only do they personally tend, in their shift from bar to bench, to acquire this habit of certainty that admits no doubt, they are almost universally encouraged to believe that the legal system itself rests on their being maintained in this quasi-godlike position. Only in the narrowest of circumstances can what they have done ever be undone. Upon that, law and politics insist, the very stability of our society depends.

In the unravelling of the Maguire case, it is the judges whose performance comes most urgently into question. Other professionals are caught up in the tale of how these people were falsely sent to prison. The police, determined to secure convictions, wanted to verify too many hasty conclusions. The scientific evidence produced by the prosecution was faulty and incomplete. Like other Irish trials of the 1970s, the atmosphere was contaminated, and the procedures fatally flawed, by what amounted to a political requirement.

The best that can be said for the judges involved is that their professionalism was not equal to the task in hand. The story is compellingly told in Robert Kee's book on the Maguires and the Guildford Four, *Trial and Error*. Kee is a hero of justice in this case, in troubling contrast to Mr Justice Donaldson and Lord Justice Roskill, as they then were. Donaldson, the trial judge, is shown by Kee to have dealt inadequately with such crucial matters as the absence of explosives in the Maguires' possession, and the serious doubts attaching to the scientific tests on which the prosecution case depended. The summing-up on which the jury based its verdict was, in other words, loaded against the accused. At the time, even without subsequent embellishments to the Maguires' case, justice was being distorted.

This defect was reinforced by Roskill's appeal judgement. Kee shows how, at every point on which the Donaldson version was open to challenge, Roskill compounded his errors and, instead of a balanced hearing, supplied one-sided support for the case against the Maguires. The court could discover no lurking doubt: only reason for endorsing, whenever it mattered, the trial judge's clarity and fairness.

These are the qualities which yesterday's decision by the Home Secretary, which he anticipated a month ago, calls into question. Sir John May's inquiry will reputedly damage Donaldson as well. And yet, we may be sure, that is not the way the judiciary wants to see it: and least of all Lord Donaldson himself, now installed these many years in Denning's old job as Master of the Rolls, from which it is above all important to declare that nothing is ever wrong which cannot be corrected by the normal procedures the system allows for.

Well, the Maguire case, like the case of the Guildford Four, shows this to be false. The trial judge presided over a corrupt trial, and nobody could or would do anything about it for many years. Minister after minister stood up to say that, since there appeared to be no new evidence in the case, the heavens would fall if any reopening of it were permitted on any other ground. Neither the misconduct of the trial itself nor the falsity of its forensic proofs deserved any credence as the source of gross injustice.

British justice is not commonly corrupt. Decent men do their duty as they see it. But these were very shocking cases, whose only saving grace is that they undermine confidence in our system. This begins with the common certitude of judges that they do not err and nor does the system they run. But they do, and it does, and we need a system as well as an attitude of mind that addresses their fallibility.

2 January 1991: Peter Lennon

Meddler after the truth

The investigative journalist, far from being a glamorous and admired crusader, is often an unloved creature. Decent people who do not wish to have their illusions disturbed are often as exasperated by him as his targets. Long before Chris Mullin gained access to the House of Commons as MP for Sunderland South to continue, in the most public of forums, his campaign for the Birmingham Six, he had been getting up people's noses.

Mullin has been crusading for the Birmingham Six for 15 years. He wrote a book about the case, *Error of Judgement*, and was a prime source for two *World in Action* documentaries. Vindication of his meddling came from a Home Office forensic report claiming that the explosives evidence of the forensic scientist, Dr Frank Skuse, was unsafe.

At 42, Mullin can still be as gleeful as an altar boy whose pranks turn out to be for the good of Christendom; but he is as fussy as an accountant in making sure his sums add up. It has taken some time for Mullin to be taken seriously. Michael Foot attacked his 'infantile leftism' when he was briefly editor of *Tribune*; the *Sun* described him as a loony MP 'who backed bombers'.

'I think I have got up my share of people's noses,' he admitted as we drank tea in the House of Commons canteen. 'But I am choosy about whose nose I get up.'

Whose nose has he got up?

'Obviously the villains in each case – the police, anyone in authority connected with the Birmingham case; it is hard to put a generous interpretation on their actions. I think we are also starting to get under the skin of the Lord Chief Justice. His resignation is the obvious way of clearing the path.'

Following the announcement that Lord Lane, who dismissed the previous appeal of the Birmingham Six, would not sit on the new appeal, there have been persistent rumours that he will take early retirement. But Mullin is not too impressed by Lord Lane's possible successor. 'Lord Taylor attacked the press for vilifying judges in miscarriage of justice cases,' says Mullin. ' "If there has been tampering or tainting of evidence, how is the judge to know without a crystal ball?" '

Well, how is he to know? 'The judge could use his common sense. Most people travelling on buses noticed there was something wrong in these cases – Guildford, the Birmingham Six. Stupidity would be one possible explanation for the behaviour of a succession of judges, but I am inclined to the view that it is a preoccupation with protecting the credibility of the legal system which takes precedence over a commitment to justice.'

Are people really disturbed by these miscarriages of justice in England – apart from immediate family and friends? 'I'm bound to say I think they are. I receive hundreds of letters from people in all walks of life. But I get annoyed when I see my book in a section of a bookshop labelled "Irish Interest". Actually –' his voice becomes crisply reproachful – 'it's a British problem. It is the British legal system which is making these mistakes and it isn't only Irish people who suffer.'

Mullin's father was Scots Protestant but his mother was Catholic, so he was educated by the De La Salle brothers. 'A very strict regime, prayer alternating with rugby, sufficient to put me off both for life.'

Was there a great emphasis on helping the weak and

seeing justice done? 'I'm afraid I don't recollect that, but somewhere along the line that has become my philosophy.'

Some people take up such causes to defend the weak, others because they are offended by the misuse of power. Which is the driving motivation with him? 'I'm a socialist and socialists are inclined to be biased – I like to think towards the less fortunate. And as a journalist I consider myself of the enquiring school.'

His enquiring began fairly early and it was mixed with some insouciant opportunism. Having hitched a ride at the age of 19 to China with SACU (the Society for Anglo-Chinese Understanding), he was smitten with the East. He got a commission from the *Telegraph* magazine to go to Vietnam and write a piece on the future of South-east Asia.

'I realised at once,' he recalls, 'that this was the end of my career with the *Telegraph* magazine because there wasn't any way that my version of the future of South-east Asia would coincide with theirs.'

The *Telegraph* magazine never ran the Mullin view of South-east Asia, but they did publish his revelation that American bombers based in Thailand had been annihilating Laos villages. However, the *Telegraph* was not amused when he campaigned to make them admit that their Saigon correspondent, 'John Draw', was in fact Nguyen Ngoc Phac, an officer in the Saigon army.

This little campaign had a useful spin-off: he got practice in pronouncing a name which was close to that of the girl he began to court, by letter, six years later: Nguyen Thi Ngoc. They are now married with three children.

Two years later he was travelling east again, to the Himalayas, this time on a commission from the *Guardian*. 'Ostensibly to cover the coronation of the King of Nepal,' he explains, 'but in fact to discover for myself the survivors of a CIA operation in Tibet.'

The *Guardian* ran the story of a disastrous CIA operation, which has since turned out to be a Mullin sleeper.

Fifteen years later it is to reappear in fictionalised form in Mullin's new novel, *The Year of the Fire Monkey*, to be published by Chatto & Windus. This punctilious tracker of the truth has also done very well with fiction. His *Very British Coup* was made into a highly acclaimed television serial, and an earlier work, *The Last Man out of Saigon*, is likely to be filmed this year.

Unlike most investigative journalists Mullin appears to have a very low level of paranoia. He has none of the usual complaints about his flat being ransacked or his phone tapped.

He points out that relatively early in his campaign some Tory MPs, notably Sir John Farr, shared his belief in the innocence of the Birmingham Six. Then Cardinal Hume and Law Lords Devlin and Scarman supported the campaign. 'That made it difficult to smear me,' says Mullin.

Error of Judgement contains interviews with the people (unnamed) he claims carried out the bombings. It is now widely accepted that Mullin knows who made and planted the bombs which killed 21 people in two Birmingham pubs in 1974.

How did he get such confessions? 'I did it by simple detective work of the sort one would commend to the West Midlands police,' he says tartly. 'I set about tracing one by one all those who had been involved in planting bombs in and around Birmingham in 1973 and 1974. There were about 50 explosions in the West Midlands alone. The police had got some of the people involved. They arrested eight people in August for some of the earlier bombings; I traced all those people and I traced others who had been arrested and were in prison. And then gradually from people I talked to I got a list of those who hadn't been arrested and traced them also.'

Why should an IRA man name other IRA men for him? 'It was not on the basis that I was seeking to put away the people who had carried out the bombing, but on the basis that I was seeking to rescue these six innocent poor sods who didn't do it. All these people know that the wrong people had been imprisoned. The IRA in Birmingham was quite a small group who knew each other. Many in jail did not know who had carried out the pub bombings but they knew they had got the wrong people as soon as they saw their names in the paper. So I turned up on their doorsteps – some in England, some in Ireland.'

Did he get a rough reception? 'I don't say anybody was keen to see me; some of these people took a lot of persuading. Very quickly I came across the man who admitted he had made both bombs, and he was willing to give me a general account of what happened. But he would not give me the names of the planters. In order to prove the wrong people are in jail you have to prove that you have met one of the planters. The police never said they had got the people who had made the bombs. In the course of three interviews with this man he let slip the name of a second man, serving life imprisonment in the Irish Republic. I went to see him. He declined to admit to any role in the bombing.

'That was the position by the end of 1985. I then started to work my way around the 17 former members of the IRA, and when I got three of them giving me the same name for a planter I moved in on that individual. Those three had no notice of my arrival on their doorstep. I moved in on him. At first he lapsed into fantasy on the question of what he was doing on the night of the bombing. He was shaking with fear; it was quite a large secret to harbour for 12 or 13 years. He would have been only about 19 at the time, the junior partner in the enterprise.

'Eventually I just said: "I think you were at the pubs", and it all came tumbling out. He was able to mark the location of the bombs, something that had never been published.'

It is possible that Mullin may find another case irresistible. 'There is the case of Judith Ward, in the 17th year of a

30-year sentence for the M62 coach bombing in 1974,' he says. 'I am told that the people who carried out the bombing are alive and well in Ireland. I have not gone into it in detail. But I draw your attention to the fact that her conviction is based on statements made in police custody and forensic evidence supplied by Dr Frank Skuse.'

15 March 1991: Ludovic Kennedy at the Birmingham Six's final appeal

The guilt of the judges

Along with the Irish ambassador, Bishop Daly of Londonderry and others of the Irish great and good, I was permitted to sit in the jury-box, which gave us a fine view of the proceedings. Straight ahead and up in the gallery were some of the Six's numerous daughters, tots when their fathers were carted off to prison, pretty girls now, who each day waved and smiled at them as they filed in and out of the dock.

Immediately below us were the seats for counsel: at the far end the birdlike Graham Boal, QC for the Crown, now playing a mostly silent role, one of his rare excursions being a damage limitation exercise on behalf of the discredited West Midlands police. At our end sat the appellants' two Queen's Counsel, Lord Gifford and the star of the show, Michael Mansfield, on his feet for most of each day and whose grasp and exposition of the often highly complex technical evidence was stunningly impressive.

Gifford and Mansfield were in this court three years ago when the last appeal of the Six was heard (though only half-heartedly) by the Lord Chief Justice and Lord Justices O'Connor and Stephen Brown. They were given a rough ride then, Lord Lane making plain from the beginning his disbelief in and hostility towards the appellants' case. But the latter-day troika of Lloyd, Farquharson and Mustill were, as you would expect from the prosecution having conceded defeat, benevolence personified. With Mr Mansfield's help they really did want to find out the truth of what had happened, and so came the nearest I have seen in a British court to the inquisitorial court that functions on the Continent. Farquharson asked the fewest questions, but they were short and sharp, like pistol shots. Mustill, who asked the most, had the air of a favourite uncle at a children's tea-party. Disarmingly, he admitted his lack of understanding of some of the technicalities, and like a tenacious but unfailingly courteous mole kept burrowing away at Mr Mansfield until he had obtained the information he required.

The fresh evidence unearthed was impressive, especially that which showed that Dr Skuse's Griess test claim that two of the Six had nitro-glycerine on their hands was nonsense; and the weirdest aspect of this was the recent discovery that soap can give the same positive reaction as nitro-glycerine, so that every time Dr Skuse washed his hands and bowls to prevent contamination, he could have been contaminating them himself. The recent technical advances in document examination, too, proved conclusively what some of us had believed for years: that the 'confessions' of the Six were fabrications.

As a result it will be claimed by those who wish to protect the legal establishment that it was *only* fresh evidence that resulted in correcting the miscarriage, and that all the judges who ever dealt with the case are blameless. Indeed this canard has already been floated, first by the Attorney-General who suggested on February 25 that all judges do is hold the ring and enforce the rules, and by Sir Frederick Lawton in a letter to *The Times* in which he stressed that it is juries not judges who deliver verdicts.

This of course is a smoke-screen, as any future unbiased inquiry into the case will confirm. Certainly it is juries who reach verdicts, but it is judges who often feel free to tell them of their profound belief in the defendant's guilt (adding so as to avoid being upset on appeal that it is a matter entirely for them). At the original trial of the Six Mr Justice Bridge (now a Law Lord) could hardly have been more hostile to the defendants if he had tried. When Dr Black, a former Chief Inspector of Explosives for the Home Office, said Dr Skuse's Griess test was *not specific for nitro-glycerine*, and that sensitive tests had failed to confirm it, Bridge was not only extremely offensive to him, but also said his evidence was irrelevant and he was wasting the court's time. Bridge then took it on himself to say that the Six's allegations that the 'confessions' were beaten out of them by the police were simply not credible, and that the police officers involved had struck him as 'honest and straightforward witnesses' (impressions that police officers always do their best to maintain). Yet the Six's allegations of police brutality were detailed, varied and specific, and the 'confessions' a mass of contradictions and inaccuracies, having been fashioned by the police before they had had time to check the details of the bombings with their forensic colleagues. It would have required a less arrogant and more open-minded judge than Bridge to see the strength of the defence's case and to give it the same emphasis in his summing-up as he did the case for the prosecution.

The second opportunity to right the wrong came a couple of years later when the Six applied for legal aid in an action against the police for the injuries they had received in police custody. This was heard by Lord Denning who, perhaps realising there might be substance in the claim and that the Six might have to be pardoned, refused to allow the action to go ahead.

And then at the last appeal three years ago Lord Lane and his colleagues, faced with convincing eye-witness accounts of police brutality to the appellants, chose to ignore them. Faced too with the discrediting of Dr Skuse's Griess test, they fell back on the evidence of a Dr Drayton, declaring that her findings of *possible* nitro-glycerine on the hand of one of the appellants was *proof* of it, adding in a total non-sequitur that this must be fatal not only to his case but that of all the other five appellants.

But the greatest sin of Lane and Co, so eager were they to demolish the case for the appellants, was to ignore the advice of the Lord Chancellor after the Stafford-Luvaglio case, that instead of judges setting themselves up as judges of the facts (on which, Michael Mansfield once said, they are notoriously unreliable) they should ask themselves what the trial jury's verdict might have been had they had the benefit of the fresh evidence (in this instance, the unreliability of Dr Skuse's tests and of police brutality). That is what Lord Devlin, a wiser judge than Bridge or Denning or Lane, said they should have done. He said the same thing of the fourth appeal in the Luton murder case when the judges, instead of asking what the trial jury would have made of the evidence of the lying crook who was the prosecution's main witness, decided themselves that he was speaking the truth. And the two wrongfully convicted appellants in that case, Cooper and McMahon, went back to prison to complete 10 years of a life sentence.

As another wise judge, Lord Scarman, has recently said, we need the services of a judicial figure early on in all serious criminal cases to prevent police manipulation of evidence. And instead of the present creaking appeal system, we need a new statutory body, not bound by the normal rules of evidence, to *inquire* into alleged miscarriages; a body similar to that now sitting under Sir John May with lay assessors, which a select committee of the House of Commons advocated in 1982, and which unsurprisingly the fossils in the Home Office rejected.

15 March 1991: Paul Hill, one of the Guildford Four, who was released by the Court of Appeal in 1989

Life without bars

The Birmingham Six have finally walked to freedom. They have emerged into a world totally changed from the one they left 17 years ago. They carry with them the deep mental scars induced by long years of isolation, now visible scars which no one could possibly relate to. Initially, they will have to temper the anger of their wrongful convictions and the irony of being suddenly cared for after many years of being deprived and vilified.

In the early days great demands will be placed upon the men by the media. I found this actually helped me to unburden the anger which I felt, because I had a voice and a story which I had to shed to help cleanse myself of an horrific experience. During this period they will experience immense euphoria at being again in the bosom of their families, many with grandchildren they will never have been with. Difficulties could arise as a result of a male being once again in a household where the female has for many years been the dominant figure. Relative vying for attention could also place a great strain on the men.

The greatest changes they will see will be changes of technology – videos, fax, portable phones, CDs. They will not understand the value of money. A simple transaction in a shop will be difficult. Having possessions will be something they will have to get used to.

The most frightening thing they will have to encounter will be the first time they have to venture out alone. After my release, I was terrified of crossing the road. Traffic petrified me to such an extent that I found it difficult even to sit in the passenger seat of a car. I felt deeply paranoid and had panic attacks while in crowds. I received much advice to have some form of counselling. I refused, simply because I felt I had to deal with my problems myself. When I saw the Birmingham Six some weeks before their release, I gave them the same advice – to deal with these things in their own way.

Psychologically, trauma can manifest itself several months after release, when the men have time to reflect on their past ordeals and begin to plan their respective futures. They will long to lose the collective term of the Birmingham Six and to be recognised as individuals.

It is imperative that the men are compensated as soon as possible in order to ease any financial problems they encounter. That they seek tranquillity and somewhere they can relax is also important. I found great solace in the west of Ireland, where I hope eventually to live.

Unlike the Birmingham Six, whose agony in the Court of Appeal is finally over, in my own case the legal system is still proving its ability to engage in legal inanities concerning the Shaw case and the May inquiry. These are totally irrelevant, as it has been proved beyond doubt to the whole world that both the Guildford Four and the Birmingham Six are innocent.

Would it be too much now to ask the judiciary to apply the same thoroughness and resolve with which they kept innocent men in jail to a public inquiry? Perhaps.

15 March 1991: Leader

Criminal justice

Suppose the present criminal justice system was 99 per cent perfect in all the convictions it achieved. That would still mean about 600 people wrongly imprisoned every year by a system which annually imposes custodial sentences on 60,000. Most of those victims, of course, would only spend a few months inside. But the Birmingham Six, who had their convictions quashed yesterday amid scenes of exultation, have spent over 16 years behind bars. Justice is important in all trials; but the bigger the offence the more crucial it is that justice be achieved. Remember. Only 18 months ago, not a single IRA terrorist conviction had been overturned. Today, all convictions in the three biggest terrorist cases Britain has staged – the Guildford Four, Maguire Seven, and Birmingham Six – lie in ruins. The only thing left slumped in the dock last night was the justice system itself. A royal commission is the right – and only – response.

Guildford began it all. Two bombs in separate pubs on one night in October 1974 killed five innocents. One year later the four defendants received the longest sentences – including one with a 35-year minimum – from a British court. The Birmingham bomb in November 1974 remains the biggest terrorist incident on mainland Britain, killing 21 and injuring 162. The six accused were convicted in August 1975, each sentenced to 21 life sentences. The Maguire Seven went on trial in January 1976, receiving sentences of between seven and 14 years for producing bombs for the IRA.

Fifteen years on, Guildford was the first of three legal 'bombs' to explode when the Director of Public Prosecutions (DPP) announced that it would be 'wrong' to sustain the convictions. The Appeal Court was told about concocted statements, the suppression of other evidence and, worse still, valid alibi evidence withheld by the police from the defence. Eight months later, the DPP reluctantly conceded that the Maguire convictions were also 'unsafe and unsatisfactory'. That after the forensic evidence in the case – the sole basis for the convictions – was shown by the May inquiry to be suspect. Now, with even more reluctance, the DPP accepts there was police perjury, discredited forensic tests, and suspect contemporaneous statements in the Birmingham case.

How could this have happened – and taken so long to correct? The short answer is a combination of inexperienced local police forces dealing with terrorism in 1974, a judiciary with an unquestioned belief in police and forensic evidence, and the enormity of the crimes themselves, which created a climate highly charged with public expectations of swift conviction. There are, however, deeper causes to the system's crisis. And its faults are far wider than these woeful failures to deal with serious terrorist cases.

Several reforms have been introduced since 1974. All terrorist crimes are now investigated by the Anti Terrorist Branch rather than local police forces. Forensic science has become more sophisticated. Prosecution decisions are taken by the criminal prosecution service rather than the police. And new safeguards in non-terrorist cases include stricter controls over police detention, improved rights of access to lawyers, and the tape-recording of all statements in police stations. But these last safeguards still do not apply to terrorist offences, even though the European Court of Human Rights has ruled unlawful the Act which allows the police to hold a terrorist suspect for seven days without charge.

It is rare – whatever conspiracy theorists think – for the police to frame a person they believe innocent. The problem is more complicated. Much more commonly, evidence is bent by the police to ensure the conviction of people they have talked themselves into believing guilty. A recent study by Justice, the law reform charity, pointed to five common threads in the wrongful convictions investigated by its staff: wrong identification, false confessions, perjury, police misconduct and bad trial tactics. The Justice committee, which included two former judges, concluded there was too little protection against miscarriages of justice in the present system. Absolutely right.

Moreover, the crisis is no longer confined to the inadequacies of the players – police, prosecutors and judges – but enfolds the procedure itself. So the root question for the new royal commission is a simple one: should the present adversarial system be replaced by an inquisitorial procedure? The commission will need to look at how each of the three separate parts of the present system – investigation, trial, appeal – would be affected. Each has serious faults.

Investigations: Crown prosecutors can point to holes in the evidence, but have no way of knowing about evidence suppressed by the police. The main impetus remains the need to secure a conviction. The police are free to formulate immediate theories on guilt. The possible innocence of suspects is left to defence lawyers, yet there is a huge disparity in available resources between the two sides. This was best demonstrated in the Guildford case where, unknown to the defence, the police did track down the alibi witness. Similarly, the defence are denied the access to forensic services which the police enjoy. Legal aid restrictions create further problems. Justice cites several cases where wrongful convictions were reached because the defence, inhibited by its cost ceilings, failed to obtain vital information.

Trial: instead of an inquisitorial search for truth, there is only an accusatorial procedure in which the prosecution has to prove guilt beyond reasonable doubt. Vital evidence is frequently never presented to the jury. Unlike Scotland, one piece of evidence – an uncorroborated confession – is sufficient to secure conviction in England. Both sides play games. Both sides bend the rules. There is a built-in incentive to fabricate or suppress evidence.

Appeal: the Appeal Court has wide powers, but refuses to use them. Its approach is narrow and restrictive. It rejects all appeals based on lawyers' mistakes, incompetence or tactical errors – like failing to call a vital witness. Journalists and battling MPs have played a bigger role in correcting miscarriages of justice than the docile, timid judges in the Strand.

There are many reforms which would improve this procedure: judicial supervision of the investigative process, an independent forensic service, a special committee to investigate miscarriages of justice. The royal commission, however, should examine the more radical alternative: its benefits and faults. A year ago the *Guardian*'s law page looked at the inquisitorial system in France. It concluded both that fewer innocent defendants were convicted, and that fewer guilty offenders were acquitted. The DPP has conceded 'the merit' of considering an inquisitorial procedure. The judiciary will be more resistant. Only the authority of a full-blown royal commission can shift them. There has not been a royal commission for 13 years. John Major is right to break this Thatcher taboo. Whitehall does not know best. Birmingham heaps further ignominy upon the procedures it holds dear. And our greatly discredited criminal justice system now clearly needs deep analysis – then radical surgery.

Strutting players

16 October 1990: Matthew Engel

Return of a legend

Leicester Races on an October Monday is the turf equivalent of the third day of a rain-affected county cricket match at Derby, or Halifax Town v. Aldershot on a cold Saturday when all the menfolk are forced to go Christmas shopping. The event is staged because the system demands it, though hardly anyone goes and only the professionals and the hard cases care. In a way, that was the perfect setting. It all helped the extraordinary man who was the centre of attention to maintain his amused pretence that nothing unusual was happening.

True, for five years he had been away; indeed, for a year of that time, owing to his unfortunate misunderstanding about income tax, he had been away with a capital A. But now he was merely back at the office. Why the fuss? And indeed, Lester Piggott had a routine sort of jockey's day – three mounts: finishing second, beaten a short head in his first race back, seventh and 14th. It was no great triumph but enough to confirm what had been generally supposed.

The most famous male bottom in Britain was in the air as he came up the straight, just as it always had been. Maybe Piggott's power and nerve have diminished but that will only become clear by imperceptible degrees, perhaps over weeks, more likely years. In the meantime, Lester is back.

It all sounded so reassuringly familiar, having his name called out: 'Jockeys in the first race . . . No. 4 B. Doyle, claiming seven, No. 5 B. Raymond, No. 6 L. Piggott.' But you had to force yourself to think how strange it was.

He will be 55 in three weeks. He rode a winner in 1948, when Attlee was Prime Minister, and Bradman, Ben Hogan and Blankers-Koen dominated the sports pages. He rode a couple of unraced two-year-old fillies here; he very probably rode their great-great-great-great-great-great-great-grandparents in the days when bookmakers stood on street corners and ran when the bobby came by.

In the stands, they saw it his way. It was a special occasion but not especially special. The crowd ran to a couple of thousand instead of the usual few hundred, but it was always bigger when Piggott was riding. And the little bets rolled in for him as they always did.

John Meredith ('Civility, prompt payment'), one of the Silver Ring bookmakers, took a few bets of two and three quid on Piggott's mount in the first. The big punters backed the winner. 'I've been watching him since the war and there was nothing wrong with the way he rode that,' said Mr Meredith. 'That song went up – Come on, Lester. It's very strange hearing it again. But it's lovely.'

It is only at close quarters that Piggott even looks different. The years and the troubles have not affected his body. He claims to have got down to eight stone five, his old weight, simply by missing Sunday lunch. But his face is extraordinary. He looks like one of those oriental martial arts mystics who could fell you at a blow.

The *Daily Telegraph* printed a seamless 1,000-word interview with Piggott to coincide with his return, though

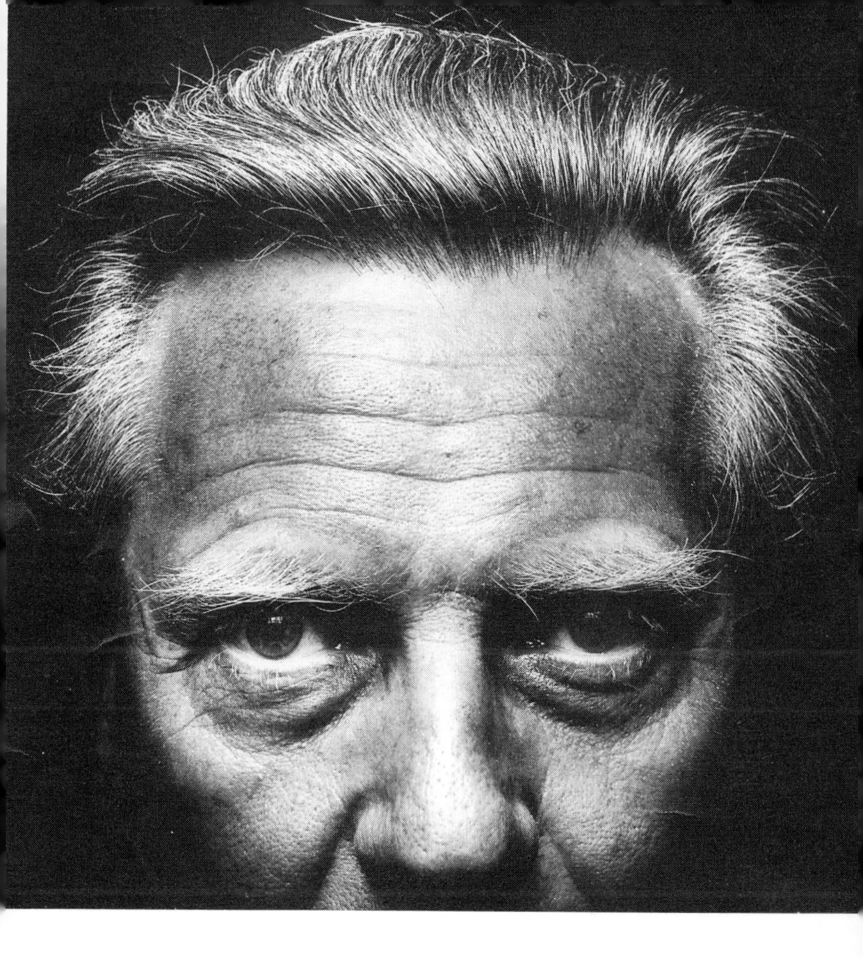

The *Guardian* won the 1991 Newspaper Focus Award for the best use of photography: the judges commented on the 'breath-taking use of original material' and 'brave cropping and treatment of pictures', noting in particular this portrait of Michael Heseltine (15 November 1990: Nigel Parry).

10

Conservative MP Edwina Currie outside the High Court after being awarded £5,000 libel damages against the *Observer* (15 May 1991: Graham Turner).

lmost the final exit: Margaret Thatcher leaves No. 10)owning Street for a dinner at the Mansion House 3 November 1990: Frank Martin).

Don McPhee was the 1991 Photo-Industrial Journalist of the Year in the BP/Industrial Society awards. His portfolio included these pictures of the Swan Hunter shipyard back in business on Tyneside (11 November 1990), and of women workers returning home from the South African factories which thrive on Botshabelo's vast pool of cheap labour (11 May 1990).

Two of the pictures which won Denis Thorpe joint second prize in the Photographer of the Year category of the 1990 Ilford awards: PC Fowewe on the beat in Liverpool city centre (31 August 1990); and a competitor in the Knutsford Great Race, a three-hour event for penny farthing bicycles (17 September 1990).

A railway special pulled by a steam train, the Duke of Gloucester, on the Settle to Carlisle line (29 May 1991: Denis Thorpe).

Poetic Grasmere: Bolton schoolchildren listening to Wordsworth's *Prelude*, part of a package tour conducted by Nancy Martin, education officer of the Wordsworth Trust (21 May 1991: Denis Thorpe).

The only breeding Bewick swans in captivity: this pair at the Wildfowl and Wetlands Trust in Arundel has produced cygnets for the second year (5 June 1991: Andrew Hasson).

More Lowry than Putney: Manchester beating Salford by 1½ lengths in the Northern Universities Boat Race on the River Irwell (7 May 1991: Don McPhee).

TILCON
Mortars Manchester

While the rest of his team collapses in a victory huddle, West Germany's Lothar Matthaus comforts Chris Waddle after his missed penalty ensured England's exit from the World Cup (5 July 1990: Frank Baron).

A bullet of a pass: Dermott in action at Wembley as Wigan beat St Helens and win the Rugby League Challenge Cup for the fourth consecutive year (29 April 1991: Frank Baron).

A young victim of the Bangladesh disaster holds her still younger brother, born on the day of the cyclone (8 May 1991: Frank Martin).

Another cyclone victim: a Bangladeshi points to his stomach to indicate his need for food (10 May 1991: Frank Martin).

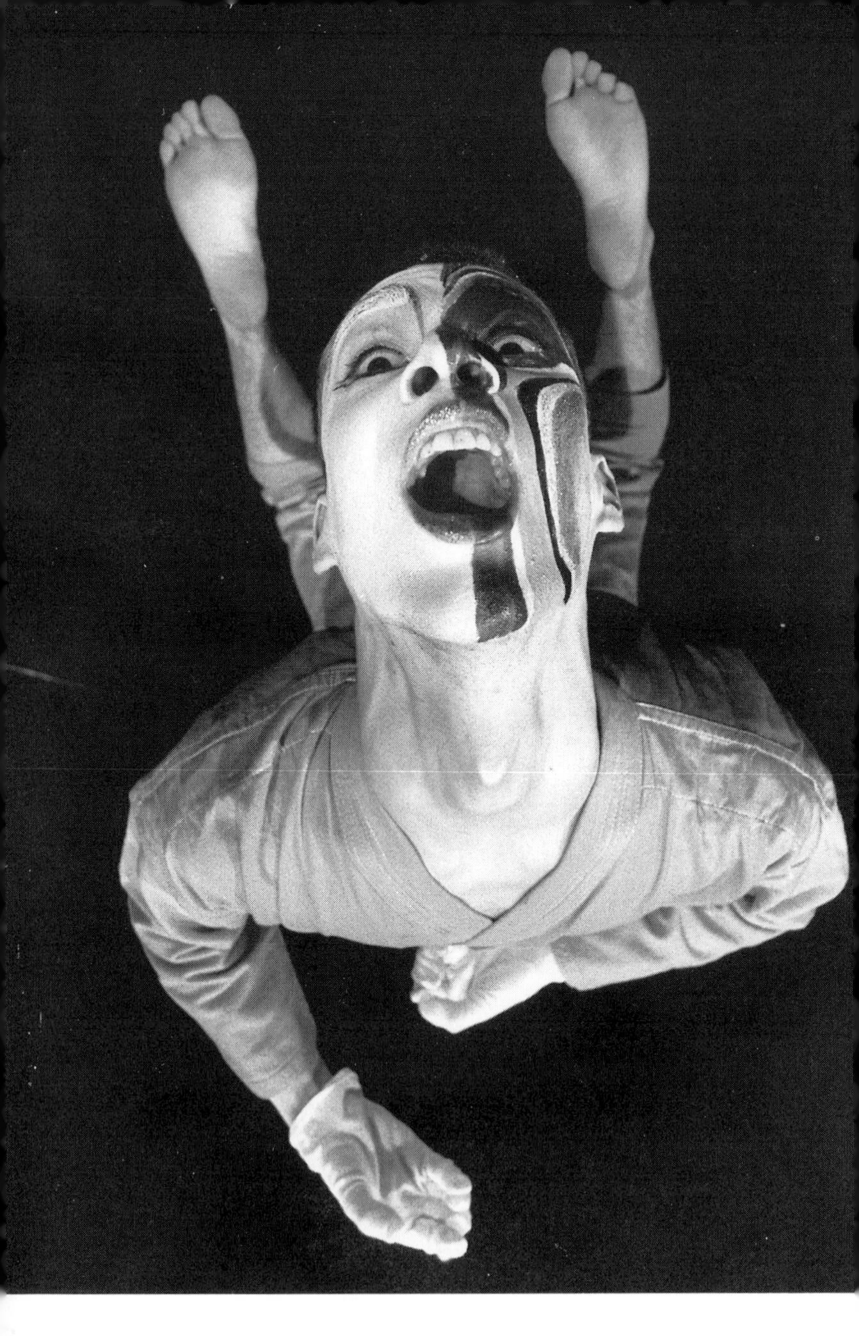

Hara-kiri: John Paul Zaccarini as Yukio Mishima at the point of death, in a play at the Battersea Arts Centre (14 May 1991: Graham Turner).

everyone in racing knows he never says more than four words at a time, top whack. Has your technique changed at all, Lester? 'One leg each side,' he replied. Did the owner give you any instructions? 'Do what I like,' he said. 'Not if you don't pay your effing taxes,' someone murmured.

But this was Piggott at his most engaging. He was loving it. He smiled when they cheered as he walked into the paddock. But it is not human adulation he is after. No one quite knows what is behind his comeback. Maybe he is broke. Maybe he thinks he is broke. Maybe he is being greedy. The most probable explanation is that he is bored, and he is back doing what he does best. No one knows horses like Piggott; but he has always seen the rest of the world in an idiosyncratic fashion.

In the paddock, the autumn winds were blowing the leaves off the lime trees, annual reminder of the passing of the years. And here was this strange man telling us that it was not so, that time could be made to stand still, and that everything could be exactly as it always was.

17 October 1990: Chris Hawkins

Just like old times

Lester Piggott rode a double at Chepstow yesterday. Put this way it sounds matter of fact and by the manner of its achievement it was. Showing all the *sang froid* and almost casual class which characterised his former career, Piggott climaxed his comeback with a wonderful exhibition of his unique, inimitable style.

It was truly vintage stuff and how the crowd loved it! A greeting of Cheltenham Gold Cup proportions acclaimed his entry into the winner's enclosure after his first victory on Nicholas, trained appropriately by his wife Susan, and there was a scarcely less muted welcome half an hour later when he returned on Shining Jewel.

Nicholas was the one he 'expected', there was no doubt about that, and the maestro certainly made it look easy. 'I was going to start on him but when I was offered the rides at Leicester I took them,' he said.

Piggott was drawn on the rails but eased his mount away from the inside to challenge on the outside of Amigo Menor. Just a switch of the whip and a couple of taps were needed to win by half a length and the colt hardly knew he had been in a race. Nicholas, owned by American Henry De Kwiatowski responsible for that great stallion Danzig, had achieved his objective and put the great man in talkative mood: 'It's just like old times. It's great. I don't regret not coming back earlier – I've had a good rest.'

Further proof of his affability came when he ended his interview with a 'Thanks for everything, lads.' A remark that had several seasoned scribes reaching for the smelling salts.

Now thoroughly in the groove, he had an even easier victory on 11-1 chance Shining Jewel in the second division of the claiming stakes. Shining Jewel, trained by Eric Eldin, had never won a race in ten previous attempts but in Piggott's hands he looked a world beater, cruising through and winning hard held by two and a half lengths.

Owner Dennis Rolt was understandably elated, commenting: 'The man's magic, I only got him by chance saying to Eric yesterday that if he didn't have a jockey in mind why not see if Lester was available. I couldn't believe it when Eric told me he'd got him. Now I understand about all those classic winners and why they rave about him.'

Looking on among the admiring crowd was Lord Hartington, senior steward of the Jockey Club, who sounded like the president elect of the Piggott fan club, saying: 'It's wonderful to have him back. People love stars. But on a more practical note he adds to the gate, I understand there are over 4,000 here today.'

By doubling attendances and putting millions on the betting turnover Piggott could be the answer to the Turf's financial problems. But don't tell him – he might want a percentage.

15 March 1991: Cynthia Bateman at the Cheltenham Gold Cup

Fading Orchid

He got his grey snout just in front as they came past the stand the first time round, and filled the bursting hearts with hope as even those who backed against him willed him on. But Dessie was no longer invincible, and as they strung out in the late-afternoon sun under the shimmering Cleeve Hill and the bright flash of grey was no longer in the frame, the belief that Desert Orchid could pull off a miracle faded.

Instead the massive – 55,897 – Cheltenham crowd, who had twittered like famished starlings before the race, roared another darling up the hill. Jenny Pitman's Garrison Savannah, ridden by the trainer's son Mark with his father Richard commentating on television, held off the French interloper The Fellow over the last lung-bursting strides to take the Cheltenham Festival's most coveted prize by a short head.

Desert Orchid, 12 years old, ears back, storming, hurting, gut-bursting in an attempt to win the crown he lost last year, came in a creditable third, 15 lengths behind. 'He still has the fight but no longer the talent,' said his principal owner Richard Burridge. On the day, the fight and talent belonged to the Pitmans and Garrison Savannah.

Savannah, named after Barbardos's famous racetrack, was well clear over the last, but as the chestnut's coat darkened with the sweat of striding out up the last cruel slope The Fellow looked to have him caught in a photo-finish.

Young Mark Pitman, his own dark hair curled with sweat, could only re-live last year's race when Norton's Coin pipped him at the post on Toby Tobias. But the cheers that greeted the Tannoy announcement that No. 6 had beaten No. 12 by a short head were as genuine as if they had been for Dessie.

For Jenny Pitman is just as great a favourite. She became the first woman to have a Gold Cup winner with Burrough Hill Lad in 1984, and the previous year had won the Grand National with Corbiere. But this had never looked to be her year. At her yard at Weathercock House in Upper Lambourn there has been nothing but bad news this season. Royal Athlete was injured, then Toby Tobias was ruled out. 'When Garrison Savannah came back from Haydock lame in January, I was totally destroyed,' she said. 'I felt as though I was in a battle. I started to build an air-raid shelter. It has been a tough season and when things go wrong people start to have doubts. But like my father used to say when we had a poor pony, "Don't tell your mother you've bred a jibber." '

Garrison was given acupuncture to heal a lame shoulder and those who stuck pins in his name on the race card yesterday walked off, if not with loadsamoney, as they had last year from Norton Coin's 100–1 shock, certainly with a decent profit on the 16–1 winner.

'This was even better than winning the National,' said Jenny Pitman. 'It has always been my ambition to train a winner of the Gold Cup or the National ridden by Mark.'

Mark had thought his number was up when Garri put him in the lead three fences from home. 'He took me in front at the third last and I thought it was too soon,' he said. 'I thought I would just sit still and try to give him a bit of a breather if that was possible. I sat on him till the second last and then I thought, "Well, it's now or never." '

It was now. Garri's three owners, who run a precision-engineering business in Cheltenham, were not so much ecstatic as numb. 'It is a dream come true,' was the best John Davies could come up with. 'Jenny asked Mark to keep him up on the pace but the question was would he stay. After the last he was dying with every step.' Would he have lasted another 50 yards? 'There weren't another 50 yards.'

Those who follow Jenny Pitman's progress and had been disappointed at the form of her horses in this year's festival were punching the air. The Gold Cup was her first win of the festival.

Nobody seemed much interested in The Fellow, although his trainer François Doumen said his owner, the Marquesa de Moratalla, was 'a wonderful lady who deserved the win', and no one seemed inclined to argue.

Dessie made a rapturous return to the unsaddling enclosure, and Burridge, who had suffered the race from the lawn in front of the main stand, head bent praying for the grey's safe homecoming, looked as delighted as if Dessie had won.

'I'm not quite,' he said. 'But he ran a wonderful race. He beat some pretty good horses. I'm very proud of him. He still draws on his battling qualities but his talent is not so great. He was very tired when he finished. But, you know, coming third in the Gold Cup isn't so bad. I think we'll give him a week off.'

His trainer David Elsworth said: 'He ran a fantastic race, but everyone knows Cheltenham's left-hand course puts him at a disadvantage.'

'You remove one of the major weapons in his armoury running him here,' said Burridge. 'He just doesn't like this track.'

It will be his last visit and after he had left the unsaddling enclosure to the victors, Cheltenham, in spite of its heaving, happy, hearty crowds, suddenly seemed an emptier place.

No doubt there will soon be a new statue, like the ones of Arkle and Dawn Run, to remind us of him, and indeed he will run at Sandown in April if the going is right. But a statue will be a poor thing next to the memory of two years ago when the tall grey with the Silvikrin tail streamed past the post with the crowd on its feet, hats in the air and the bookies in tears.

6 May 1991: Matthew Engel

Kentucky fried

Three weeks after the Masters, a young man from Faldo country failed by a fraction of a second on Saturday to storm an even richer, more famous and more impenetrable citadel of American sport. He failed gloriously and came back with a hard-luck story so heartfelt that, even in a sport of hard-luck stories, it sounded pretty convincing.

The event was the Kentucky Derby and the young man was Ian Jory, the 33-year-old son of a radiologist from Tewin in Hertfordshire and now training horses in Southern California. He only went into racing because he read a Dick Francis when he was looking for a job and emigrated here eight years ago because it was a cheaper place to start on his own.

Last year Jory trained the fourth and another Briton, Chris Speckert, had the third. In 117 years, no British trainer ('someone who speaks English,' as Speckert put it), based on either side of the Atlantic, has ever won America's greatest horse race. But our boys are getting closer. And so they should: the course is, after all, called Churchill Downs.

Jory's horse, Best Pal, was beaten a length and three-quarters by Strike the Gold, a good name for a winner, which paid just under 5–1 to his backers and £400,000 to his owners. Best Pal was just over 5–1. Hansel was favourite, the 12th in a row to get beaten; he was 10th.

The whole thing took just over two minutes – the longest two minutes in sport, since everyone who matters gets to the track before breakfast and the race starts around 5.35pm. But the Derby (or rather Durby, as opposed to Darby) is not just a race or a day at the races. They began gathering way back in April and this has been the most rigorous week of the racing year, of preparation for the horses – all stabled close to one another in the barns behind the back stretch – money-making for the locals and boozing for the visitors.

Kentucky has not yet succumbed to the new American puritanism. It still grows tobacco and makes bourbon and is the one state in the union, aside from casino-run Nevada, where horse racing is regarded as a respectable and important business rather than the pursuit of a depraved minority.

It is a business in deep trouble. The recession has hit hard, the tax laws have been adjusted unfavourably, the Arabs have pulled back. And now the great stud farms of the Bluegrass are struggling: Spendthrift Farms, appropriately enough, went bankrupt; Calumet Farms is said to be $65 million (£39 million) in debt.

As the mint juleps went down at Anita Madden's party, the poshest of the Derby-eve thrashes, some of the guests may well have been seeking oblivion with more determination than usual. It is a nice question which country's racing is in bigger crisis, the British or American.

The essential difference is this: the big British bookmakers are captains of industry; in America they get jailed. The result in Britain is an economic set-up hopeless for everyone except for the bookmaker but a sport that can still produce a Dessie who can touch everyone's lives.

America has a tote monopoly that even in bad times pumps money back into the sport to provide sumptuous racecourses, good prize-money and a sport that leaves most of the population entirely cold. The US has fallen as out of love with horses as it has with the nation's other forefather, the iron horse.

But not at the Derby, not in Kentucky. The biggest party was not at Anita Madden's, it was on Central Avenue, right there on the street outside the racetrack in the inner suburbs of Louisville and only just finishing when the early risers arrived on Saturday morning. The street party was a celebration of the extraordinary properties of American beer, which fits the classic definition of a catalyst: it passes through the human body without undergoing any noticeable change.

On the sound principle that folks should be able to do what they like as long as they do not do it on the street and frighten the horses, the party-goers should all have been arrested. They were doing both, shrieking obscenities through the fences at the stables barely 30 yards away. One shooting, one stabbing, 100 arrests: a quiet year, said the police. But several horses spent an uneasy night; it was the first part of Jory's hard-luck story.

And so the 117th Kentucky Derby Day began. It was an overcast, muggy one, threatening wet. The crowd poured into their respective positions. It is a two-nations event, like Epsom. Here people's positions are not necessarily assigned at birth but there is a huge difference between the clubhouse and the infield. The top three tiers of the stand are known as Millionaires' Row and the women make an effort to reproduce something of the front and fashion that the O'Haras maintained at Tara circa 1859. The infield, meanwhile, is populated by people in T-shirts with folded chairs and rugs. By mid-afternoon it looked like Tara after General Sherman had marched through.

The first race began six hours before the big one,

almost in a vacuum. American racing is so different, so foreign. The horses, bolstered by drugs and whipping that would get the trainers and jockeys banned for centuries in Britain, are trained by the stopwatch to leap furiously out of the stalls; they are nearly always going slower at the finish than at the start. The dirt-tracks have less individuality than the average greyhound circuit. The horses are anonymous.

The Derby rises above all this because, like the Masters, it had a presiding genius who understood marketing before anyone used the word. Colonel Matt Winn took over Churchill Downs in 1903, when the Derby had been going for 28 undistinguished years. He invited the top sportswriters, cultivated their company, fed them stories, picked up their bar tabs and reaped the reward. The golfers at Augusta did much the same thing. Both acquired that most prized American quality, tradition, almost at once.

Churchill Downs has twin towers (more elegant than Wembley's, with the vague whiff of a Bavarian schloss). There is a garland of roses for the Derby winner and as the big-race runners emerge on to the track from the parade ring, the band strikes up 'My Kentucky Home'.

The sun shines bright in the old Kentucky home,
'Tis summer, the people are gay . . .

There is a problem with this song. No one knows the words which, anyway, have changed: in more insensitive Kentucky times it was 'the darkies are gay', and one day they will probably be forced to change gay as well, which will cause havoc with the rhyme structure. None the less, it is one of those spine-tingling moments in sport, like 'Abide With Me' in the old days at Wembley.

They were even trying their hardest to sing along in the infield, though by then most of the people were well out of it. They had been out of it since at least the fifth race, when thousands were diverted by an impromptu display of tit-flashing from girls sitting on their boyfriends' shoulders. Unlike square-dancing, balloon-racing and the Annual Salute to Black Jockeys, this is an event which the Louisville city fathers have yet to include in the fortnight-long Derby festival.

But by 5.30, everyone who could still stand was attentive. The army band was inspected by the guest-of-honour, one H. Norman Schwarzkopf, who I think is someone in showbiz. American racing may be troubled, may be dull. But as one looked down from the roof on 135,554 people, 20,000 flowers, 16 thoroughbreds, one four-star general, the fountains, the tote boards recording millions of dollars' worth of betting, the frankfurter, nachos and mint julep tents and the honour guard standing to attention, one sure as hell knew one was not at Market Rasen any more.

Jory's horse was drawn on the outside, by far the worst position of any fancied runner. Best Pal started slowly, was checked on the bend and then boxed in by an outsider. By the time Gary Stevens was able to make him fly, Chris Antley on Strike the Gold was going too well. The draw alone is said to make two-lengths difference.

The achievement of coming second seemed lost on Jory. A security guard refused to let him through to his horse ('If I'd won, I'd have punched him') and the handler almost got lost on the way to the winners' enclosure, which would have meant disqualification.

'Look at him, he's a fresh horse,' said Jory. 'He's hardly had a race. We couldn't really run until we got out of the rails. I think we had the best horse.' He shrugged. 'You know. Racing luck.'

The winning trainer, Nick Zito from New York, gave the credit first to his horse: 'I had to make him happy and he told me what to do.' This sounded promising, as victorious American sportsmen usually say God was responsible for their victory and, by implication, their opponents' defeat.

What was he shouting down the home stretch? 'Show me the way,' said Zito. Sorry? 'I always look to the guy upstairs. This game will humble kings.' Back at the stables, he explained further. 'You see the sun up there. Strike the Gold comes from the special person upstairs. Good is better than evil.' He was not being personal about Jory. With the winner watching from his stall they embraced each other. 'Nice guys finish 1–2,' said Zito.

He went on to the winner's party, another tradition. Jory walked slowly away to fly back to California – but only for a couple of days. The horse goes straight to Maryland for revenge in the Preakness, the second leg of the Triple Crown, on Saturday week and Jory will follow him there to continue the strange, nomadic, almost circus-like life that is the American trainer's lot.

He was not the only one out of luck. This should have been a great triumph for the successful but hard-up breeders Calumet Farms. But the stud sold Strike the Gold last autumn. And the win will not even raise the value of his sire Alydar; he died in November. So it goes in racing these days.

Strike the Gold was bought by a syndicate including the man who brings out Trivial Pursuit and headed by one B. Giles Brophy, who breeds Holstein cattle. His wife Gale, in a red floral hat, said winning the Derby was better even than when she shot a crocodile in Africa. 'It's the greatest high honour. The closest thing for a woman is probably having a child.' Schwarzkopf was pleased too. 'I've had nothing but winners today,' he beamed. 'Lemme tell you, I've had nothing but winners for the past nine months.'

Meanwhile, as dusk fell, the rain finally arrived and the last of the drunks lurched slowly and damply through the litter out of the infield.

6 June 1991: Frank Keating at the Epsom Derby, won by Generous at 9–1

Running on flat batteries

The oldest horse in the field prevailed resplendently, but not the oldest jockey. The youngest jockey did that – with a punching whoop of triumph as he passed the post: new-style horsemanship.

Lester Piggott may only have been seventh in the field of 13, but the wizened maestro can certainly claim to have been involved with another Derby winner – for young Alan Munro, at 24 over 30 years younger than Piggott, spent two hours on Derby eve in Piggott's house watching films of the former champion's nine winning Derbys and being talked through them by 85-year-old Keith, Lester's father. 'Be in the right place at the right time,' was the tenor of the old man's griff.

'Everything sure went to plan,' said the young jockey, full of himself at the end, and fair enough. 'There was not one frightening moment. Everything was smooth and sweet. I switched him off for the first half – and switched him on for the second half. Simple. End of story.'

If confidence is a prerequisite for going the whole way in professional sport, then young Munro is going far. You bet. Dark, swarthy, beetle-browed and cocksure, he is like a swaggering little Welsh scrum-half of the legend; playing behind a really good pack, mind you; as in a way he most assuredly was yesterday.

'That's my business,' snapped Munro to two or three questions at the end about contracts and so on – adding fiercely: 'Not that I want you to think me brash.' You could have fooled a few of us on that one. But, for sure, we are going to be hearing a great deal of – and from – Master Munro in the future.

Perhaps, as Piggott's did through four decades (and

now into a fifth), Munro's strut and confidence might sustain for a little longer at least the very English myth that Derby Day at Epsom remains one of the wonders of the world.

From dawn yesterday we were all at it – in the public prints and on radio and television. You know the sort of stuff. 'The greatest horse race in the world . . . the blue riband . . . the finest happy-go-lucky social mix of plebs, debs, queens and commoners known since the Magna Carta and democracy were invented.'

Who is conning who? All of us are. True, the pewtery skies and angry spits of drizzle did not help yesterday – but the vaunted boast, plucked out of the air by PR men, that half a million folk were jostling together in merry, funfair fandango on the Downs just could not be true. It looked to be less than a Cup final crowd.

As for this 'revered national institution watched by the world' lark, well, just over two million clamoured around their TV sets to watch the race yesterday. What does that make *The Archers* with over seven million three hours later on the radio?

One has to say the Ever-Ready Derby has flat batteries indeed. Even as a race for global zillionaires it is decidedly loose-change stuff these days – around 20th in the world in the big-race prize-money list.

Epsom's ancient 1½ miles is still the most perfect of testing courses – but it is diminished for sure when the world's, even the continent's, even the country's, finest thoroughbreds are happy to pass it up. Simply because business is business and horses are bred at this level not so much to dare to race but to breed.

There were only 13 runners yesterday – and, to paraphrase an Irish rugby forward in another context: 'Boy, we were lucky to get 13.' There had also been just 13 starters in 1989; there were 18 last year, most of them second-stringers. Indeed, all in the know were saying yesterday that if you want to see some real international championship flat racing go to the Irish Derby.

Thank (to coin a phrase) God for the Sheikhs of Araby. Only three of the 13 owners yesterday could count Britain as their home – Messrs Bill Gredley and Charles St George, and Lady Beaverbrook. Cry God for Milady, William and St George: we few, we happy few, we band of brothers.

The always zanily xenophobic *Daily Mail* and a couple of other nationals yesterday, in a half-page colour show of the runners and riders, never even mentioned the names of the owners of the 13 horses; only in big bold type the English trainers and English jockeys. Over half the horses were owned by eight various gradations of Sheikhdom. Prince Fahd Salman pronounced himself most happily fulfilled at tea-time yesterday. 'Ah, we meet again, sir,' said young Munro, sticking out a hand in the winner's enclosure.

The prince is as handsome as Errol Flynn in his dashingest days, with a saucily thin moustache to match. Prize money? Last year, he said, he gave all his prize money to charity. 'This year I'm putting it all back into racing and sponsoring two big days on English racecourses.'

He could do worse, if nothing else strikes him, than to give Epsom a hand-out. If we thought the Edrich-Compton stands at Lord's took a long time to get up and ready, Epsom's yesterday seemed scarcely padded up. All day long as the furiously keen March-like zephyrs zapped off the Downs they took with them dust and debris from the builders' skips behind the grandstand. Not to mention a few crisp packets.

Men in morning coats on the posh side tried to look even cooler than they felt as they hung on to their toppers. The millineried molls on their arm had to take both hands to their spaceship hats at the same time as pretending to look glam. Don't these dames ever deign to listen to the weather forecast?

A blustery day and, generally, a disappointing one. The only plus is that the winds might just have blown in an exceedingly bold new character in Master Munro.

2 July 1990: Ian Ridley in the Olympic Stadium, Rome, at a quarter-final of the World Cup

Exit Jack's giant killers

'Tis a tale of a magic night that will be told for generations to come from Main Head to Mizen Head, of how Ireland took on the mighty Italians in their own colosseum and had them on one knee before losing 1–0. There are defeats more triumphant than victory, as Montaigne said.

Actually, the story of Ireland's World Cup was more Barbara Cartland: romantic but not particularly well written. The broad brush counts more than the detail; the joyous presence of the team, after 56 years of trying, and its 15,000-strong green party of enlightened followers overshadow some unflattering facts.

The little things stick in the mind: Jack Charlton prowling the pitch before kick-off, a manager wishing he could still play; the team turning their backs on TV cameras to face the flag during their national anthem; Chris Morris shaking each Romanian's hand before penalties; Pat Bonner in tears of relief and nervous exhaustion after them.

But when intellect takes over from emotion, the Irish look less attractive, playing some tedious, ugly football which failed to yield a win and produced a goal on average every four hours.

One of the myriad banners accompanying the Republic proclaimed Booterstown United. This may be the name of a real club back home, but it seemed more appropriate for the national team.

'Maybe the type of game we play shows a little bit of merit,' said an unusually humble, polite and complimentary Charlton after the defeat by Italy. 'Maybe it's shown the way that other people can go.' Are you watching, Brazil?

Charlton, who has made himself a larger figure than any of his players, confirmed himself a stubborn and uncompromising leader. He would have us believe that his credo – 'Don't put the ball at risk in your own half, get it upfield high and quickly and see what develops' – is designed to mirror the strengths of his players.

It is more a way to cover up deficiencies – he admitted to 'laxities', including the laxity of a good winger – especially in defence. It is also an insult to the ability of such players as Ray Houghton, Kevin Sheedy and – although it was rarely allowed to be exhibited – Andy Townsend.

Ronnie Whelan, though he insisted he was fit, was never given the chance to show his true value, the manager attempting to prove his theory that system is more than individual. That cut to Whelan may take time to heal.

Charlton frequently proved himself boorish, most recently in his manhandling of a TV camera crew after Saturday night's match. There was a time in Palermo when it seemed the daily grind might lead him to walk away from the job as he had done at Sheffield Wednesday and Newcastle. His advancement as a potential president of the republic owed nothing to his diplomatic ability. His inability to take criticism of the sort he used frequently to dispense on television himself became ridiculous.

The curmudgeon could be a charmer, however. And the achievement of reaching the quarter-finals will not be minimised in the republic. For them his only mistake was perhaps not discovering that Robert O'Baggio fellow first.

Charlton said last Thursday in a press conference of rare good humour that he intends to honour an agreement to stay in charge for another 18 months. It will, though, be difficult for him to alter the angle of attack and take the Republic to another European Championship finals from a group containing England, Poland and Turkey. He took the oldest squad to Italy and it is likely to be the end of the affair for some, notably the 34-year-old Kevin Moran. Nor, unless some more Irish ancestry is discovered, does Charlton have ready-made replacements, particularly in central defence.

The Republic's strength has been their single-minded belief in their own game irrespective of the opposition, be it, say, Finland or Italy. On Saturday night it became a weakness as they proved unable to adapt.

Italy were in discomfort midway through the second half and in the first 10 minutes, when even Baresi was giving the ball away, but as much due to their own anxiety as the Republic's stomach for the fight.

Quinn's towering header from the excellent McGrath's cross had Zenga leaping to save and please the crowd, but moments later Schillaci headed just wide at the other end.

When Schillaci did score after 37 minutes – 'I know little about the Irish but I think I will score,' he had said before the match – the Republic were expiring like mosquitoes in the Roman night. The briefly unsighted Bonner parried Donadoni's shot, but Toto's eye, touch and aim were sure.

Schillaci, having already scooped a good chance over the crossbar, might have had a hat-trick. His breathtaking shot from 30 yards bounced down from the underside of the bar on to the goalline and with seconds to go he was denied a goal by a linesman's erring flag. And for each half-chance that Aldridge squandered, Italy spurned two.

As ever with the Republic, the scoreline covered up. But their heart was never in question, certainly not from the applauding Italian audience. Like a faithful flogged horse, it had taken them as far as it could.

26 January 1991: Mike Selvey in Adelaide

Jewel among the Ashes

Just occasionally there occurs an individual performance so perfectly sublime it transcends the contest itself. Yesterday on Australia's most lovely ground and in front of a capacity holiday crowd, Mark Waugh in his first Test innings for Australia made a century of such stunning, rounded perfection that, for a while in the afternoon sunshine, batting was elevated above the level of the purely functional modern mode and transported back to the Golden Age.

At six o'clock, when the last ball of the day had been bowled, Waugh turned on his heel and marched briskly from the middle, through the applauding throng and up the stairs to the Australian dressing room. He had made 116 undefeated runs, every one of them a pearl of timing, elegance and grace.

Ten minutes before the close, after three hours less four minutes at the crease, he had rocked on to the back foot and punched a short ball from Phil Tufnell precisely, mathematically, between the cover fielders for his 15th boundary, and it took him to 101.

A roar rose from the crowd and Waugh, in sheer genuine delight, whipped off his batting helmet and bathed shamelessly in the standing ovation accorded him by every man, woman and child on the ground, Australian and English alike. For a brief minute, nationalism had taken a back seat. Those who witnessed this innings knew that they were a privileged few.

In all, Waugh hit 16 delicious boundaries from 144 balls. His first 50 used 74, the next only 52. In a glorious final session, when the cloud cover that had lingered over the ground for the first part of the day finally rolled away, he scored 95 out of 125 and his partnership with Greg

Matthews for Australia's sixth wicket produced 145 runs, taking Australia from the depths of 124 for five to 269 for five; Matthews made just 29 of them.

'Well batted, boy,' said Graham Gooch to his county colleague as he shook Waugh's hand. He knows a class act when he sees it.

So Waugh joins an elite band. Few batsmen have the nerve, skill, temperament, technique and luck to make a century on their Test debut. The last Australian to do so was Wayne Phillips against Pakistan almost eight years ago. Fewer still do so in an Ashes Test. Keppler Wessels was the last, in Brisbane in 1983, and before that one has to go back 20 years to Perth when the young Greg Chappell first stamped his elegance on the Test scene.

Comparison with the latter is not inappropriate. Chappell had played 98 first-class innings for his state and Somerset before making his Test debut: yesterday's was Waugh's 101st innings, many of them for Gooch's Essex. It was also his 25th century, each meticulously marked totemistically on his bat in black ink. Chappell, of course, went on to make 23 more blissful centuries for his country: who knows how many Mark Waugh may make?

His innings, though, had a significance over and above pure statistics or even aesthetics, for finally, after five long years, he has emerged from the shadow of his twin brother Steve to become an international player in his own right. Steve made his Test debut in 1985, ahead of his time maybe, when the going was hard in Australian cricket. It took him 27 Tests and 42 innings to make a century but, when it came to that magic day at Headingley in 1988, when he dissected the England attack to make an unbeaten 177, it was a repayment of faith.

Never, one thought, had there been such a maiden century as this. Until now. And there is the true irony of it. While Steve was fretting away, frustrating those who recognised talent worryingly unfulfilled, Mark played the underling. He became known as Afghanistan – the forgotten Waugh. In status, Steve might have been his elder brother by four years, not four minutes.

But hard times have hit Steve once more. He was omitted from this Test; and Mark took his place.

Yesterday Waugh had arrived at the crease rather sooner than he would have liked after Allan Border had won the toss for Australia, for England, playing five bowlers and omitting Jack Russell after 20 consecutive Tests since his debut to make room for them, had reduced them to 124 for five by midway through the afternoon session.

Only Marsh, who had appeared impregnable until he was caught at second slip, and Boon, who spent more than three hours over 49 before slicing a catch to third man, looked capable of shrugging off the constraint applied by the English seamers.

Taylor had been run out early on, Border spent an hour and a quarter over a dozy dozen before edging down on to his stumps and, in the same DeFreitas over, Dean Jones was given out lbw, much to his annoyance; there seemed to be an element of bat in this.

Waugh came in as Jones went out, and from his second ball, which he creamed effortlessly past the bowler for three, to the end of the day he never looked in the slightest trouble.

'I respond to pressure,' he said, as he conducted his press conference with a shy, bemused air, 'and four for nothing can get you going better than four for two hundred.'

This was some response. His footwork was effortless, his timing as immaculate as a Swiss chronometer. His strokes through midwicket off the seamers were steel-wristed economy, his strokeplay to Tufnell, down the pitch one second, laying back to cut the next, was calculated and cruel, his cutting of Malcolm savage and emphatic, the rifle-crack of his bat echoing under the stands.

In the end, it was not a question whether he would

score his hundred, merely when, and England's flagging bowling in the final session eased his way.

This was a theatre and he was centre stage. The audience was not going to be denied. Mark Waugh is a very fine batsman: he is also, it seems, a showman. Forgotten no more.

18 March 1991: Frank Keating sees England win the grand slam at Twickenham by beating France 21–19

Blanco's try

Four momentous tries gilded Saturday's climax, with the first possibly the most opulent since old men with memories were themselves at their grandfather's knee. That takes in all the rich history of the Five Nations Championship.

The very context sharpened the grandeur of its daring, dotty conception and the nerveless joy of its execution. For the challenge, in bold relief, matched England's substance, nous and penalty power against France's airy *élan*, spontaneity and dextrous tricks and treats.

At once the two philosophies collided. England missed a long penalty and all eyes and senses, certainly those of the England XV for a moment, relaxed and prepared for a 22 drop-out.

Suddenly all hell broke loose or, rather, the incomparable Blanco, dusky warrior-captain of France, did. '*Moi, moi*,' he shouted to Saint-André. Blanco has always put his trust in gods who favour the foolhardy. He was now across his line but still only ten yards beyond it. In a trice the ball was with Lafond outside him and the wing's left hip took out Andrew, first to spot the danger, and an instantaneous fingertip pass allowed Sella, at speed, to round his own despairing white marker.

Sella was over the 22 and momentarily clear as England regrouped and frantically funnelled back. The stalwart Probyn had tanked across to confront him on the 10-metre line. Sella feinted to knife inside him, so stopping the prop in his tracks, and as he did so, he turned in a dummy-scissors loop and fed on the outside again the delicate Camberabero. The pit-a-pat fly-half could now snipe across the halfway mark.

Then, with dainty exactness, he slippered the ball over the head of the retreating Hodgkinson, caught it in full-pelt stride and was now up to England's 22-metre flag. Though England's bold general Carling had remarkably made it across the field he could only fling himself at Camberabero a split-second after the Frenchman had dapped the most perfect cross-kick to within five metres of the posts.

This took out the corner-flagging Hill and left Saint-André to compose himself, collect and triumphantly launch himself at the line as Guscott's all-in, last-gasp dive lassoed his ankles. The palpitating thing was done.

From line to line it took 17.25 seconds, four more than the previous collective marvel of the age, for the Barbarians at Cardiff on 27 January 1973, when the dancing Bennett dared and set in train that breathtaking passage down another touchline. For Dawes's phoney dummy then, read Sella's phoney scissors here; for Quinnell's genius slip-catch from David then, here was Camberabero's chip-and-catch.

But that Barbarians epic was done with licence to cavort. If daring failed, no matter. Saturday's audacious try was inspired by all the vivid intensity of the grandeur of the Slam.

Memories of another inspired collective score, touched by angels, came to mind when the cockles calmed themselves: in 1980, high on the veldt of Northern Transvaal in May, the Lions were losing 16–19 with minutes to go. With defiant courage Quinnell (again), Patterson, Richards,

Renwick, Woodward, Hay and nine others poured themselves in desperate tides at the opposition line through five rucks, 33 pairs of hands and a minute and three-quarters of optimism until Slemen plunged in the killing thrust under the posts.

But that was no Grand Slammer and those who were there that day agreed this weekend that the palm was now for France – the grandest of the grand. As the Barbarians' score in 1973 will always be 'Bennett's try', so will Saturday's be 'Blanco's try'. What a way to go.

Two hours after he had showered, and easily into his tenth cork-tipped cigarette, he was shruggingly explaining the sweet 17 seconds. He was in his *je-ne-parle-pas-Anglais* mood but the translation is roughly this: 'The try? It is communion. The team is a sacrament. No one man scores a try, the whole team scores it. The communion made this try, because all of us opened our minds to score it. No one man has the vision, the whole team has the vision, fifteen as one man.'

Had he seen the English momentarily drop their guard? '*Non. Il est instantané, il est spontané, instinctif. C'est le rugby. Finis.*' His dark eyes glistened. He smiled and lit another cigarette from the glowing stub of the previous one.

Along the corridor the heroic, relieved English were rightly celebrating. All they had wanted was to win *something* tangible, they had insisted, and dedicated their victory to their grandchildren. 'Is it true, Grandpa, that you were in the Grand Slam finale way back in '91?' 'Yes, my child, I was.' 'Tell me, Grandpa, was Blanco's try as good as the history books say?' 'Argghhh!'

16 April 1991: Matthew Engel at the US Masters at Augusta

Master Woosnam

Up the airy mountain
Down the rushy glen
We dare not go a'hunting
For fear of little men

Ian Woosnam, being 33 and British, fits the average age and average country of origin of recent Masters winners; at 5ft 4½ in he just happens to be almost a foot under the average height.

There is a great tradition of pocket battleships in sport. There was Bobby Collins ('the Wee Barra') of Celtic and Leeds United, who wore size 3 boots and kicked like a bad-tempered mule. There was Harry Pilling of Lancashire, as fearless as any batsman except when he batted with Clive Lloyd, who he kept thinking was going to tread on him. There was, or possibly still is, Maradona.

Woosnam is extraordinary. Sandy Lyle always appears to be playing golf having set out to do something else but forgotten what it was; Nick Faldo plays as though he is doing The Most Important Job In the World and only his eight-foot putt can save humanity from destruction. Woosnam looks as though he has come out for the Red Lion's annual trip to Stableford, 18 holes and a crate of Mackeson on the coach home.

If Faldo is golf's Geoff Boycott, we have now moved perilously close to Jocky Wilson. On Sunday night someone asked Woosnam a technical question. 'I think that's a lot of twaddle,' he said. 'I just stand there and hit it.'

He and his wife Glendryth (who is even tinier) were sitting between two representatives of Mark McCormack's organisation who looked like a plain-clothes police guard.

Then one of them announced that Woosnam could expect to make $5½ million (£3.1 million) as a result of this win. 'It opens up a whole new worldwide market for Woosie.'

The Woosnams wore the expressions of pools winners and made pools winners' remarks. Ian said it was a dream come true at least four times. No, he said, there wasn't anything he wanted but perhaps his mum and dad might want to go round the world. 'My friends are my friends. I don't see why I should change my life for anybody.'

There might just have been a 'We'll see about that' expression on one of the McCormack men's faces; but it will take a lot to spoil Woosnam. He is gloriously unglamorous. Even the smallest available green jacket hung loose on him. He marched up the fairways puffing his fag. After winning he promptly sent a message to the lads back in Oswestry to get the beers in. He is totally different to the American pros, with their designer-teeth. And he beat them.

The American press and public have no idea what to make of him. This is partly because the nation only has a limited capacity for absorbing foreigners into its consciousness and it has had Lyle, Faldo and Saddam Hussein in fairly short order.

Many of them have not heard anyone say anything like 'I kept me head down' since the Beatles' heyday. And they are bewildered how a man with his physique can consistently outdrive all the men who look the part. The power appears to come from his big rear end and his farmer boy's thighs. But that hardly does him justice: he is a lovely instinctive golfer and a competitor in the best bantam-cock tradition.

They are still mighty confused, though. Nearly every paper yesterday placed Oswestry in Wales. One radio man enquired whether Wales was in Scotland. Well, you never know what the next local government reorganisation might throw up, and several papers took up the same theme of mixed-Celtery. 'Play a chorus of God Save the

Queen and raise a glass of Britain's best stout to Wee Woosie,' said the *San Francisco Examiner*.

Ah yes, Wee Woosie. It's a braw bricht moonlicht nicht tonicht, iachy da, for the broth of a boy, begorrah. Which reminds me: it's Ronan Rafferty's turn next.

7 June 1991: Matthew Engel

Sweeping death under the carpet

Bill Smith, chairman of the Auto Cycle Union, and I were standing in a garden belonging to a lovely lady called Beryl, waiting for the riders to come by in the Supersport 400 event, the third race of the Isle of Man TT week. We were on Bray Hill in Douglas, which to the untutored eye appears to be a street of detached and semi-detached 1930s houses like thousands of others in the British Isles, though the TT course guide talks instead about 'an ultra-fast right-left hander with a sadistic bump just out of sight over the crest'.

Smith was apologetic. 'They're not very quick, the 400s.' Suddenly, the first rider came by, a flash of man and motorbike. He was doing 130 miles an hour on a line precisely seven feet from Beryl's front gate.

The rest streaked through at intervals of a few seconds, silencing conversation and birdsong, whooshing past Armleigh and Monaveen, past the pebbledash garages and the rock gardens and the birdtables and the rose trellises, down past the newsagents and the beauty salon, up the next hill and out of sight.

It does not require much imagination to work out what the attitude of most people in similar streets in Dorking or Doncaster would be if motorbikes were doing 160 mph seven feet from their front gate at five in the morning. I asked Beryl what she thought. 'Oh, love it,' she said.

Beryl spoke for everyone. On the Isle of Man and among the motorcycling fancy the TT Races are a matter of huge interest, intense pride and no controversy. The TT made the island famous; otherwise, there are only cats, kippers and the birch. The races are the basis of a tourist trade which in other respects has been in steady decline, but the TT ceased to be part of the Grand Prix circuit 15 years ago. The top track riders no longer come here, nor do most sports-writers.

Non-Manxmen and non-bikers now hear little except the statistics: of the 535 competitors entered in this year's TT, four are already dead – Ian Young, Petr Hlavatka from Czechoslovakia, a father of three, Frank Duffy, and Roy Anderson. This brings the total killed on the course over the past 80 years to 160. For reasons we shall come to, this is a strictly unofficial figure.

The event, however, is not declining. It has turned into the world's greatest bikie-festival: 40,000 enthusiasts flock here, bringing with them 14,000 motorbikes. But two of the fans have also been killed this year, one of them on an occasion known, with reason, as Mad Sunday, when anyone can ride round the course. No one knows how many people, competitors and others, have been injured, crippled or rendered senseless over the years. But an informed source estimated that there are between 20 and 50 major injuries – broken legs and worse – during the fortnight every year. These are subjects which no one on the island wants to discuss. They want to talk about Steve Hislop's chances of winning the big race today and whether he might push the lap record to over 125 mph. It is not exactly a conspiracy of silence, but there is a conspiracy to talk as quietly as possible.

Forty per cent of the Isle of Man's declining tourist industry depends on motor-sport events; the Manx weekly papers did not even name all the dead riders. There must be Manxmen who oppose the whole business, but they keep quiet and take their holidays when the TT is on. For motorcyclists the island is a haven of tolerance in a hostile world and they hate the bad publicity as much as their hosts. *Motor Cycle News* shoved the deaths very quietly on page two.

People here – nice, helpful, friendly people – begin to shuffle uneasily when they meet a journalist who does not want to write about the torque ratios on the 750 Honda. In the early 1970s in the United States, 30 people were killed every year playing American football; last year no one was. Grand-prix racing drivers used to die with horrific regularity; the last death, touch wood, was in 1982.

There is a modern obsession with avoiding risk of any kind: James Dean and Jim Morrison are modern icons but no longer role models. Most westerners now want to grow old. The Isle of Man prides itself on being behind the times.

Roy Anderson, the fourth rider to die this year, was a Scot. At once a Scottish Labour MP, Tony Worthington, demanded that the whole thing be banned, as Labour MPs are prone to do when they know nothing about a subject.

'He wants to mind his own business,' said Michael Jopling, the former Conservative chief whip and agriculture minister who is president of the Auto Cycle Union. 'The Isle of Man is not part of the United Kingdom. They make their own laws and they are grown-up boys. It really is nothing to do with Westminster MPs.'

Is this so? Well, up to a point. The Isle of Man is a 'Crown dependency' like Jersey and Guernsey. Its parliament, Tynwald, existed when the Saxons and Celts on the two big islands nearby were running about in woad. If its 70,000 people did send an MP to Westminster it would undoubtedly be someone not unlike Michael Jopling.

The TT – which stands for Tourist Trophy – started here in 1907 because Westminster even then refused to countenance the idea of closing public roads for racing. It fits into the island's prevailing philosophy, which might be defined as selective libertarianism.

The tax laws are famously generous. There is no breathalyser and no general speed limit. Seat belts are not compulsory. On the other hand, hanging and birching are still on the statute books, homosexuals can, theoretically, be locked up for life and a TT fan from Nuneaton was jailed this week after disembarking from the ferry with the grand total of 1.3 grams of cannabis.

In practice the laws are less draconian than they sound. The lad with the dope will be released when the races are over, the police do not charge into homosexuals' bedrooms, and no one will ever be hanged or birched again – quiet pressure from Westminster sees to that.

Manxmen just like to maintain the pretence that they could do it if they wanted, and that their strictness keeps them free of the modern world's impurities. This is total rubbish, as even the island's Minister of Tourism Alan Bell admitted: 'We kid ourselves that we have the moral high ground. We have exactly the same problems for our size as any rural community anywhere.'

But when it comes to road safety, the island is different. Driving down the hill to Creg Ny Baa on Tuesday, which was not a race day, we were overtaken by a motorcyclist doing at least 140. He was committing no offence.

Everyone admits that the race kills people. The famous Mountain Course, almost 38 miles round the centre of the island and along the fringe of lovely Snaefell, has been in use since 1911. Victor Surridge was killed on Creg Willey's Hill that year, when the machines were little more than pushbikes with engines attached and the fastest lap was clocked at 50 mph. Competitors have been dying ever since, but there is no discernible pattern. Victims include brilliant riders and other riders who should never have been there. They have died through their own errors and mechanical failure. They have died in obvious danger spots and on the most ordinary stretches.

Safety measures have improved over the years and injured riders are now picked up by helicopter and rushed to hospital much faster. But the motorbikes keep getting faster too. Obvious hazards are cushioned with bags of hay, but on a course of 38 miles and 400 bends it is not possible to soften every tree, telegraph pole and stone wall.

'I would have to accept that the TT is dangerous,' said Bill Smith of the ACU. 'Bloody dangerous. There is no doubt about that. I think people accept the risks.'

Not everyone does. Among the race's most forceful critics is the former world champion, Barry Sheene. 'It is totally impossible to make the course even reasonably safe,' says Sheene, who raced here once and never came back.

The islanders are scornful. 'It's easy to go on a bike and ride round a track five or ten times with plenty of spin-off areas,' says Paul Quine, who lives just by Bray Hill. 'It takes a motorcyclist to ride this. Barry Sheene wasn't man enough to ride the course.'

The arguments of the TT's supporters become a bit repetitive. They endlessly claim that other sports are just as dangerous. They have been known to argue that considering the number of riders and the miles they travel, the race is really rather safe.

The most astute point was made by Peter Sheen of the Motor-Cycle Industry Association, who said the course was such a superb test that it contributed hugely to bike-development and thus saved lives elsewhere.

One enthusiast was talking less intelligently: 'Look at all the rugby players in Stoke Mandeville. Compare it to other sports. I think it's safe.'

'I've covered a lot of sports,' I said. 'I don't think it is.'

He sighed. 'Well, that's what makes it. I'll tell you what. You put hand rails up Mount Everest, you'll get ice picks in your back.'

And that's the point, of course. Even seat-belted, low-fat,

look-after-yourself modern man has a deep-seated urge to test himself. Among road racers it just lurks nearer the surface.

'These marvellous young men queue up to come here because they want to,' said Jopling. 'The vast majority of these nice guys who ride round the track lose money. It is inherently dangerous. People go into it because they know it is dangerous. I think the world is a more vigorous, interesting and exciting place when young men have the opportunity to meet this sort of challenge.'

The challenge of saying this loudly and meeting the objectors head-on is something the event's supporters find more daunting. If the ACU does keep a record of the deaths and injuries, it has never made it public. The figure of 160 comes from a little green notebook kept since 1965 by a Manx journalist, Terry Cringle, who discovered that no list existed and set out to compile one, he says, out of youthful enthusiasm and bloody-mindedness.

'I'm seen as a TT wrecker. Nothing could be further from the truth,' says Cringle. 'The only thing that annoyed me was that they kicked death under the carpet. These men had died and they dishonoured them. At one time they were really obstructive about giving out information on deaths. Now they do at least give it out in a professional way.'

But not very professionally. For a major sporting event, the TT is rather shambolic; that is part of its charm. There is none of the commercialised, security-conscious slickness of most modern sports events.

It is easy to drive up to the Grandstand and wander round. It is an event for fans, even in the press room. When Steve Hislop came in on Monday, he had more requests for autographs than interviews.

The organisers do care about the deaths, but they are bikers and bikers know the score. Could they do more? 'Not a lot, to be honest,' said Smith, 'not a lot.' But there are dangers that are obvious to the most casual observer.

At Creg Ny Baa, where the riders scream down the hill at 160-plus and take a right-hander with their right knees almost scraping the tarmac, they straighten up and take a line a few feet from kids dangling their feet over a bank. A mistake there could kill not just the rider but many spectators. I mentioned this to an official.

'Sore point,' he said. 'I've told them.'

The TT's appeal, however, lies not only in its challenge to competitors but in the freedom it offers spectators. Bike fans love to ride up to their own favourite spots, watch the racing, then get together with like-minded people afterwards.

On Douglas seafront the horse trams clip-clop incongruously past thousands of bikers of both sexes and a remarkable range of ages, caressing their machines and lovingly pointing out to new friends the twin-cams on their Kawasaki ZX-10 or something. Later they will earnestly discuss the Suzuki's cooling system over a pint of Okell's before revving up to go to the BMW Owners' Rally, say, or the nightly Miss Wet TT-shirt competition. About 6,000 of the visitors come from Germany. Everyone gets on famously. There is hardly any violence.

Motorcyclists see themselves as an oppressed minority. Other road users hate them. In their space gear they look frightening. Old ladies cower and imagine them all as Hell's Angels. In fact, they are often shy and solitary, which is why they ride motorbikes.

'It's an opportunity for motorcyclists to come somewhere in complete freedom where they're not hassled,' said Bell. 'They can go into the bars at the Palace Hotel and the Empress in their leathers and they're more than welcome.'

The TT offers freedom on many levels. Smith rode for 27 years, losing many good friends but doing no damage to himself until his gearbox locked in 1982 and he broke both arms, both legs and his back. But the thrill has never vanished for him.

'The early morning practice is the best, climbing the mountain on a clear morning. Even on the bike you can see the five kingdoms – England, Scotland, Ireland, Wales and Man. It's the best feeling you could have in your life. Better than sex. A lot of the guys used to say they would sing when they were riding, they were so elated.'

And at the start line next day, you could see the current generation lined up, eyes intense behind their helmets, at ease with their machine but anxious to get going. The first away was number two, Brian Morrison.

There was no number one. Number one was meant to be Ian Young, and Ian Young was dead.

2 January 1991: Bob Fisher

Winners losers

Uncertainty has always been the lifeblood of ocean racing. No matter how careful the planning or how meticulous the pre-race study of meteorological data, those who venture off shore know that the sea does not always deliver what is expected. Would the crews of the 303 boats which set out from Cowes for that fateful 1979 Fastnet Race have gone if they had known that there would be Force 11 winds and huge waves in the Irish Sea?

The Sydney–Hobart is one of the world's classic ocean races and each year more than 1,000 yachtsmen take up its challenge. So, when the opportunity to compete came, it was short work to accept. Ocean races are described as the breaks between parties and the Sydney–Hobart has the biggest party of all; it also has the greatest uncertainty.

Boxing Day, 1pm. The New South Wales Premier Nick Greiner fired the starting gun for the 110 yachts from Shark Island in Sydney Harbour. A case of champagne was offered for the first around the Heads and, in 20 knots of south-easterly breeze, there was a full-blooded charge up the three miles of the harbour.

Lawrie Smith chose Rothmans' place on the starting line with care. Clear air and room to manoeuvre are all-important. The 80-footer was up to full speed as the guns fired and shot into an early lead. She was, however, challenged by the ultra-light Bobsled of Geoff Bush, a downwind flier which did not quite make the break-through to windward and could not find her way through the shadow to leeward. The champagne was ours and, as we began to make our way south, Bobsled's challenge evaporated fast.

For 12 hours we beat dead into the wind, keeping an eye on the whereabouts of our closest rivals: Ragamuffin, Condor and Brindebella. There is no sense in going off alone and allowing the others to find better winds. But the gaps began to grow and the wind began to change.

Early on the second morning we raised a light spin-naker before peeling to a heavier one at 7am as the wind backed to the north. It blew at more than 20 knots and our search for stronger north-easterly winds took us about five miles to the east of the Rhumb line course. We hoped they would come, but no one wanted what finally arrived.

At first, in mid-afternoon, the winds gave us the most exhilarating sleigh ride. The 38-ton yacht took off like a speedboat, surfing down the faces of the waves at more than 20 knots with a full-sized spinnaker and unreefed mainsail. The tension on board was electric. This was what we had come for – the slithering of a big yacht on the brink of control.

The seas of the Bass Strait are not the long rollers of the Southern Ocean for which Rob Humphreys had designed Rothmans; they are short and more suited to smaller boats. Rothmans was sliding down the face of one straight into the back of the next.

On one wave she stuck her bow into the one in front and tried to become a submarine. The boat seemed to stop dead although everything is relative – the speedometer, which had read 23 knots, now showed 10. A wall of water, three feet deep, was brimming over the foredeck and the stern was lifting out of the sea. Rothmans was in danger of cartwheeling.

The deck watch were all clipped on with safety harnesses as 10 tons of water hurtled towards them. It was a horrifying moment. Suddenly we were all waist deep and the smile that had been on the face of the helmsman, Gordon McGuire, faded. Mike Spies was trying to come up the companion hatch as the water cascaded down the steps. He later compared himself to a spawning salmon battling upstream.

In those terrifying seconds we all held on, uncertain what would happen next. The yacht continued to drive through the wave and came out the other side. She accelerated again as the 10 tons of water poured over the stern and off the sides of the deck. There was much down below to be pumped out and we knew we had too much sail up.

That led to another moment of horror. The wind had climbed further up the scale and was gusting over 50 knots. The spinnaker had to come down before we could give it the protection of a jib. It was a dicey move but the risk had to be taken. Just as all seemed well, the sail tore on the end of the boom. It was only a small hole but as the sail flapped viciously in the wind the tear extended across the sail.

Hauling the spinnaker in became difficult and it trailed in the water. Everyone on deck was holding on to it but was being dragged aft; the struggle was one-sided and it was decided to cut the sail free and ditch it. By then there had been another disaster: two crewmen had fallen on and broken Don Buckley's arm as the sail took charge.

Eventually we began to control the boat and charged on with just a fully reefed mainsail, still peaking at over 20 knots. At dawn on the third day out there was enough moderation in the wind for a jib to be hoisted for a while, then after another 40-knot blast, the wind faded to six knots. That effectively ended our chance of breaking the race record and we had to wait until the end of the day for any real wind again. The finish was eight hours away, rounding Tasman Island in the dark and arriving off Cape Raoul, with its famous fluted cliffs that resemble organ pipes, at first light.

When the wind continued as we sailed by the Iron Pot lighthouse at the entrance to the Derwent river, we all crossed our fingers, recalling the times when race leaders had been 'parked' here and passed by others.

But this time there was wind all the way to the finish. The spectator fleet grew – close to 100 boats were around us as we crossed the line. It was then that we learned of the race committee's intention to penalise us for using an 'illegal' spinnaker with our sponsor's logo.

But we knew they could never take away the fact that we had finished first, and we smiled.

11 December 1990: Peter Lennon watches Gary Kasparov on his way to retaining his world title

Endgame at Lyons

As in the old Odeon cinemas, you walk up a short carpeted flight of steps and an usherette with winged *Dynasty* shoulders leads you to a seat in the vast stalls sloping towards the stage. Nine hundred customers are already there for a matinée performance. They are looking down in silence at a man on the stage below sitting in a black chair and doing strictly nothing, unless using his chin silently to count could be judged a performance. The first shock for a newcomer to world chess is to find Anatoly Karpov alone, playing to an empty white chair.

Did he do something wrong? Was he told to stay in after school, in front of all these people, until he got his sums right? You experience that shiver of vicarious humiliation which goes with school memories.

A good 20 minutes later, he moves a piece and begins writing diligently in his jotter.

Now Gary Kasparov, 27-year-old world chess champion, strides across the stage and occupies the white chair. Upon which Karpov stands up and walks away into the wings.

We are now made privy to the fact that Kasparov wipes his nose on the back of his hand. More than that Kasparov is not willing to do for some considerable time. Even that we are only able to see because of the two giant television screens on either side of the stage.

Where is the baleful forehead-to-forehead aggression between the two men we read so much about? Where the goading glances? When they are together Karpov's eyes flick continually over Kasparov's face but their eyes never meet. Kasparov pays no attention to his rival, his fierce restless concentration always on the board.

There is only an occasional whisper from the men, women, youths and small children in the auditorium, nothing more than a sucked-in breathy bubble filleted of consonants. But the crowd creaks continuously like a great, half slumbering pachyderm. There are no courting couples at this Saturday matinée.

As the hours deepened into Saturday night and drowsiness dragged like bags under the brain, I began to have the hallucination that I was in an enormous Jumbo jet flying the Atlantic around 2am, with nothing to do but watch the in-flight movie. Only someone had fouled and put on a minimalist symbolist mittel European play of the Thirties translated by Auden and Isherwood from Serbo-Croat.

The two protagonists finally got together, flanked by a frowning man and stern lady stage right and a bald man with a black beard in a black chair stage left. The middle-aged man and woman stared into a segment of the auditorium, no doubt delivering a message to the audience at dog whistle pitch. The Chief Arbitrator, the bald bearded man in the black chair, looked into the distance, his demeanour announcing unflinching authority. At one point he stood up, buttoning his jacket bureaucratically to indicate that he was not bent on mundane unbuttoning business, such as a visit to the john, but on a Grave Errand. Then he too returned and sat in silence.

As we went into the fifth and final hour a question gnawed: how was this audience going to applaud? Were they capable any longer of drawing noise from their cork-lined Proustian silence? Could they bear to smash palms together?

There was once a fey little cave in St Germain des Prés where they performed eighteenth-century folk songs, and the squirmingly cute convention was that you applauded only with your thumb nails. Perhaps here they would just blink their eyelids?

As it turned out, the applause when Saturday's game was adjourned was conventional but bisected, since Karpov had already left the stage leaving Kasparov to hang his chin over the board alone.

The 18th game in the 24-game contest re-started belatedly on Sunday. It was plain to all that Karpov was in a desperate situation, and on Sunday morning his camp tried to postpone play on the grounds that the challenger was snowed up in his hillside villa – thereby buying time for further computer analyses of the overnight position.

The referee, Geurt Gijssen, cannily decided to investigate. He found little difficulty in negotiating the road up to Karpov's house. Karpov duly made a delayed and sheepish appearance at the Lyons Palais. Kasparov duly cornered him with a Spanish game rather than the Scotch – a nineteenth-century variant never previously used in a world title contest – which he disinterred to stave off defeat in the 14th game. After 30 minutes Karpov resigned.

Lyons at the weekend was rather more preoccupied with the Immaculate Conception than the chess championship. On Saturday night Catholic families put rows of flickering little *lumignons* out on their window-sills, declaring that the Faith still flourished.

There was satisfied chat among the locals about how a modest town such as theirs had succeeded in taking over from New York as host for the world chess championship. They gossiped eagerly enough about what they called the *coquette* sum of 2.5 million Swiss francs for the winner and of the 'interesting' 2 million the loser would take away. And they were moderately thrilled at what is developing into one of the greatest battles in chess history – Kasparov now leading 3–2 with only six games remaining. Kasparov would keep his title on a 12/12 draw but Karpov has to have a clear win to regain the crown.

The locals had to admire the bold stroke of their Mayor, Michel Noir, in winning the venue from Wellington, Seattle and Toronto. But they were distracted this weekend by Noir upstaging his own international event by announcing his resignation from the French Parliament and the neo-Gaullist RPR party with the declaration that 'French politics is sick!'

This was a Sicilian game in Noir's political chess match with the Presidency of the Republic as coquette prize. He had gauged the *crise de foie* that an indigestible dose of crassly self-interested and premature presidential campaigning by Giscard and Chirac has induced in the citizens.

Noir was able to make Lyons a plausible venue for the chess championship because he is a player himself, and has even played Kasparov. He also laid on a tremendous gourmet meal for Florencio Campomanes, powerful chairman of FIDE, the International Chess Federation.

Noir had to produce extra balm for Kasparov, who has

never forgiven Campomanes for abruptly halting the world championship match with Karpov six years ago, declaring a draw when Kasparov looked like taking the crown. Kasparov won the title from Karpov the following year and has twice since kept Karpov at bay.

Now the mollified Kasparov, with his entourage of 10, is guest in a palatial mansion of a property development company, while Karpov has to pay his own rent (£10,000 for the six weeks) for a villa on the Croix Rousse hill.

2 April 1991: Leader

Kiss of life

All those who took the result published in yesterday's *Guardian* to be part of the celebrations of April Fool's Day will now kindly write and apologise to the players, directors and staff of Runcorn Highfield Rugby League club, preferably enclosing an appropriate donation. For what we reported is true. The team which went from October 1988 to 3 March this year without winning a single match, which completed the season 1990–91 without earning a single point, scoring 218 points and conceding nearly 1,000, before gates which dropped at one point to little more than 100, is suddenly transformed. The harbinger was that epic draw with Carlisle on 4 February. That was followed on 4 March by victory (9 points to 2) over Dewsbury, ending a run of 75 games without victory since their thrashing of Fulham nearly 18 months before. Then on Sunday an astonishing, and no doubt astonished, crowd of 1,002 saw them humiliate mid-table Keighley by 56 points to 10.

Such a margin cannot be argued with. The mantle unwillingly worn by Runcorn over the past two years as the least successful professional sporting club in the country passed in that moment of triumph into other hands. Having struggled on in some form or other for almost 70 years, first as Wigan Highfield, then successively as London Highfield, Liverpool Stanley, Liverpool City and Huyton, they must have feared going the way of such earlier titans as Belle Vue Rangers, Brighouse and Merthyr Tydfil, into unmourned extinction. But not any more.

What's more, they have achieved this renaissance without any help from the *Guardian*. That marks them out from Sheffield United, whose fortunes have been transformed not, as is sometimes supposed, by the signing on loan of Glyn Hodges from Crystal Palace, but as the direct result of a comment in this space on 20 December alerting them to the danger that they might become the least successful side in the history of the first division, surpassing even Stoke City, who ended the season 1984–5 with the lowest number of points (17), the lowest number of wins (3), the lowest number of goals (24) and the most defeats (31) in this division's history. In 16 games before our comment appeared United garnered four points, with seven goals in their favour and 30 against. In 16 games since they have taken 34 points, scoring 22 goals and conceding only 17. This cannot be a coincidence. Our unstinted congratulations go this morning to both these grand old clubs. What a shame that Runcorn got so horribly walloped at Leigh yesterday afternoon.

Screen time

Watching with Nancy Banks-Smith

8 September 1990

Bernie Winters was once doing his stuff to a peculiarly porridgy audience. The face, the voice, the dog, the lot. Nothing. With a brotherly backup commendable in the circumstances, Mike Winters arrived on cue. 'My God!' said an appalled voice from the audience. 'There are two of them.' I was reminded of this by **Talking To Myself** (BBC 2), a fetchingly lunatic idea, in which people interview themselves.

'I have a guest with me this evening who needs no introduction to me nor I to him. It is, yes it is, Enoch Powell!' said Enoch Powell. He was wearing a light grey three-piece suit. Enoch Powell, on the other hand, was wearing a dark grey three-piece suit. Both had a matching grey moustache and spoke on the same flat, nasal note like the whine of wind in telephone wires. Enoch Powell is one of the last great parliamentary orators. Oratory does not suit television. He opposed televised parliament to the end.

'I have to tell you,' Mr Powell said to Mr Powell, 'you are not the man you were. You've become old. Putting it another way, there is not so much left as there has been. Can you tell me what it's all been about?' A generous invitation, briskly accepted. Like Othello, upon this hint Enoch spake.

'The most important thing I ever did, and perhaps the only important thing I ever did, was in 1939 when I threw up my position in Australia, came home and joined the army. It was the recognition of something to which I belonged, which had an unlimited claim upon my obedience, my allegiance. And that thought has been with me ever since.' Surprisingly for so logical a man, his life seems to have been a headlong love affair with the British Empire, the Conservative Party and 'this wonderful place', the House of Commons. He lost the lot.

I was enthralled by the classical architecture of his sentences. People don't talk like that. Well, of course, the Romans did. Listen to him on British entry to the EC: 'So strong was my objection to it in parliament when it was introduced and so strong has been my objection to it ever since that I have accepted 16 years in exile.'

You can't interview yourself any more than you can tickle yourself. It is almost bound to turn out something like Frank and Ernest, a couple of American missionaries whose powerful encounters I used to enjoy on Radio Luxembourg. Frank would ask frank questions like 'How do I know I shall be saved?' and Ernest would give earnest answers like 'It says so in Corinthians'. You could not but feel they were both on the same side.

Still and all, *Talking To Myself* is only 10 minutes long. It is worth 10 minutes of anyone's time to find out what well known people don't want to tell you about themselves.

24 October 1990

Twin Peaks (BBC1) is logging country. The mountains

wear firs; the men tartan shirts. Apart from a rather high incidence of insanity, adultery, addiction and stuff like that, Twin Peaks is pure as a mountain stream. A clean and wholesome environment, as Benjamin Horne, the richest man for miles around (and there *are* miles around) says while trying to sell it to some Norwegians. I never thought the scheme was on, as Norwegians already have more environment than they know what to do with. It was thoroughly scuppered ('The Norwegians are leaving!') when Laura Palmer, the purtiest gel you could wish to see if it wasn't for her cyanotic lips, was found gift-wrapped in plastic on the lake shore.

This caused Andy, a deputy, to burst into passionate sobs. The menfolk of Twin Peaks are surprisingly prone to tears, but none is so damp as Andy. A policeman's lot is not a happy one and one wonders if he wouldn't be happier governing New South Wales.

Sheriff Harry S. Truman, usually referred to as Hairy or Shurf, is made of sterner stuff. I particularly like the way he gestures with his hat in his hand like someone bringing a plane in to land. Hairy is given to expressions of simple astonishment: 'Holy smoke!' and 'What the hell is goin' on here?' He looks clean as several whistles but he may have secret depths. I was disconcerted to discover, towards the end of this episode, that he is having an affair with an exotic Chinese widow with a mouth like a poppy. It says here in the publicity that he has a passion for doughnuts. No mention of Chinese widows with mouths like poppies.

What with Andy crying such a lot and Hairy being indistinguishable from a tree in trousers, the FBI send in the supernaturally brilliant agent, Dale Cooper, who can spot the reflection of a motorbike in the videoed pupil of an eye. A neat variation, this, on the old belief that the eye of a corpse retains an image of its murderer.

Cooper is very taken with wherever-we-are and country sanity: all that scenery, cherry pie and damn fine coffee. I would not myself call Twin Peaks *normal*. The local psychiatrist, who must be kept busy, wears cotton swabs in his ears and an improper tie. Big Ed's wife seems to have one eye and an obsession about noisy curtains. Johnny Horne, who is fully grown, wears a Red Indian head-dress and bangs his head against a doll's house. Hank Jennings is in gaol for slaughtering someone. And there is the Log Lady. 'Who's the lady with the log?' asks Cooper. 'We call her,' says the Shurf with characteristic succintness, 'the Log Lady.'

You seem to hear, like a moose calling another moose in the mountains, the faint cry of the director, David Lynch. 'Keep it in!' The head of a deer falls off the wall – keep it in. The lights in the morgue flicker – keep it in. These things give a certain thickening to the surreal soup and they certainly keep the viewers off balance.

I'm inclined to think *Twin Peaks* is about Marilyn Monroe. David Lynch and Mark Frost, who wrote it together, met when they collaborated on a script about the death of Monroe called *Goddess*. They could not find a producer, but no writer throws anything away. *Twin Peaks*, a title with slightly sexy overtones, is about the death of a disturbed young beauty. Somehow connected with nude modelling. Into drugs. Under a psychiatrist.

It is, of course, a cult craze in America where they are halfway through the second series and still no nearer discovering who gift-wrapped Laura. It has flashes of quite striking acting, is much better looking than your average soap, and far funnier.

Tell you what, though. It is made by someone who doesn't take soap seriously. Like romantic fiction, soap has to be sincere. Twin Peaks is just down the road from Tongue in Cheek.

3 December 1990

Right. Hands up. Who at the BBC turned down *Corona-*

tion Street 30 years ago? Nobody leaves this building until somebody owns up.

The first episode of **Coronation Street** (Granada), grainy and grey, returned from the vaults to haunt us with the way we used to be. There only seems to be one TV in that Coronation Street, a 14-inch set belonging to the Barlows, an upmarket family with a table cloth.

Frank Barlow, quite amazingly like Mr Glum, is toasting his trousers, snapping his braces and washing down the HP sauce with rich tides of tannin. David Barlow is dismantling his bike in front of the fire.

Kenneth Barlow, a sensitive lad, is trying to conduct a fledgling romance under these unpromising circumstances and getting it in the neck all round: 'That college has turned you into a proper stuck-up little snob, Kenneth Barlow.' Nobody watches the TV.

Meanwhile, at the corner shop, to be gloriously revamped 30 years later as Alf Roberts' Mini Market, Florrie, the new owner, is being reassured about the locals: 'They won't eat you.'

On these ill-chosen words Ena Sharples arrives in a double-breasted battledress.

She is not, you notice with some surprise, wearing a net. Her hair is, however, terrorised into immobility, each little strand curled up with its hands over its eyes.

She settles down – they had chairs in shops then – and in short time has discovered that Florrie is widowed, C of E and childless ('Oh, you're better off without them. A bottle of bleach. They're more bother than they're worth'), has advised against cremation and Mrs Tanner in that order and bought six fancies without eclairs on tick.

What one wants to know, even at this late stage, is whatever happened to that crematorium just down the road and what was the matter with the eclairs?

Set against this rock of propriety ('I'm the caretaker at the Glad Tidings Hall') is Elsie Tanner, her strings of improbable pearls laid out on the shelving beach of her chest like Woolworth's jewellery counter and her smalls hung on a string by the fire. Elsie was the sort of woman brush salesmen always hoped would open the door. Ena was the one who generally did.

Conversation in Coronation Street was like going over the top in the face of machine-gun fire. 'You know what your trouble is, don't you?' 'Whatever did you want to do that for?' 'What time do you call this?' All questions expecting the answer 'Er'.

There was nothing evocative or decorative about Coronation Street then. No sleeping cat. No cherry blossom. It was quite astonishingly true to life in post-war Lancashire, where my parents kept a pub near Queen Victoria Street.

When I think about our snug I am no longer sure if it's Ena Sharples's face I see, slamming down a milk jug to be filled with stout. The snug was for old women only as the bar was only for men, short, bandy, belted men with whippets shivering under their seats.

Surely that was Mike Baldwin's face I caught sight of in the snooker room, which was reserved, according to my mother, for a better class of person all together, bookies' runners who hid their betting slips in their trilbies during a police raid.

Is that the Glad Tidings Hall I hear on full song or only my father changing barrels in the cellar singing that the common round, the daily task, could furnish all he needed to ask?

Is that Annie Walker or my mother adding an H on to everything, just to be on the safe side? It all blurs.

And the Coronation Street faces seem to merge. Albert Tatlock dies and comes back as Percy Sugden, Annie Walker changes into Bet Lynch, Elsie Tanner into Rita Fairclough. They even use the same red rinse.

'House to let, apply within. If I go out, Mrs Jones comes in,' as the little girls chanted, playing hopscotch outside the corner shop.

If you are tired of *Coronation Street*, you are just tired.

The Street itself always had comic resilience. 'Ee, Elsie, you're just about ready for the knacker's yard,' said Elsie Tanner in that first episode. And spat indomitably into her mascara.

21 January 1991

Quite the most cheerful note of the Gulf campaign was Alex Brodie's report for the BBC that Iraq had dropped a damp squid on Israel. The first casualty is, of course, comedy. **'Allo 'Allo** (BBC1) fell as if struck by a sand-filled sausage, fast followed by **They Never Slept** (BBC2), both Second World War comedies. British pilots in the Persian Gulf, however, were watching Monty Python between forays, their nerve unshaken even by the parrot sketch.

'Tell me you're not going to pull Ruby Wax,' I cried, in the voice of those waiting on the New York dock for the last instalment of *The Old Curiosity Shop*, who shouted: 'Is Little Nell dead?' **The Full Wax** (BBC1) got there, a little late, but got on to the air.

Little Nell was in the street shanghaiing people for a low-budget, late-night discussion programme like *After Dark* without the Scotch and sofa. She zoomed in, laser-guided I shouldn't wonder, on a small woman in a hard hat (if you can imagine a helmet with a bobble or Boadicea off to Tesco with her trolley). 'I'm wondering if you could take part in a discussion group? Perhaps air your little opinions, tell us the problems of being an elderly person.' She placed a hand on her arm. 'Oh, bugger off,' the woman in the hat replied.

A youth was cradling a ghetto-blaster. He was entirely surrounded by dreadlocks. 'Excuse me, I'm doing a show and we need someone from a minority group and you seem to fit the bill.' He parted the dreadlocks doubtfully like the first Red Indian peering through a thicket at the first American as she landed shouting: 'Let's get this show on the road.' 'Minority? What do you mean: minority?' 'Well, are you gay?' 'No, but I'm black.' That was unquestionably true and he was bundled into a transit van with the elderly woman, seduced with specious promises of Kilroy, a barrow boy in an apple-patterned waistcoat, a large woman with a loo brush ('I've got to do the toilets.' 'There are plenty of toilets where you're going.'), and a couple down for the day from Bolton.

The theory was that, if you lock a representative collection of people in a room, they will eventually produce conversation. Or, of course, children.

Ruby Wax and her co-host, Jennifer Saunders, were both heavily pregnant, which made Zsa Zsa Gabor recoil as if it might be catching and Kathleen O'Connor, a former nun, described her honeymoon. 'We were three days and three nights trying to figure it out.'

Meanwhile, back in the bunker, daylight was dawning on the discussion group. 'It's just come to me 'oo she is,' the barrow boy said, indicating his forehead with his finger. 'She's that Ruby Wax.' 'Ruby Wax? She's horrible,' the man down for the day from Bolton said.

After some vague but viperish threats from Little Nell, the barrow boy kicked off: 'I was reading an article this morning. There's 2,400 gallons of methane gas emitted every day into the air in New Zealand.' 'Thank God it isn't in Bolton,' the man from Bolton said. 'Where do you think it comes from? I'm 100-per-cent serious now. Sheep. I'm telling yer.'

'I want to see some passion; I want to see some anger. Get yapping,' snarled Little Nell.

The woman in the hat, it turned out, could take direction. 'It's time the country woke up to the truth,' she cried. '*And* the Channel Tunnel, I 'ope somebody blows it up. Armies could come through it overnight. *And* I think it's time the British people had the guts to say it.' The minority representative parted his dreadlocks, sighed, and let them fall again. 'We've no friend in Europe; not one; only

Portugal. We never had salmonella until we went into the Common Market. They're coming from all over. They even come from Egypt and buy 'Arrods. This realm set in a silver sea shall never,' and she stamped her lace-up on the barrow boy, 'be under the proud foot of a conqueror.' 'Elderly woman!' Little Nell cried enthralled: 'Do you have an agent?'

30 January 1991

There's Something About A Convent Girl (Thames), like a well trailed worm, hauls up strange fish from deep places. I had forgotten for 50 years that I must sleep on my back with my hands folded so that, if I died in the night, I would not be found looking as though I were caught on the hop but composed like a statue of Our Lady. Only horizontal, naturally. 'Mother of God,' they would say when they came to lay me out, 'doesn't she put you in mind of somebody?'

In case I did not die in the night, I was to bang my head seven times on the pillow and ask Our Lady to wake me at 7am. Oddly enough, that works.

If one worm-word seems to trawl up more memories than most it is knickers. Ellie Laine, here seen whipping off her whimple as a Naughty Nun Strippergram, may have been introduced to this bizarre business by youthful knicker inspections at St Mary's Woodford just as Alison Halford, Assistant Chief Constable of Merseyside, was introduced to identification parades when every girl at Notre Dame, Norwich, was paraded before her.

For knickers, read sex. 'It was like a light switch. Nobody knew where it was. You might put your hand on it by mistake and set World War III in motion,' said Frances Donnelly.

At my convent every girl had to know how to make a stout pair of navy serge knickers and a high-necked nightie. This would stand her in good stead in later life.

Shipwrecked on a desert island, surrounded by sharks, she should be able to set to and make a stout pair of navy serge knickers and a high-necked nightie. What helpless tears I wept over the gusset. Why did the sleeve of the nightie always end up in the neck?

My almost imbecile inability to do needlework was treated with surprising indulgence. I was a Protestant. Nothing, not even knickers, applied to me. In catechism I sat at the back while Marie Thérèse got it in the neck again for not knowing that a sacrament was an outward and visible sign of an inward and spiritual grace. I was much better at this kind of thing than Marie Thérèse, but nobody asked me about the nature of God.

Hearing sister say one day that only Catholics could go to heaven, I did ask if my parents would go to hell. I can still hear the long silence while she wondered what to say. Soft and strong, these memories push up like toadstools under paving stones. I was not unhappy. Is a goat unhappy in a flock of sheep? Nobody is going to eat it.

Something About A Convent Girl, not altogether accidentally, coincides with the publication of a Virago book of the same name. Of all the convent girls who appeared, some as implausible as Anne Robinson and Germaine Greer, none seethed like Carmen Callil, who founded Virago. 'It scarred me so terribly. Everything else that happened to me in my life pales into insignificance beside what those nuns did to me. No, I don't think God approves of those people. I think he's on my side. In fact my Mother Superior left in disgrace. She ended up . . . ' she spat out the word and, ping, it hit the spittoon, 'in Queensland.' As Carmen Callil's convent was in Melbourne this is not as penitential as it sounds.

There was a scalding head of steam about some of the testimony that made you whistle like a kettle. 'There was a kind of violence underneath the habit all the time, simmering away, never quite boiled over. Everything we did was wrong. You lived in fear of being found out,' said Mary O'Malley, who wrote the play *Once a Catholic*. It was shown in delicious snippets. The priest killing invisible beetles with his crashing fist: 'When you've got the wedding ring on your finger you can fire away to your heart's content.' The nun transfixing a girl with an eye like a fork: 'Eat every single bit and offer it up for all the souls in purgatory. Think of each grain of rice as a poor soul in agony.'

Grief is the best basis of comedy, but terror and rage will do nicely. *Once a Catholic* is undeniably funny, but Detta O'Cathain, director of the Barbican, was so furiously offended by it she walked out, trailing the confused non-Catholic friends who had paid for her ticket. As George Kaufman said during an anti-semitic conversation: 'I intend to walk out and I hope Mrs Parker will walk half way out with me.' (Dorothy Parker was half Jewish. I shouldn't have to tell you these things.)

You carry for ever the fingerprint that comes from being under someone's thumb. Patricia Hayes, who was at St Andrew's Convent, Streatham, in 1914 still remembers her lines: 'God made me to know him, love him and serve him in this world and to be happy with him forever in the next.' There are worse things to remember as you fold your hands so death doesn't take you by surprise.

10 April 1991

If you live in Leeds and have a toy wooden penguin in the attic, congratulations. You are probably the owner of an original Walter Bennett. I would very much like to see an Antiques Roadshow from Leeds in which hundreds of Bennett penguins emerged from their dusty roost, each on its little green, four-wheeled cart, each more pristine than the last. Bennett penguins were rarely, you feel, played out, worn to the wood, loved to death. They didn't, well, *chirp* or anything. Even the penguin-maker's son thought them a rather dull toy.

The penguin-maker's son, Alan Bennett, stood in the County Arcade, Leeds (**Building Sites**, BBC2), in a woolly scarf and wilting raincoat and talked to us as if he had met us out shopping. The whole point of an arcade is that you don't *need* a scarf or a raincoat. Outside the sharp sleet is waiting to beat you with a hairbrush. Inside all is golden and enfolding. Newly renovated, County Arcade is festooned with swags of glowing oranges. A mosaic, so high you can only see by opening your mouth, shows a golden-breasted woman, wearing a perfunctory towel, flourishing a melting ice-cream cornet. The ice-cream streams like flame. It might, of course, be a cotton bobbin. She could be Industry. I can only say that that is not the impression she gives.

In this hot house Alan Bennett is dressed for a downpour as if someone had sent him out saying 'Mind on, don't catch cold' and tied his scarf with a throttling knot. He has the peculiar property of seeming to move immediately from seven to 57, without touching 20. It is as though he has drawn an unusual card in the board game of life. 'Go straight to middle age.' He can also move effortlessly back to seven years old. It is all still vivid for him. 'At the start of the second war,' he said, 'toys were in short supply and my dad, who was a butcher with the Co-op, invested in a fretsaw and started making toy animals. His speciality were penguins and on his afternoons off he'd hawk them round the toyshops of Leeds. Though without much success.'

When Smart's toy shop in the arcade offered to take his entire output at a sharp discount, he did not haggle. By now the house must have been like those blizzard whipped ice floes where a thousand Emperor penguins clump together for months, shifting stoically from foot to foot. 'Every week after that my Mam and Dad and sometimes my brother and me would come down with carrier bags and the week's output of penguins.' Walter Bennett was, perhaps, temperamentally behind the times like his son. Penguins were extraordinarily popular *before* the war. 'Pip Squeak and Wilfred', a *Mirror* cartoon about a dog, a penguin and a rabbit, was a national catchphrase. Squeak, rather implausibly, was the penguin. I was very attached to a penguin pyjama case called, more suitably, Percy. My father, who liked a joke, called him good old Percy Verance. Penguins were everywhere and then suddenly, as if their floe had melted, they weren't.

Walter Bennett took a shy pride in his unpopular product and, if he ever saw a child trailing one about, would loiter with intent, wistfully hoping to hear something to his advantage. 'Experiencing the same frisson,' said his son 'as an author does when he catches someone reading one of his books.'

Unlike Smart's toy shop, Chapman's the Corsetières has breasted the onrush of years. In their window an iron-clad girdle, stoutly laced against all eventualities, leads a colourful flotilla of frivolous knickers. 'A corseteer' Bennett calls them to rhyme with charioteer. Corseteer. A Yorkshireman does not pander to the preferences of the French in the matter of pronunciation. Besides, if you imagine Boadicea driving her bacon slicer chariot straight at the Romans, she is definitely wearing a firm-control corset, which Roman lances bounce off blunted. A fine figure of a woman like Alan Bennett's Aunt Evelyn, a corseteer who measured ladies in their homes. Ah, Spirella!

Alan Bennett has the tap root of a dandelion. It goes down into hiding-places 50 years deep and comes up golden.

Country Arcade was only 10 minutes long. It is astonishing what a good time you can have in 10 minutes. But then you knew that, didn't you?

16 October 1990: Derek Malcolm

A perverse way of doing business

Martin Scorsese is now 48 and has been making films for over a quarter of a century. He is one of the most admired directors in the world, and certainly in America, where his *Raging Bull* won the influential *Premiere* magazine's poll as the best film of the Eighties.

Yet he is still deeply suspected by the money men of Hollywood – as a New York film-maker who is not really 'one of us' and as a man generally incapable of delivering truly popular films to the public. Only one of his movies has actually hit the jackpot, and that was *Taxi Driver*, in which Robert de Niro, almost a constant in his films, played a New York cab driver who murders a pimp and others in a nightmarish final blood-bath.

The terrible violence of that study of urban alienation and sexual repression is reflected again in *GoodFellas*, his new examination of the Mob and its minions, as is the street anarchy of *Mean Streets*, and it has caused considerable controversy. But this big-budget film has also opened well enough in the States to prove at last to Hollywood's doubters that Scorsese is still capable of making properly commercial films. It is a brilliant piece of direction that could not have been achieved in anything like the same way by any other director. But it does raise the question of how you can make an entertainment that has to appeal to millions because of its cost and still say something relevant about the deadly corruption and violence that is part and parcel of a certain area of American life.

On one of the first occasions I met Scorsese, I had just seen *Taxi Driver* in a Los Angeles cinema in front of a baying crowd who, when de Niro's cabbie ran riot, screamed their approval in much the same way as they would have at a faked-up wrestling match. It was a disturbing experience which, when I told him about it, worried Scorsese, nothing if not a gentle man. What he said then was that this particular audience had clearly misjudged the film. And that, anyway, it was impossible to make movies that took note of the susceptibilities of every inadequate in the audience.

In fact, his films are always highly personal, and invariably reflect his own background of Catholic guilt and repression. And *GoodFellas*, above all, mirrors the life he knew from the streets of New York's East Side. He is talking in the film not about Godfathers but about Godsons – the lower orders of the Mob for whom it represented the way out from under an impoverished and exploited lifestyle. Some of these people, he says, do terrible things in the film – things any normal person could not possibly even contemplate. But they also have a good time. To make an honest movie, it was not enough to paint a bleak and black-as-pitch portrait of crime and eventual punishment. He had to show the attractions of the lifestyle too.

The question the film constantly poses is – what sort of life would these mobsters have lived without the protection and support of the Mafia? And here Scorsese knows exactly what he is talking about.

He grew up, small and asthmatic, mad on movies but at first planning to become a priest, in an Italian-American neighbourhood which was the opposite of the more cosmopolitan Greenwich Village next door. The East Side was full of Sicilians, Neapolitans and Calabrese, and his block (Elizabeth Street) was purely Sicilian. He never went near the West Side, despite the fact that it was only six blocks away, until he enrolled in New York City University.

He was, he says, around eight years old when he

became aware of a group of people within this tight little community who were somehow different from the rest.

'They were in bars, talking privately in corners. And all I knew is that what they were talking about wasn't legal. My father would say, "Be very careful. Don't go with that person, go with that one." I saw people who were so powerful that it was obvious from the way they walked. I saw how they used that power, and how other people behaved around them. These people didn't have to yell. They behaved like Gian Maria Volonte did in Rosi's *Lucky Luciano*. They behaved nicely. They were quiet. But they had control over life and death. It was the lower echelon who were the loud ones, and fortunately they liked me. I was small, I had asthma and I couldn't fight. So I was no threat, especially since, when I did get punched up once, I didn't cry and I didn't tell anyone either. Between the age of 13 and 17 – a very delicate period – I could very easily have got into their clutches and become one of them. Fortunately, I went the other way. But I had friends of both kinds.'

GoodFellas is, for Scorsese at least, as much anthropology as thriller. It is a remembrance of things past, almost Proustian in its love of tiny detail – look at the eating scenes – but hardly Proustian in its regret. It is also a morality play, which insists that the glory days of the thugs we see is usually less than 10 years, after which one of two things happen: either they get jailed, or they get out of line. In the latter case, they die, or have to run.

'They can't live that crazy lifestyle for all that long. Things catch up on them sooner or later. It's a very attractive thing, and I have to show that. What I also have to show is the price they have to pay for it. Violence is the means of expression, the way of keeping things under control. I don't romanticise it. I just show it. And I've tried to show it like it really is – cold, horrible and unfeeling. Almost incidental. A perverse way of doing business. And I've attempted to show what it means at both ends – to those who actually do it, and to those on the receiving end. Yes, it's a little about the banality of evil. Because some of these characters don't know when to stop. I've seen it happen – when someone goes by, scrapes his foot on your shoe and doesn't say he's sorry. So he's dead. Now, if you show this, you may be accused of reckless violence, and exploitation. But if you don't, you're not telling the truth. And the truth is that this is the way part of our system works.

'The Mafia think they found the perfect way to deal with the American Dream. But you can see what happens – how it all crashes in on them in the end, because all they want to do is get as much as they can as fast as they can in any way they can. And that way of life becomes a nightmare.'

Scorsese knows full well that a lot runs on *GoodFellas*, since it cost a lot of money and the future of several other projects is bound up with it. One of his most cherished concerns is a special fund, to be set up by his own company and that of Spielberg, to encourage young and independently-minded film-makers, in America and elsewhere, to make the films they want to make without undue commercial pressure.

Scorsese recently spoke at the memorial service for his friend, Michael Powell. He said then that the cinema of imagination was paramount. His own particular brand of it, like Powell's, has often been fraught with danger, as *GoodFellas* is.

But he still believes that the cinema has awesome responsibilities. 'We aren't here to make money. We're here to tell the truth as we see it. It's got to be a personal vision. And if it is, people will recognise it sooner or later. That's the only way.' In a strange sort of way, he still wants to be a priest.

20 December 1990: Derek Malcolm

Walt's golden wonder

On Boxing Day one of the greatest animation films ever made and certainly the most expensive, is relaunched in Britain. Walt Disney's *Fantasia*, reviled by some and adored by others, is finally on the march again after a long and difficult struggle to restore it to its full glory. Its cost in 1940 was more than two and a quarter million dollars and it was drawn entirely by hand (which has never been done since with a full-length feature). It was a risk only Disney could have even contemplated. What is more, this astonishing pot-pourri of classical music and Hollywood storytelling was a financial failure for years. It did not make its money back until as late as 1969 when it was taken up as a 'trip' by the younger generation who were seeing it for the first time. They smoked so much pot as they watched that the old publicity line '*Fantasia* will amaze-ya' took on a new meaning.

When the film was released, the critics raised eyebrows and the American public raised yawns, particularly at the abstract summing up of Bach's *Toccata and Fugue*, even though it was lushed up by the Stokowski arrangement in a way the purists frowned upon. It had a good many supporters too. But *Fantasia* was never taken to the world's bosom like *Snow White, Pinocchio* or *Dumbo* and was heavily criticised for its lack of taste. Even so, constant screening, as often as not in countries other than America, had wrecked all existing prints by 1980, both visually and aurally. Very few of the technicians consulted felt the film could be successfully restored because of general wear and tear. Yet, after the spending of far more money than it originally cost, here it is with us again, looking and sounding as good, if not better, than it did in 1940.

Restoration work started in earnest in 1988, and there is

little doubt that the huge success of *Roger Rabbit* was a factor in the studio's burgeoning confidence that it was worth doing. If a film like *Roger Rabbit* could make a fortune, what would the new generation of film-goers think of the infinitely superior *Fantasia*? And, as it transpires, *Rabbit* was no one-off fluke. This year's new Disney, *The Little Mermaid*, has taken another fortune at the box-office and animation seems back in fashion.

Even now, the original 'Fantasound', with speakers placed behind the screen and at the sides and rear of cinema halls, is past reclaiming. It had been recorded optically on nitrate prints that have gone for ever. Instead, it was decided to restore the basic three channels and plop them into modern sound systems through a series of technical miracles.

To restore what we see, the negatives were taken from the studio's Burbank vaults and the original material sorted from the duplicated copies several generations removed. The task took weeks. Finally, after considerable trouble with certain sections of the film, restorers using microscopes cleaned each frame by hand, often with razor blades. Every 10 minutes of screen time meant cleaning 3,000ft of film. Cropping by projectionists of the new Technicolor print, graded with enormous care, will be impossible, so all cinemas screening it will have to get it right or not play it at all, which in itself will be a welcome change.

Despite all this, the new *Fantasia* still has its technical blips. The images are not always entirely perfect and nor are the high notes on the soundtrack. But the colour is now marvellous and the details are often clearer. What is also noticeable is that Stokowski's score is now perfectly synchronised with the pictures.

What should we now think of *Fantasia* as a concept? Many contemporary animators – and the younger they are, the more they think it – believe that it was at once ahead of its time technically and regrettable artistically.

They feel the Disney sentimentality, melodrama and kitsch, so obvious in the recidivist *The Little Mermaid*, gave its watchers an idea of what animation should be that effectively murdered any thoughts of popular experiment. They at least would not put *Fantasia*, or any of the Disneys, in their top 10 animation films. Their shadow is too long for comfort, dominating public taste.

And there is the same feeling among many who like classical music. In an era when so many are obsessed with authentic instruments and back to the past orchestration, it is hardly likely that centaurs making moo to Beethoven's *Pastoral* and ostriches and hippopotami balleting about to Ponchielli are going to be received with unalloyed admiration. Nor are Stokowski's edited and sometimes souped-up scores going to cause a sudden spate of joy.

But the fact is that *Fantasia* has probably brought millions of people all over the world jogging gingerly towards classical music, and that it remains a quite astonishingly detailed tribute to the ability of the cinema to create a world of sight and sound that is almost indivisible and certainly unique. Personally, I can never hear Tchaikovsky's *Nutcracker Suite* without visions of those dancing mushrooms and flowers, nor Dukas's *The Sorcerer's Apprentice* without recalling Mickey Mouse practically drowning in all that water. And the more the kitsch flows, the better I like it. Reverence of classical warhorses might profitably be kicked in the teeth more regularly (though Disney, of course, had no such thing in mind). A dose of sacrilege is no bad thing.

What doesn't now seem so great are the more serious episodes, though surely the pterodactyls of Stravinsky's *Rite of Spring* are a pardonable excess, and so are the imaginative Bach abstracts.

The critic Pare Lorentz wrote to Disney: 'I advise you to disregard the howls from the music critics. *Fantasia* is a Disney and not a classical conception of a concert . . . You can dismiss the complaints of the little hierarchy of those who try to make music a sacrosanct, mysterious and obscure art. You have brought it out of the temple, put it in carpet slippers and an old sweater, and made it work to surround, support and synchronise a brilliantly drawn series of animated colour sketches.'

But you can't look at *Fantasia* without looking at Disney himself, who was not only an artist who sought, and achieved, technical perfection, but also a man who wanted desperately to be accepted as something other than an entertainer. *Fantasia* was, to him, his magnum opus, proving his credentials as a great American. He said the film was timeless, and so it has undoubtedly proved, thanks to the work of the restorers.

9 May 1991: Derek Malcolm, who was president of the Festival's international critics' jury

Cannes noir

For the next twelve days, the centre of the film world will not be Hollywood but an expensive seaside resort on the French Riviera where an ugly (and unfortunately British-designed) conference centre plays host to the best new films from all over the world. The 44th edition of the Cannes Festival opens tonight, with David Mamet's *Homicide*, in front of an exceedingly well-dressed audience of celebrities who, if they want to get in, have to possess not only a highly sought-after ticket but the clothes to match the occasion.

The police will ring what is laughably called 'the new Palais'. Press photographers and television cameras will have a field day jostling hysterically for the best position. Loud-speakers will blare celebratory music – probably the theme from Stanley Kubrick's *2001* yet *again* – as the favoured walk up the steps. Crowds of gawpers will strain to see if you really are Roman Polanski or Whoopi Goldberg (both on the jury this year), and they will probably entirely ignore the less recognisable and terminally shy Mamet and his leading player, Joe Mantegna.

But these two, and any others from the cast and production who turn up, will get their moment when, at the end of the performance, the lights will seek them out as the audience turn to pay them homage. If the film is really liked, the applause and cheers could last almost as long as those for Mrs Thatcher at Tory conferences of yore. If it isn't, there are unlikely to be any boos, at least on the opening night. Later on in the Festival, however, there is no such politesse.

But though this is a terrifying ordeal for any film-maker, there is an even worse one earlier. This is when something like a thousand critics and journos sit down at the unearthly hour of 8.30 in the morning to see, and prepare to pronounce upon, the same film. It is not so demonstrative an audience but the brave film-makers who look in on that screening can either leave very happy indeed, completely nonplussed or utterly miserable.

What is this thing called Cannes? The real answer is that it's what you choose to make it, capable of almost anything. There is art for art's sake – no director is too obscure to be fêted if his or her film is good enough – commerce for commerce's sake – no director is bad enough *not* to be fêted if his company spends the money – and almost everything in between.

The power of Cannes lies in its ability to attract not just the best, but very nearly the worst as well. Hopefully, the best is somewhere to be found in the official programme, though not necessarily the competition section, where politics sometimes intrudes into the realms of pure culture. The worst is generally represented outside the programme, at the stands in the basement of the Palais, unaffectionately nicknamed the Bunker, where frenetic sales-persons show unutterably awful movies to fat wallets out to make a quick buck in the strangest of territories, primarily with unconvincingly orchestrated sex 'n' violence.

Cannes is the most important film festival in the world because it manages, without losing its very French pride and dignity, which some people call arrogance, to suit everybody. No philosopher king of the cinema – or very few of them – would refuse an invitation. Not many hucksters like to admit they have no intention of going.

It can be an immensely costly exercise, and it isn't cheap for anyone. If you want to make a mark in one of the best hotels, like the Carlton or the Majestic, with an office there as well as a bedroom, you are certain to have to spend thousands of pounds, food and entertainment included. If you are a major Hollywood company, wishing to bring over a few directors, stars, executives and their partners, you could finance a film or two on the amount you end up spending. Even the prostitutes put their prices up during the Festival, and everyone else follows suit. For pickpockets, it's total heaven.

The question is – is it all worth it? Not necessarily. At the highest level, a Cannes Palme D'Or winner like Roland Joffe's *The Mission* or David Lynch's *Wild At Heart* (last year) may not make a cent more at the box-office worldwide because of the accolade. Or it may be just what's needed to start the ball rolling. A bad reaction at Cannes can kill a film stone dead, and often has.

Yet Cannes consistently makes and confirms reputations and, for a young film-maker in particular, can set the tone of a whole career. It helps even more if he or she is presentable and gives good interviews because if you don't put yourself about and talk yourself hoarse, there is not a lot your publicity people can do for you unless you've made an inalienable masterpiece. When the unheard-of Indian, Mira Nair, won the Camera D'Or for the best first film with *Salaam Bombay*, the projections were packed at every performance partly because it was a genuinely popular (and good) film but partly because she was the toast of Cannes as a personality.

Finding your way round this giant jamboree can be a mortifying experience for the uninitiated (you start off trying to find a bed), whether they are film-makers, critics or buyers and sellers. But old hands, though they can never relax, know that the golden rule is not to panic but to do what you can and no more. For critics, that means combing the programme for likely movies, marking them down a day ahead and trotting off to see them with time enough to push your way through the crowd, preferably waving your pass and shouting simultaneously.

A lot of the time you will hear on the grapevine that the film you are going to see is *awful* and that you should be somewhere else seeing something else. The trick is to ignore such advice unless it comes from someone you can trust. There are, however, not many of those around.

Each day, there are two competition films that it's obligatory to see, for who would want to miss the winner? But that's only the half of it. There are a lot of other hopefuls in a section called 'Un Certain Regard', which means that the Festival Director, Gilles Jacob, likes them but not enough to put them in competition. There are more in the Directors' Fortnight, which for years has taken its own line about what constitutes an interesting movie and has often proved absolutely right, and a further selection in the Critics' Week, which concentrates on the promising and hitherto unheralded. Almost always, there are at least half a dozen films in these sections that are better than all but the best in competition.

Added to all this, there are the special screenings, usually at some untoward hour, like midnight, and a huge programme of market screenings of films that either didn't make it, weren't quite ready in time or are there in the hope of a sale, sometimes retitled from previous years.

Then, of course, there are the parties – overpriced lunches on the beach, dinners at a restaurant you can't find, drinks here, there and everywhere, vast celebrations out of town in a grand château somewhere you can't get back from and small gatherings for the cognoscenti on the roof of a hotel somewhere. If you don't go to some of them, people will be hurt. If you try to go to all of them, bang go the films. It is almost as important who you see at Cannes as what you see.

What you have to remember is that the whole thing ought to be fun and that Cannes can provide anyone connected with the film business with a host of good contacts and a wonderful bird's eye view of world cinema as a whole. Many film festivals do that, with Berlin in February and Venice in late August vying for prestige with Cannes. But Cannes comes out top because it has the money, it has the history, and no one could seriously deny that it has the glitz and the seriousness that satisfy both wings of the film world.

This year, the glitz will be provided by Madonna, who arrives on the scene a few days in with her revelatory concert film, *In Bed With Madonna*. She will be stationed in full glory outside Cannes in the exclusive Hotel Du Cap where Clint Eastwood stayed last year and Meryl Streep the year before. *In Bed With Madonna* is said to do all the things concert films never do, which is to give away backstage secrets by the basinful. It isn't in competition but the gossip writers will be, since ex-husband Sean Penn rides into town as she leaves (it is rumoured into the very same hotel suite) for his first feature as director, *The Indian Runner*. He will be giving a press conference. She won't. Though if she arrives at the Palais for the film, the Festival may well come to a dead halt until she is swept away. Meryl Streep complained this was one of the worst experiences of her life, but Madonna may actually *expect* the mobbing.

People

18 October 1990: Tom Sutcliffe

Lenny the lionheart

The world into which Louis Bernstein was born (he adopted the name Leonard when he was 16) was a world where American music – by which I mean musical composition in the United States – meant nothing at all. There were nineteenth-century American writers to reckon with, and a few painters. There was concert life, and an eager audience for operas new and old. But broadly speaking American art had still to be invented. The great conductors were imported, like Mahler. Novelties came from Puccini: *Girl of the Golden West*. Even 50 years ago, when Benjamin Britten was finding the US and American critics little to his taste, the process had not gone far.

It is one of the wonders of the twentieth century that, in such a short time, all-American music has come to dominate the world in the popular field above all. And it is one of the nicest ironies that the greatest and most recognisable national composer of the United States, Aaron Copland who will be 90 on 14 November, should have been not only a Jew, but homosexual and a communist. Copland (for all his supposedly unAmerican activities) gave the US a musical soul, inventing a national idiom that could reconcile the black and white influence, the jazz and the country, and yet be an absolutely authentic element in the repertoire of serious composition. Copland is home to the US, the way Elgar and Vaughan Williams are home to Britain. And Copland, who was Lenny Bernstein's creative mentor, made Bernstein's achievement possible.

Confidence, dancing exuberance, blessed vulgarity, a means to contain and heal pain: these characteristics of American music, none of them present in the anxious masterpieces of Britten, were behind Bernstein's composition. Bernstein was not a great composer, outside the musical theatre. But he did produce a range of worthwhile pieces often quite small in scale, like *Prelude, Fugue and Riffs* (for Benny Goodman). Though I regretfully conclude that *Candide* is a theatrical failure as a whole, its overture is a glorious romp and a popular concert-hall work. Whether or not the three symphonies and Mass will hold a place in the repertoire, there are real joys in Bernstein's early ballet score, *Fancy Free*, and in his short opera, *Trouble in Tahiti* (which he incorporated in his last bizarre but fitfully brilliant autobiographical operatic effort, *A Quiet Place*). Bernstein wore his compositional schooling a bit stiffly and unfluently in his attempts to create serious stuff. He is at his most natural in the Broadway masterpieces, *On The Town* and *West Side Story*.

American composers in the 1930s were not in the Schoenbergian avant-garde. But like Kurt Weill, Stravinsky, Poulenc and Shostakovich, they were inspired with a strong social conscience, an obligation to the needs of ordinary people as well as with a certain neo-classical revivalism. This was as true of Elliott Carter as of Samuel Barber, George Gershwin and Copland. And it explained the magnetism of the New World for Britten, as for Auden and Isherwood.

With *West Side Story* Bernstein provided a work that could speak to everybody. Twenty years after Copland's *Billy the Kid* ballet, 15 years after *Appalachian Spring*, five years after Bernstein's own score for Kazan's film *On the Waterfront*, Bernstein blended ballet and social realism into a tragedy that brings the conflicts of the global village into everybody's heart. This is a unique piece, profoundly unconventional in being a sort of operetta, yet devastatingly sad, and concluding with death. It covers a spectrum of feeling, with happy dancing and jokes and satire as well as the racial bitterness. Yet it manages to be completely serious about its Shakespearian subject matter. And the music is unmatched in the way it fits the subject. I have no doubt that *West Side Story* is Bernstein's greatest achievement, and contains the key to his life.

For he put his talents and his 'ham of genius' personality to single-minded use for the service of the people. He was a liberal and a democrat, a homosexual who married happily but never stopped expressing both sides of his sexual nature, a Jewish humanist who refused to behave decorously or compromise with the requirements of the New York Jewish establishment. We should never forget that he was the first all-American conductor to break through as a world figure, and that he did it not through hype and personal promotion (though he was a gift for the PR men) but through extraordinary and acute genius as a technician on the podium. He may have looked as if choreographed by Jerry Robbins, baton in hand, but he knew exactly what he was doing with the orchestra in front of him.

And that genius for manipulative gesture means that the figure he chose to cut in public was absolutely calculated as a political phenomenon. If Lenny was a notorious manizer, it wasn't just personal indulgence or weakness. It was a libertarian statement, like the chain-smoking that killed him. He demanded freedom. (Incidentally, not all his acolytes must be regarded as bedfellows, according to

Scottish Opera's John Mauceri, a similarly 'out' bisexual: 'Everybody thought I was that to Lenny, but I wasn't,' Mauceri says.) That conscious registering of his identity is why those who affected to be shocked or 'sympathetic' with him about the frank exposure of Joan Peyser's brilliant biography missed the point.

Like history, biography always has a hidden agenda, and Bernstein's tell-all biography was a marvellous tribute to the age of Aids. It was, I believe, Bernstein's act of penitence for his betrayal of his ideals in the McCarthy era (where his record was so sensitive that Peyser wasn't allowed scrutiny – perhaps the 'truth' can now be known). Of course Bernstein could make his vulgar confession naturally, where our native equivalent parable (the respectability of Benjamin Britten's homosexual marriage, leading to a peerage for himself and a knighthood for his 'wife', Peter Pears) is shaded in darkness by the Britten estate.

Bernstein's attitude was healthier. New York was always more open, as the diaries of Ned Rorem have long shown. Jewishness and homosexuality and music go together in the USA like a surrey and its fringe on top (*Oklahoma*). Dimitry Mitropoulos had 'Greek' tastes. Marc Blitzstein was queer-bashed to death by sailors in a bar in Martinique. The present 'born again' Christian attempts to suppress the homo-erotic art of Robert Mapplethorpe as obscene and shocking are a bit late in the day. But the Jewish homintern of US musical life is not an obligatory mafia, and the Peyser biography's attempt to class Bernstein's straight classical music-making along with his marriage as parallel bids for respectability is narrow-minded and uncomprehending. No doubt Lenny's corpse will be fought over by those who want to make him posthumously more respectable than he was. But his genius doesn't need protecting by such as Peter Gradenwitz, whose biography dedicated to the memory of Lenny's wife Felicia contains no entries for 'homosexuality' or 'sexual promiscuity' as Peyser's does. Yet even Gradenwitz's Euro-centred view of Bernstein the international conductor has its useful aspects. He pins down the link between Bernstein the composer and Bernstein the interpreter of other people's music. Most great conductors in the past have been composers (however bad). The act of re-creating means more to somebody who knows what it is to create. And Gradenwitz reports what should be a wonderful epitaph for Lenny from Nikolaus Harnoncourt, who was in the Vienna Symphony Orchestra for years before he became a star conductor and period instrument guru. Harnoncourt heard Bernstein's Mozart concert with the Vienna Symphony in 1948 and hails the interpretation: 'Nobody,' says Harnoncourt, 'can know what is and what is not Mozart style. If a musician has such an insight into Mozart's world as Bernstein has and interprets his music so convincingly, then that is Mozart style.' A lesson for the age of authenticity.

Leonard Bernstein, born 25 August 1919; died 14 October 1990.

14 February 1991: Michael Henderson

Simon Rattle: man of the Millennium

The Schauspielhaus, tucked away off the Unter den Linden, is the Berlin Philharmonic's home from home for the next two years, until the roof of their Philharmonie is repaired. It is a hall of sumptuous beauty where every concert should be an event: Mahler's *Resurrection Symphony*, the concert that launched the orchestra's 'East Berlin season' in the reborn city last month, certainly qualified as one.

Such a magnificent hall on so historic an occasion deserved a performance of distinction. As if they had been challenged to prove themselves worthy of it, the Berliners responded with playing which is not likely to be heard anywhere else this year. It was one of those transforming experiences which a music-lover can expect to hear only half a dozen times in a long life.

Rapturously as the audience received the orchestra, choir and soloists, no one doubted who was the true hero. After the players had left the stage, Simon Rattle was obliged to return to the platform where, with due modesty, he held up a copy of the score to acknowledge the cheers. The audience were not done, Rattle came back again, clutching the baton between his teeth as he presented Arleen Auger and Alfreda Hodgson, the soloists, as collaborators. Although he is a man of considerable will, Rattle is not one to blow his own trumpet, so the *Berliner Morgenpost* did it for him. Their headline read: 'Britischer Wündermann'.

As the doorman at the Uffizi Gallery is reputed to have told the American tourist: 'Remember, signor, here it is not the paintings which are on trial.' So it is in Berlin where the world's greatest orchestra provides the litmus test for any conductor. Of British ones, only Sir Thomas Beecham and Sir John Barbirolli, who is lovingly remembered for a famous recording of Mahler's *Ninth Symphony*, have passed it.

Rattle's reception was no great surprise. When he first appeared with the orchestra in November 1987 to conduct Mahler's *Sixth Symphony* the acclaim was, if anything, more insistent, prompting an old orchestral hand to mutter, as he left the stage: 'I am going to have to take this young man very seriously.'

Four years on, a younger musician used the metaphor of a conduit to describe Rattle's command of the orchestra. 'With Simon the music comes in here,' he said, holding one arm vertically above his head, 'flows through him and' – extending his other arm – 'comes out here.' Or, as Douglas Miller, Rattle's earliest teacher, said of his teenage pupil: 'Simon seems to have a direct line to the composers.'

It is Birmingham, not Berlin or Boston, where he goes later this month, which continues to see the best of Rattle. His contract as music director of the CBSO expires in 1994, when he will have completed 14 years, but the decision to move the main family home to Edgbaston suggests he is in no rush to leave.

In his time the CBSO has developed from 'what was a fine symphony orchestra', in the words of Ed Smith, its chief executive, into the outstanding band which Rattle is now invited to take all over the world. However strict the criteria, the CBSO/Rattle partnership must be the most notable success story in British musical life since Barbirolli's days with the Hallé. What Rattle has proved in Birmingham is that whenever talent and energy are aligned to a common will and good planning audiences will benefit.

Comparisons can be misleading, but Rattle approves of the one often made with Barbirolli's work in Manchester after the war. 'Glorious John' let the Hallé grow with the music – 'and that is what we have tried to do, except that in Birmingham we have better players.' What is undeniable is that in an age which favours cosy 'accessibility' above the pursuit of excellence, Rattle has transformed the musical *éclat* of a city by stretching audiences, not patronising them. In Birmingham, Bartók, Stravinsky, Sibelius, Janáček and Debussy form the core of the repertory, not an exotic sideshow. Moreover the CBSO play to full houses week in, week out.

'People often say that home entertainment will kill live performance,' says Smith, 'but we have found that is not the case at all. The perfect performance on a compact disc is not nearly so involving as a slightly imperfect one in a concert hall.'

When the 2,200 capacity Symphony Hall opens, giving

them an additional 450 seats they desperately need, the CBSO will have a home to rank with any in the world. Russell Johnson, the notable acoustician, has been involved from its inception: the acoustic canopy and reverberation chambers will enhance the sound of any performance, be it a Schubert recital or a Bruckner symphony.

Rattle has planned musical festivals before but 'Towards the Millennium' is his boldest idea yet, juxtaposing the contrasting preoccupations of artists working at the same time as each other in this fractured century. Performances of Schoenberg, Webern, Elgar and Suk – to be heard at the Royal Festival Hall in London as well as in Birmingham – will be set alongside *The Ragged Trousered Philanthropists* at Birmingham Rep, and a debate on 'Imperialism and the Modernist Consciousness' in Birmingham Central Library.

'I am not suggesting that you have to study Impressionism in order to play Debussy – obviously Bernard D'Ascoli [the blind French pianist] gives the lie to that – or that you must be a Christian to conduct the *Missa Solemnis*, but it is important to try and relate music to other forms.' As an obvious example Rattle draws a parallel between the music of Mahler and Viennese Secession painters like Klimt and Schiele. 'For instance I never knew that *The Cherry Orchard* and *Peter Pan* were both written in 1904. Interestingly, although there have always been mavericks like Rameau, Berlioz, Janáček and Messiaen, music has tended to lag 20 years behind the other arts.'

Birmingham's willingness to take the lead in the Millennium celebrations is another example of the City Council's admirable support of the performing arts. Part of the CBSO's job, according to Ed Smith, is 'musical education in the broadest sense, building an audience for the future.'

One of the ways in which the CBSO has sought to touch that audience is through a scheme which sends musicians into local schools to introduce a work the orchestra is about to perform and to invite the children along to hear it. Smith initially had reservations about noise and attention levels, but now says: 'They have been absolutely rapt, sharing the delight of a live performance with an adult audience.'

With council backing, and the encouragement of interested audiences, the CBSO has opened two very different outlets, the Contemporary Music Group and the Birmingham Ensemble, which plays baroque and early classical music. The orchestra also has a composer-in-association, Mark-Anthony Turnage, whose *Three Screaming Popes* was heard at last year's Proms.

No wonder that London-based musicians look enviously at the Birmingham revolution and their managers covet Rattle, who could have had any of the music directorships up for grabs in the past decade. When Smith claims that his orchestra offers musicians 'a more civilised life than any other orchestra in the country' who would disagree?

When the millennium arrives what will the by then knighted Sir Simon Rattle be doing? Nicholas Kenyon, who has written the first work-in-progress biography, would like him to be the man 'who turns London round into a city where one superb orchestra performs the kind of challenging programmes he does in Birmingham. But Simon would regard that as metropolitan prejudice.' There is certainly no danger of returning from foreign engagements, as Barbirolli once did, to complain: 'Ten ovations in Berlin . . . and no-one is in Manchester to meet me.' At 36, Rattle is already such a national asset that his judgement can appear almost infallible. Kenyon, though an admirer, believes he is 'an archetypal product of our times' who still has a lot to prove.

'Any conductor growing up in the past would have been brought up on the Beethoven symphonies and Mozart operas. Although Simon is an admirer of Furtwängler, who took a long romantic view of the classical repertory, his own instincts are in the opposite direction. Mahler has been the perfect bridge between these polarities but something which requires a bigger arch may be more difficult. There are many conductors who can give beta-plus performances but Simon can produce more outstanding ones. He knows the problems and has not approached certain works until he is ready to do them.' That was the way he tackled Beethoven's *Ninth Symphony*, and last year's performances justified his gradualist approach. He is not a pushy man; neither is he one to be pushed. In Berlin his independence led to a misunderstanding last year which reflected the differing aims of a strong-minded conductor and an orchestra locked into the international music industry. Rattle scrapped a Bartók recording after orchestra members who had not attended rehearsals turned up for the session.

To the players this arrangement was business as usual, and Rattle's decision was seen by some of them as an indication that he was not ready to record with the orchestra.

Significantly, Rattle received an endorsement from the *Suddeutsche Zeitung* which commented, 'If more people followed Simon Rattle's line conducting would become an honourable profession.'

Last month, the Berliners pulled the plug on the scheduled final rehearsal of a Ravel-Mozart-Haydn programme: again, 'business as usual'. Fortunately it did not diminish the actual performance, a wonderful Berlin debut by Imogen Cooper who gave a luminous reading of the K.595 concerto.

Simon Rattle is a man of many contradictions: a conductor who has built an international reputation by staying in Birmingham, a risk-taking programmer whose choice of accompanists is generally risk-free, a self-confessed shy man who communicates easily, a friend of music who relishes time spent away from it and who has already taken two lengthy sabbaticals to preserve the sanctity of his personal life. 'It can get ridiculous. I know what I'm doing in 1994 but sometimes I don't know what I am doing next Thursday!'

In particular, he abhors the froth-and-bubble world which readily seduced a showbiz chameleon like Nigel Kennedy. 'I am very concerned for Nigel because he is one of the most musical violinists we have produced, but really, you just can't do *The Four Seasons* like that.'

Rattle's humility, based on his belief that music is the *Ding an sich*, is entirely genuine. He is not afraid to lean on a confidant like Alfred Brendel – with whom he will perform the Beethoven concertos later this year at Symphony Hall and the Barbican – or listen to Carlos Kleiber 'if I want to know how something should go. I was sitting next to Bernard Haitink at Covent Garden when Kleiber conducted *Otello* and Bernard leaned over to me and said, "You know, Simon, I think my studies are only just beginning."' There might be a Rattle *Tristan* before the Millennium. 'I would love to do it, but where is there the *Heldentenor* to sing it? Philip Langridge perhaps. There may be one or two Isoldes. Possibly the answer is to do it in a smaller house, as more of a chamber piece.'

In Berlin, Rattle can afford to bide his time, and anyway he is not an empire-builder. This season he has conducted more concerts there than anyone except Claudio Abbado and Daniel Barenboim but suggestions that he would become the effective principal guest conductor behind Abbado – there is no such post in Berlin – have been greatly inflated by gossip. 'The orchestra does not want to create special jobs,' says Dr Helge Grünewald, 'but the cooperation with Simon will continue and may be intensified, although we realise he is very busy in Birmingham.' Next year's Berlin plans include an all-Schoenberg programme with the orchestra's chamber music group.

Rattle, meanwhile, pursues his intention of making every concert in Birmingham an event. Ed Smith, who has known him since the early days in Liverpool, is best placed to summarise his achievement. 'Simon spends 26 weeks a year with us, far more than any other music director in the world spends with his orchestra, and the repertory will sound as fresh at the end of that time as it did at the beginning. What people may forget is that Simon's appearances here would be major highlights for other orchestras. We must never take him for granted.'

17 June 1991: Jocelyn Targett

Clever git with a violin

Who likes Nigel Kennedy? John Drummond doesn't, for starters. The Controller of Radio 3 labels Kennedy 'the Liberace of the Nineties', and calls his record company stupid, his image unnecessarily vulgar and his record sleeves ludicrous. John Peel, the Radio 1 DJ, is no fan either: 'Does the word "wanker" suffice? I was at a press conference once where he said that Paul McCartney was "a real cool cat to hang out with". Anyone who says that nowadays is as close to a total wanker as it's possible to get.'

The two Johns disapprove of Kennedy for the same reason: they don't like the way he looks. But they disapprove in opposite directions. Drummond (John snr) scorns downwards. He thinks Kennedy is a punk who is debasing classical music with the clothes and coinages of rock 'n' roll. John jnr hates upwards. He thinks Kennedy is another Chris de Burgh, an unhip, middle-of-the-road twit who rolls up the sleeves of his jacket in a morally reprehensible attempt to palm off his soft-centred records to gullible teenagers.

In between John and John is a nation of people who buy next to no classical music and who dress like Chris de Burgh: easy-listeners, Radio 2 types who have probably never heard of the two BBC Johnnies. These are the people who do like Nigel Kennedy.

Kennedy currently has the top three records in the classical LP charts. His version of *The Four Seasons* ('by that cat Viv Vivaldi') has sold in excess of a million copies and is the best-selling classical LP ever. It even reached number three in the pop LP chart, pipped only by a Phil Collins album and the reissued *Carpenters Golden Greats*. He was voted Showbusiness Personality of the Year for 1990 ('monster news'), succeeding Jimmy Tarbuck, Wogan and Cannon and Ball, and he is widely regarded as the most extrovert violinist since Paganini, who used to snip through three of his strings and encore on just the one ('clever git that Pag').

His latest release, the Brahms *Violin Concerto* which came out in April, has already sold 100,000: more in its first 10 weeks than even the Vivaldi achieved. Classical music hasn't shifted this fast since Richard Clayderman's fuel-injected K-Tel special offers; and many at the posh, wing-collared end of the classical business, accustomed at best to low-lit successes, are growing suspicious of this new neon Nigel of the People.

Some are inclined to credit the sales to the ingenuity of EMI, to the David Bailey publicity photos, to the hairgel, wisecracks, and throwaway celebmanship of a pop star. The music, they are beginning to mutter, isn't that good: in fact, the music is vacuous, in parts cynically pretty, elsewhere melodramatic. This is especially sad, they say, because Nigel Kennedy was once such a promising young violinist.

'The Elgar concerto he recorded in 1984,' says Sigmund Nissel, a founder-member of the Amadeus String Quartet, 'had such virtuosity and a wonderful innocence. I was very moved to hear it, and it is still in my ears as one of the most miraculous things I have ever heard. But *The Four Seasons* I did not agree with. I could see why it was very popular. It did what it was meant to do: it gave a show. But he wildly exaggerated the rhythmic element. He used it – and these are strong words – as a pop session.'

Even Andrew Keener, who produces all Kennedy's recordings with EMI, is 'not convinced' by the Vivaldi or the Brahms. Keener too, however, covets the Elgar, which was Kennedy's first EMI release, recorded when the violinist was 25 and which – a year or so before Kennedy swapped his tails and white tie for a razorcut and an attitude – sold more than 100,000 and won two industry awards. In a market where a target of 8,000 to 10,000 sales was ambitious for a popular work by a well-known soloist, these Elgar figures by a virtual unknown remain outstanding.

Nigel's mother, Scylla, was a piano tutor, like her mother before her, and his father, John, was principal cello in the Royal Philharmonic under Sir Thomas Beecham. His grandfather, Laurie, had been first cello in the BBC Symphony Orchestra, and even his great aunt Daisy, genetically twice-removed, managed to lead a string band at the Regent Palace Hotel. So, from the first nano-second of his conception, Nigel Kennedy was going to be a musician: his DNA spells out no alternative career.

By the time of his birth, just after Christmas 34 years ago, Nigel's parents had already parted. John Kennedy settled in Australia, and has seen his son only on a few far-between occasions. Nigel was brought up by his mother and grandmother in Brighton. An only child, he was often left on his own while Scylla went out to teach. When she was home practising he used to clamber on to the piano stool to be next to her. From the age of three, he too was given piano lessons, and at six he learned to play the violin.

Scylla describes him as being almost monosyllabic as a child and, convinced he was being mollycoddled, she applied for him to be taken as a boarder by the Yehudi Menuhin School. 'I knew,' she says, 'that I wouldn't want to go on teaching him.'

Sir Yehudi was very taken by Nigel's audition. 'He played his own composition on the piano – a very excellent little piece – and he played the violin perfectly in tune. It was clear that he had a strong rhythmic personality.' Menuhin persuaded his own father to stump up the fees for the chubby six-year-old. Scylla, meanwhile, remarried and moved to Solihull.

Nigel made meagre progress over the following five years, becoming increasingly withdrawn. Several times, his teachers recommended his scholarship be annulled. 'Even at his best,' says Peter Norris who taught him chamber music, 'he didn't communicate much. He was efficient, but he never had a lot of flair.' Only Menuhin, and Menuhin's father, stuck by Nigel: the money was never pulled.

'As a boy he rather lost his heart to Stephane Grappelli,' says Menuhin who arranged for Nigel to jam with the old French jazzer. Grappelli was so impressed that he invited Nigel, still only 14, to gig with him at Ronnie Scott's in Soho. He played there several times as a teenager – with the school's blessing, but not his mother's. 'She was not pleased,' says Kennedy. 'I was meant to be the next Heifitz.'

In the holidays Nigel used to take the bus to watch Aston Villa, sneaking under the turnstiles at the Holt End for free. These days he is a senior vice-president of the club, and is the only one allowed in Villa's men-only boardroom without a tie. Shrill blasts of his Vivaldi are Tannoyed to the stands when the team wins.

In the early 1970s, BBC2 approached Sir Yehudi with the idea of making a documentary to map a musician's progress from teens to twenties: Nigel was nominated as the subject. The programme, *Coming Along Nicely*, shows Nigel at 16, as a small, podge-faced child with glossy, shoulder-length hair flattened into an immaculate parting. He enunciates cleanly – very Home Counties, all his consonants intact – and his voice didn't break until he was

18 and studying at the Juillard School of Music in New York.

Nigel introduced the Juillard students to soccer and spent evenings in Greenwich Village jazzing with Stan Getz. He busked for pocket money outside Tiffany's on Fifth Avenue. When punk raged in London, Nigel Kennedy's untopiaried head and wide eyes made him about as dangerous as a welcome mat. But he was, says his Juillard tutor Dorothy DeLay, already 'playing around with accents', trying to find one to set him apart.

At 20, and scarcely adult, Kennedy married Joanna, a nurse, and at 21 he soloed at the Royal Festival Hall. By 22, he'd slurred into the accent he favours at the moment, his loose-lipped cityspeak, a kind of Stanley Unwin down at the old Bull and Bush.

Within a year, he'd signed an exclusive recording contract with EMI, toured America and the Far East, and slid behind the music unions to perform in South Africa. He also began to fall out with his management at Holt Associates, upmarket classical purists who were as unhappy as his mother about him moonlighting with jazz.

Soon after the Elgar, Kennedy severed links with his adolescence: after 10 years at Holt's, he signed up with Terry Harrison, James Galway's manager; after seven years of marriage, he split up with Joanna; and after a lifetime of nerdiness, he went for a haircut. Then, on the night of a concert, he left his tie and tails in the boot of another violinist's car and had to go on as he was. By a combination of good and bad fortune, he'd scratched himself a niche. He didn't bother picking up the suit for six weeks.

Two robust but unremarkable recordings later, EMI's Rupert Perry decided Kennedy's career needed special handling and he put him in touch with a new manager: John Stanley, who used to look after the Bay City Rollers.

John Stanley is the classical music industry's idea of the biggest problem with Nigel Kennedy. It's Stanley who cancels his concerts at the last minute; Stanley who orders light shows for his recitals; Stanley who calls in the graphic designers; Stanley who hires the bouncers for the Royal Albert Hall; Stanley who talks not of records but of 'units sold'; and Stanley who whisks Nigel away from the other musicians and off to the nite-spots in a stretch Bentley.

'The classical world,' says Ginny Macbeth, formerly Kennedy's press agent, 'is peopled by a very particular type. Low-key, not flash. You get a different sort in the pop business – people like John Stanley.'

Kennedy has replaced his Stradivarius with a Guarnerius: 'That shows he's become interested in power, the power to ride over the orchestra,' says Sigmund Nissel who plays a Strad. And Kennedy has replaced Joanna ('she's normal, she's OK') with a peroxided rock guitarist, Brix Smith ('my top animalette'). His autobiography was bought by Weidenfeld's for an estimated £300,000, and is going to be serialised in *Today*, a paper without a music critic. Nigel, some conclude, is being led astray.

Stanley hadn't even met Kennedy when the Vivaldi was recorded in 1986, so its Kylie-esque breeziness can't be his fault. Two years on, Kennedy's high glucose *Four Seasons* – 'the most marketable of the classical repertoire,' says Barry McCann, EMI's strategic marketing manager, 'by our most marketable performer' – was promised a £100,000 advertising budget. His Elgar had been launched on £3,000.

The record, released in September 1988, did solid trade until the New Year when sales waned. Then a promotional documentary, commissioned by John Stanley and Janet Street-Porter, was screened on BBC 2, and the record shot back up the charts. In Kennedy's own estimation, the programme established him as 'not a totally boring kind of cat'. It showed him as chatty and unpretentious, a sweet man, and it captured some of his stage presence, his jabbing arm, his juddering legs, the metronomic sway of his body. And it made a great deal of his unsavoury appearance.

'He looks like a polytechnic student,' says a concert soloist – a compliment to how completely Kennedy has achieved his downward mobility. Sir Yehudi, his mentor and advocate, understandably disapproves too: 'He delights his audience, but he shouldn't look so different from the orchestra. It is not respectful or discreet.'

Kennedy, however, revels in his difference. When he meets people he embarks on a crazy hand-jive designed to disorientate, not greet. He dunks his biscuits in other people's tea. 'He arranges to see you,' says the pianist Peter Pettinger, 'then he doesn't show. It is exasperating. He's very charming afterwards, but charm is easy for him, easier than saying he can't make it in the first place.'

Nigel is always being forgiven. The only child with no one to play with now has too many friends. He hasn't the heart to leave them behind, so they tag along, accepting what crumbs of friendship he offers, and growing a little bitter about his fast life and John Stanley.

'Stanley's bloody impossible, frankly,' says Doug Ellis, the chairman of Aston Villa, 'but Nigel's a great kid. I'm so proud of him.' Ellis takes Nigel pheasant shooting and they've plans – fluid, of course – to go salmon fishing in Ireland. 'He confides in me, calls me "Monster". I like to think he looks on me as a dad.' Menuhin met John Kennedy, Nigel's real father, on a recent trip to Australia. 'He embraced me and cried, thanking me for what I have done for the son he doesn't know.' Scylla, however, who has gone back to Sussex, isn't so delighted. Nigel gave her the gold disc he won for *The Four Seasons*, but it clashes with the decor so she keeps it in the spare bedroom.

He has the talent but not the temperament of the son she wanted. 'He's got this view,' she revealed in a tabloid newspaper, 'that you're not special if you're a classical musician. So he pretends he's like one of those football players. It's a bit disappointing really.' Fancy thinking you'd bred a little prince and have him turn into Gazza.

9 October 1990: Joan Littlewood

The divine Bunnage from Chorlton Rep

Drop a flower, or say a prayer if such is your persuasion, for Avis, the most talented, wittiest actress who ever came into my life. You could have passed her in the street. She didn't dress to kill; but when she sang, or told a story, or walked on to the stage, she was beautiful. She shone. She held the whole audience in the palm of her hand. She could bring down pomposity too, deflate anyone with one well-timed wisecrack – a true Lancashire lass. Her mother had been a Tiller girl and later became known as 'The Dainty Soubrette'.

Her father was a keen musician – and a dentist – but it was the music which dominated his life. He would travel to Birmingham just to take part in a concert in the park. As a little girl Avis danced for her mother, sang and played the piano for her father. Inevitably, she gathered other children round her, formed a concert party and gave shows in the Bunnage backyard.

This was in Manchester, at her home in Chorlton-cum-Hardy. She never lost her love for the place, nor her ear for the true accents of the north. True is the operative word. The characters she created were always true – as she was. When she left school she didn't find her way in the world easily. She tried various odd jobs and went to the theatre as often as she could, in a town which was lively theatrically in those days. Even the quiet suburb where she lived had its repertory theatre. It was there, at the age of 24, that she first trod the boards, in a play about the Brontës.

Chorlton Rep harboured budding talent. Jimmie Lovell who was there became an excellent director and its doors were open to guest artists, such as Theo Bikel from Israel, and David Scase when he had a week off from Theatre Workshop. Harry H. Corbett made his debut there and met Avis. They became friends and that friendship lasted for life. David introduced Harry to me, and in 1952 Harry joined Theatre Workshop. Avis hesitated. 'She's better than me,' said Harry. She was, he depended on her. Avis was the one person who could make him laugh at himself.

Theatre Workshop was playing one-night stands all over the north-east when Harry joined us. For him it was liberation, but home-loving Avis did not relish the prospect. Nevertheless, she came, and played miners' halls, welfare halls, clubs and chapels – for all the world like some eighteenth-century barnstormer, except that Theatre Workshop standards, technically and artistically, were as high as, or higher than, those of any other company.

Harry was constantly announcing his forthcoming marriage to Avis; a bridal chamber would be prepared, the local JP alerted – but always there'd be a slip up somewhere; either Harry would have forgotten to get a licence, or he'd be broke, or Avis would have been recalled to the parental home because Mrs Bunnage, who was by now crippled with arthritis, needed her. Avis loved her mother and was often torn between theatre and family duty. In the end theatre won.

One of the most amazing transformations was to see this young woman, anything but bookish, and fresh from weekly rep and revue – plunging into:

You will accuse him? You will bring him in
Within the statute? Who shall take your word
A whoreson, upstart, apocryphal captayne,

Whom not a puritan in blackfriars will trust
So much as for a feather?

She had Ben Jonson's Dol Common word perfect in a matter of days, and went on to an education in the language of Marlowe, Shakespeare, Marston, Lope de Vega and Vanburgh – then to Shaw, Synge, Sean O'Casey, Pirandello, Julius Hay and Jaroslav Hašek. In all the plays the divine Bunnage played a leading role.

Strangely enough, when she turned her attention to the dishevelled scripts we were then receiving – she took to editing and witty improvisation like a duck to water – the wealth of English she had at her disposal must have helped her.

A Taste of Honey would not have made sense without Avis. 'Send it back and wait till she can write a play,' she said, but when we agreed to try to make the script stand up Avis was superb. The young author understood her heroine and black lover, but the 40-year-old mother only came to life through the wit and art of the actress – Avis.

It was the same with Brendan's lodging housekeeper, Meg, in *The Hostage*. There was little to go on in the original script, but with Brendan's help Avis brought the character to life.

Her gift for improvisation became known in the profession and TV and film directors vied with each other for her services. Critics, on the other hand, seemed to have no idea how much the Workshop and its performers contributed to the success of these shows.

Avis was that rare bird, a creative actress: few recognised the species, now dying out like the red kite.

When I knew that I couldn't put up with the horrors of Theatre Royal, E15, much longer, I decided to stage a tribute to Avis, something which would show her gifts to advantage. I knew that she loved Marie Lloyd's songs. Someone had sent me a Marie Lloyd script. On the spur of the moment I accepted it. With the bright company I had –

headed by Maxwell Shaw, Jimmy Perry and Gaye Brown we could always improve on it – but to my horror, when we came to play the songs, they weren't the old originals: the author had engaged a composer to write modern songs. That wouldn't suit my purpose at all. We cut them and dug out the Marie Lloyd tunes, then still part of the Cockney heritage . . . they were not to my taste, but when Avis sang them they gained a freshness and vitality which I hadn't heard in them before. At the end of the show, we couldn't bring down the curtain.

It was the same night after night. The audience yelled for more and Avis sang the songs again. They wouldn't let her go. Neither should we. I know that I, for one, will hear that glorious voice till the end of my days.

Avis Bunnage, born 22 April 1923; died 4 October 1990.

10 January 1991: Peter Lennon

Mother outrage

When Glenda Jackson stood behind the railings of St Eldridge's, Greenwich, to pose for the photograph her whole posture declared: 'I will prevail.' Her head among the spikes suggested: 'Discomfort is my chosen way.'

She would make a wonderful Joan of Arc, exhibiting the same indifference to the flames as she did to the gawping locals dragging anchor as they passed with their shopping. Even her docility as she posed had a commanding quality; she had chosen to submit and did so without special aid from camera angle or fad which any thespian anxious to maintain an image – particularly one such as Jackson who has turned politician – would demand. With Glenda Jackson the image comes from within: resolution, with a dusting of weariness at people's stupidity; an iron determination to serve, sauced with a taste for chastisement.

She has served and chastised the best in theatre and cinema – among them Peter Brook and Ken Russell. 'Ken doesn't know anything about acting,' she remarked casually about the man for whom she writhed nakedly (but consciously introducing a repellent dimension) in *The Music Lovers*.

She described London audiences as 'steamed puddings'. Glenda Jackson is dedicated to rebuking humbug, shallowness and wobbly commitment. Over the years this bricklayer's daughter who graduated from behind the counter at Boots to international renown has laid her brand on *Hedda Gabler*, given the asp's bite to *Cleopatra*, and put steel into the heart of *Mother Courage*.

But as you sit tentatively feeding some timid compliments to this rather glum tigress, referring to her success (acclaimed in the theatre; two Oscars) – the figure that most comes to mind is Charlotte Corday advancing on you with a (verbal) knife while you sit like poor Marat insufficiently (ethically) clothed, scratching about for a bit of frivolous relief.

Success? The mouth, slightly down at heel, savoured the word with scorn: 'The work is the work that you do at the time that you do it,' she intoned. 'Whatever has gone before is irrelevant. The work is the work.' (Maybe she should try her hand at Gertrude Stein?) Did the feeling that the theatre had no longer any great satisfaction to offer influence her decision to accept nomination as Labour candidate for Hampstead and Highgate? 'That presupposes that there is satisfaction and of course there isn't,' she said, squeezing out that comforting word 'satisfaction' as if it were a blackhead on the face of her escutcheon.

Will there be satisfaction in politics? Yes, she will have 'the temerity to say to people "I can help you".' If elected she will not divide her career between politics and the theatre, but there is still a living to be earned so in February she will be in the Glasgow Citizens' Theatre's new production of *Mourning Becomes Electra*.

During her selection, a Labour MP cast doubt on the ability of a woman to cope with politics. She scorched this idea. 'If you can show me an MP,' she retorted, 'who has touched as many bases in a lifetime as a woman has to cover in a day I'd like to meet him.'

She is not lost for a word when it comes to Tory-dominated England. 'The Tories have made a virtue out of the worst aspects of the English character: narrow-mindedness, mean-spiritedness, lack of generosity, and spitefulness have become virtues.' And this was only in peace time.

Her immediate concern was the orphaned children of Romania for whom she will perform in an all-star gala, *Kids At Heart*, at the Palladium tomorrow. Her attitude to charity is clear-headed: charity works, she says, when 'what people are being given is a hope that things might be made better partly by their own efforts'.

As for the situation in the Gulf, she felt sanctions should be given longer to work. 'The idea of going in, almost as a dare, is monstrous,' she said. It was shortly after the Iraqi Foreign Minister had spent six hours instead of the expected five minutes with Secretary Baker at Geneva. There seemed still be to hope that the Theatre of Cruelty proposed by the warrior politicians might not have an opening night. But the monstrous dare came about.

29 October 1990: Ian Mayes

Freda Jackson's people

The first time I saw Freda Jackson was on the Hammer Films set at Bray Studios in 1960. The film, not one perhaps to go down in history, was *Brides of Dracula*. Freda was to come on and, at the foot of a grand staircase, discover the empty chains from which the unfortunate vampire had been misguidedly released. Minutes earlier someone had been round the set putting up cobwebs from a hand pump. The clapper boy was lying on a coffin reading a comic. In this early morning atmosphere of total artificiality, the rising crescendo of Freda's hysterical screams chilled the air and raised the hair on the assembled necks.

In private life she could be a bit scary, too. It took visitors to her home in Northamptonshire some time to realise that she and her husband, the artist Henry Bird, quite normally expressed their mutual devotion in an exchange of ferocious pleasantries. In her professional life this full-blooded approach incredibly lifted her from the asthma which plagued her all the time I knew her into extraordinarily physical performances as her Mother Courage in the early 1960s.

But while she could be disconcerting in her more combative mood she was also loved for the warmth and generosity of her friendship. When I began working at Broadcasting House in the late Seventies she insisted I use her room in St John's Wood, kept since shortly after the war for occasions when she was on the stage or filming in London, and later retained as a kind of insistence that she had not retired (in fact she appeared on the West End stage as late as 1982, in *Uncle Vanya* at the Haymarket). Freda's room was in a house in Marlborough Hill, a place of brave decrepitude amid the splendour, as conspicuous as though Charles Addams had designed it. On the landing there was a bathroom which had a geyser plastered with warnings that ignition might destroy the better part of St John's Wood. The only person who used it regardless was Raymond, a retired civil servant who occupied the next room. The crump as the gas came on shook the house. Water from the bath, due to a plumbing defect, drained directly through the ceiling of the entrance porch, so that Raymond's ablutions were always marked by a small pile of moist plaster on the doormat. Beneath the bath itself there was a bicycle saddle, some cigarette ends in a saucepan, and a dead mouse.

By the time I began to use it, Freda's room had assumed a decadent grace which Miss Havisham might have recognised had not she, like Freda, been more or less oblivious of her surroundings. An enormous window from near floor level to the ceiling was too precariously balanced in its frame to stand cleaning. Paper sagged on the ceiling and peeled tentatively from the tops of the walls. Oriental carpets covered the floor, and the furniture included a sideboard stuffed with the scripts of the films and plays in which Freda had appeared, including *Tom Jones* and *Bhowani Junction*. At night the mice had free range and in the morning their tiny teethmarks patterned the plastic bag in which the loaf was secured.

Freda's was the only occasional room in the house. The others were occupied by residents who all seemed to be 73: an Irish couple in the basement, the widow of a *Punch* cartoonist on the ground floor, Raymond next to Freda, and on the floor above a retired schoolteacher. They all struggled valiantly against the creeping decay and the harassment of successive landlords for whom the controlled tenancies represented an intolerable frustration. I remember having to haggle over the rent with Freda. In the end she said, 'All right, make it £3.' 'That doesn't sound much for a week's rent.' 'Good God,' she said, 'I meant £3 a month.'

Anxiety, insecurity, loneliness, or something, sometimes took its toll. The woman from the ground floor appeared on the landing one night and invited me to take her in my arms like a man. When I demurred she threw herself down the stairs, although carefully, sliding on her back and complaining that the world was 'out of kilter'.

Freda was very fond of all these people. The range of

feeling she had explored in her work, from her early days at Stratford and the Old Vic onwards, was not irrelevant to her life outside the theatre. Art and life were hard to separate. In Northamptonshire, with her husband Henry, she belonged to a small group of people pitted, in what now seems a rather old-fashioned way, against the philistines, not for what they were but for what they were missing, and for what provincial life might otherwise have been.

Freda Jackson, born 29 December 1909; died 20 October 1990.

4 April 1991: Leader

Odd genius out

Hale knew, before he had been in Brighton three hours, that they meant to murder him . . . . That, as it happens, is the opening of *Brighton Rock*; but turn up the opening lines of the rest of his books and they won't disappoint you. Graham Greene, who died yesterday, rich in years and rich in honour, was first of all a storyteller, gripping the reader's mind with skilled and relentless fingers before his first page is out and not letting go thereafter. Unusually, he segregated his novels into two distinctive categories: some had serious purposes, some were 'entertainments'. But the categories weren't exclusive. Even the entertainments are full of ideas and the novels of high ideas never forget they are also stories.

Because he travelled so much, and absorbed all he saw, the array of locales is dizzying: yet they all reflect a world, transcending geography, which is uniquely his; a world where the day is almost always too hot; a world where duty, or faith, pull one way, and inclination the other; whose anguished, faltering heroes have left undone what they ought to have done, and have done what they plainly ought not to have done, and know there is no health in them; where in consequence the sense of guilt hangs like an imminent thunderstorm and a drink seems some form of relief, even if not for long. Perhaps we are in West Africa, Vietnam, Central or Southern America: but even in places of blameless gentility, the possibility of human trial and potential horror lurks not very far away. Rose, at the end of *Brighton Rock*, walks rapidly in the thin June sunlight towards the worst horror of all. 'And in the end, this – horror,' Mrs Scobie exclaims to the priest in the closing lines of *The Heart of Matter*. 'He must have known he was damning himself.' Greene had lived from his earliest days with a sense of menace. The misery of his schooldays at Berkhamsted School – where instincts which prompted rebellion had to be stilled because his father was headmaster – drove him to escape (followed by psychoanalysis). As he recounts in *A Sort of Life*, even somnolent Chipping Campden, to which he retreated after the publication of his first novel, was not immune from this sense of the dread: 'the old man who sells the *News of the World* on Sunday mornings', he was soon recording, 'was found yesterday by his wife hanging dead; he was seventy-three and Greenall, our daily, says that he could no longer stand his wife's nagging . . . '

Greene was 86 when he died, though he might have perished in the autumn of 1923 when he heard about Russian roulette, put a gun to his head and missed by only one barrel. He adventured on his own behalf and on ours. Official tributes will now be paid in abundance, but none will be any more eloquent than the regiments of his books marshalled along the shelves of the high street shops. We can say of him with certainty that the best of his books will still be read and enjoyed in an age that none of us now alive will live to see. No writer could wish for a higher accolade.

Graham Greene, born 2 October 1904; died 3 April 1991.

9 April 1991: John Ezard

Dead certainty

'That must be the mistress,' a Swiss journalist murmured as a chic woman in black signed the mourners' register outside the church of San Jean.

A quick peek at the register, which was open under a blossoming cherry tree – and, no, it was the irreproachable wife of the British ambassador, Chris Long.

Graham Greene's widow, Vivien, was already in church. And so, it emerged later, was his mistress, Yvonne Cloetta, an equally chic woman in black.

It was just that so many journalists were peeking at the register yesterday that she had been unable to get through to sign it. There was no friction in church. 'A peculiar lot, we Greenes,' the clan spokesman, Graham Carleton Greene, murmured in clarification.

The novelist's funeral and burial in the coniferous dignity of a hillside looking across Lake Geneva to the Alps was an affair as happily complaisant, in his sense of the word, as it was comradely and loving. It was led by a bevy of Greenes, right down to his grandson, Andrew Bourget. Its supporting cast included one of the world's greatest leprosy specialists, Michel Lachat, whom the author met while working on *A Burnt Out Case*, and the resonantly silver-haired real-life Honorary Consul for Nice and Antibes, Ronnie Challenor, a friend for 20 years but not, he hastened to add, the original of the maritally tortured consul of the book.

Most of all there was Father Leopoldo Durand, Spanish original of M. Quixote in one of his old theological sparring partner's last novels. 'Farewell, sweet prince, and flights of angels sing thee to thy rest,' the father chanted exuberantly while splashing – sprinkling is not Father Durand's way – the coffin with holy water.

In the pulpit earlier he acknowledged briefly that 'Thomas the Doubter' had been one of Greene's lifelong names for himself. But the priest went on to leave no single hairline of doubt in his sermon. He told the congregation that to avoid misinterpretation it was important to make clear the 86-year-old novelist had taken the initiative in calling him to his bedside: 'His physician said he had never seen such an extraordinary character in the presence of death. He had been unwell for about 15 months. I told him most directly, "Graham, God is waiting for you just now – pray for us where you will be for ever in God's blessing. I now give the last absolution." This I did. He passed away in the most peaceful manner. Without a gesture, he fell asleep. My faith tells me that he is now with God or on the way there. He was a loyal friend who would risk his life if truth or justice demanded it. His work remains as our legacy.'

Mr Carleton Greene, the author's nephew, said afterwards that he did not think anybody in the family would mind the certitude of Father Durand's remarks. 'After all it was Graham, who knew what kind of priest he was, who asked him to come.'

When Greene developed leukaemia, he moved here to an apartment in the parish of Courseaux from Antibes, where he had hoped to die. It brought him to the town where Charlie Chaplin is buried, and close to Greene's daughter, Caroline Bourget. But it also brought him to a neat landscape of hypermarkets, sensible houses and tiered vineyards, to the country which, as his Harry Lime said, enjoyed 500 years of democracy and peace, 'and what did it produce: the cuckoo clock'.

His grave near that of a town doctor is in the posher part of a small cemetery built in steps up a hill. The only section of this view which broods like his books is the Alps, their high snow lines hidden in cloud even in yesterday's sunshine.

'He liked it here,' Mr Carleton Greene said. 'He'd visited most of the turbulent places of the world. Maybe one needs peace.'

Courseaux cemetery was dominated by the fortitude with which Vivien Greene, aged 85, walking slowly along gravel paths, kept her wedded husband company on his last earthly journey after more than 40 years' marital separation. Greene wrote to her in a 1925 letter: 'You carry magic with you always.'

She led the family in sprinkling water on the grave. Then Greene's biographer, Norman Sherry, left a final red rose. The press wanted to know whether Vivien knew that the last of several mistresses was present. 'We'll leave that to analysis in Professor Sherry's next volume,' Mr Carleton Greene said.

5 July 1990: W. L. Webb

Pornbroker extraordinary

Maurice Girodias, pornbroker extraordinary – or the most literate and discerning publisher of erotic literature in our time, if you like – died of a heart attack in Paris while being interviewed on the radio about the publication of his memoirs. 'A calling to be a troublemaker', was how he once described what drove his extraordinary career, but actually it was bred in the bone. Girodias's Olympia Press, with its austere-looking olive green paperbacks, set Beckett and the likes of Nabokov and Genet cheek by cheek with *Whips Incorporated* and *The English Governess*. But a generation before, his father, Jack Kahane, a refugee from gray Edwardian Manchester, had founded the Obelisk Press, which in the 1930s, with Radclyffe Hall and Henry Miller and his friend Lawrence Durrell's *Black Book* on its list, had rather a similar literary and scandalous reputation.

For scandalous scope and sheer audacity, though, there's no doubt that the second generation had the edge. Who else could have fled the hot clutches of the French police to turn up smiling 18 months later as guest of honour at one of Christina Foyle's literary lunches at the Dorchester. ('I think almost anyone who is radical and English,' said Angus Wilson, beaming on the ranks of bemused W. H. Smith minions and other booksellers, 'must think this a very exciting moment.')

That memorable moment for the British book trade establishment occurred in 1966. (It was the more remarkable in that many people believe that the Home Office had been pushing the French to close Girodias down because he had lately committed the near capital offence of publishing Roger Casement's 'Black Diaries', the account of his homosexual loves during his time as pro-consul in the Congo and elsewhere which the Home Office was said to have circulated in a limited edition to favoured journalists at the time of Casement's trial.)

For this moment in the Swinging Sixties, Maurice Girodias became almost respectable, but soon it was back to more familiar kinds of excitement. In November 1971, after the police had raided his London office, he confided his thoughts on byways of the English psyche to Jill Tweedie: 'There is a peculiar tension in the English character that expresses itself in destroying people in very intimate ways by getting at their ego.' This expressed itself in 'the whipping of schoolboys and torturing of servants so standard in British pornography'. In fact, he said, he published flagellation books 'almost entirely for the English'.

It was not long before the English retaliated. In May 1972 police raided his warehouse and seized nearly

40,000 books, 98 per cent of the stock. Once again Girodias was back where he had been in 1964, when he had been expelled from France. Two years later, after trying to publish a novel in which Henry Kissinger was an all too thinly masked principal actor (and, almost as effectively dangerous, some of his friends believe, after publishing an exposé of the Church of Scientology), he was expelled from the United States, and his publishing days were substantially over.

Whatever his various chastisements, what Girodias did, especially in the early days, made an enviable list. He started on his own in 1953, having the luck to get hold of Kazantzakis's *Zorba the Greek*, and acquiring Henry Miller through his father's friendship (Maurice, who had taken his French mother's name, had designed the cover for *Tropic of Cancer* at the age of 14). Beckett (*Watt and Molloy*, the first novel of the trilogy) came to him through *Merlin*, the expatriate magazine edited in Paris by Alexander Trocchi, whose staff and hangers-on were able to eat by supplying Girodias pseudonymously with some of the pornographic stuffing of the list. Nabokov himself, unable to place it elsewhere, brought him his immortal nymphet.

There were William Burroughs and Genet, and there was the relatively innocent book which was the beginning of the end of him: *The Ginger Man*, the fierce comedy with which the young J. P. Donleavy wrote himself into the canon (the Manchester connection was revived: parts of it had already been published in the *Manchester Guardian* as 'backpager' sketches). The breach of contract suit Donleavy brought sank Girodias, and when he attended the auction for the title of the firm and tried to buy it back, Mrs Donleavy sank him again by outbidding him.

Another scarred bruiser in the censorship wars described him as 'a wild romantic of the libertarian left, hopeless about money, but he would go into any cause he believed in head down, all the way.' Girodias's view was that freedom to publish was not to be qualified. When the 1960s were only just over, and before Knacker made his call on the Olympia Press's London warehouse and an age before Aids, he was prematurely welcoming the victory of the sexual revolution, leading us into a new era of freedom in which 'we shall be obliged to behave as free people'. That, however, added the voice of experience, 'is no bed of roses.'

Maurice Girodias, born 12 April 1919; died 3 July 1990.

1 May 1991: Suzie Mackenzie

Clipped Wings

I got to quite like Geoff, Linda McCartney's publicity man, in the dozen or so phone conversations that preceded the interview. 'Allo Sue, it's Geoff,' chirped his voice daily on my answermachine. 'Don't worry, it's cool. Linda is cool. Paul's cool. Ask her anything you like. Take as long as you like.'

And so we sit. Linda, Geoff, Heather, Linda's 27-year-old daughter by her first marriage – 'To Harry, or was it Mel?' 'It was Mel, Mum' – and I, in Paul's newly converted recording studio in a windmill in west Sussex. Linda has made the tea. 'No, Geoff, I'll make the tea. I'll do it.' I have been introduced to all the workmen. 'Chris, this is Sue. Sue, Chris.' And now there is little left to do except talk.

Perched anxiously on the edge of the sofa, her eyes fixed on her mother, her arms wrapped tightly to her body, Heather chain-smokes. Geoff, I notice, is also looking decidedly less cool. He, too, chain-smokes. There is a man, I know, posted at the bottom of the stairs, who regularly nods at Linda, who amiably nods back.

'Tell me about the veggie burgers,' I say to break the ice.

The veggie burgers – or what Geoff endearingly calls 'Mrs Mac takes on Big Mac' – are Linda's latest attempt to convert the world to vegetarianism, her own idea, her own recipes, resulting in six frozen products of textured soya concentrate – lasagne, pasties, chicken nuggets – all made to taste and look like meat. 'Why don't you ring Chris, Geoff, and get him to cook a bit for Sue?' Geoff makes a note.

The McCartneys took the idea to Ross Youngs, a subsidiary of United Biscuits, who seized it and packaged it along the same lines as Paul Newman's sauce products in the States. So it's a straight endorsement deal – they buy her name. 'Don't be defensive, Geoff. I can answer.' And to me, 'I'm doing it for the animals, I don't need the money.'

Linda is talking. Heather is twitching. Geoff is sulking. There is something uneasy-making in the contrast between Linda's exaggerated vivaciousness and Heather's fragile and trembling nervousness. She seems to be almost pathologically protective of her mother, constantly reminding and with mounting urgency: James, Linda's 13-year-old son, will be home from school. Or Dad's on his way. 'We're going to have to wind this up,' says Geoff from his corner.

'Linda, Paul on line one.' It's the man on the stairs.

'Why aren't we talking about food?' beseeches Heather. 'You said it would be about food.'

At the centre of this, Linda, with her bony, tomboyish appeal, lying back on the sofa, flicking her hair. Fifty this year – 'Fifty years of knowledge,' she says, musingly. It is the eyes that get you, the hooded, half-closed, sexy eyes. The eyes that met Paul's across a crowded London club 22 years ago when she was an unknown freelance photographer and he was, what? A god? 'Instant karma' – this said romantically. 'He thought, who's that dishy blonde over there.' This prosaically. For she tries on attitudes like a child dressing up in front of a mirror, amusing itself while the grown-ups are out.

'Was he still with Jane Asher?' A bit mischievous, but why not. 'I think he was with lots of people. I don't think he was with anyone.' Down-to-earth Linda: so far you may go and no further. A flurry of flunkies on the stairs.

'I think we should split,' moans Geoff.

'Carry on,' she says jauntily.

It is hard to get a handle on Linda McCartney. For a start, she denies there is any tension between her public and private image. She is, she would have you believe, wholesomely complete. She has a strong line in that sort of fatuous and meaningless sincerity: 'We're all human beings. I bleed. I go to the toilet. Just like everyone else.'

She would like to see the world enfolded in one loving embrace. She is an ordinary person. But what does this mean? She sends her children to state schools, she makes sure that they live 'well but not grandly'. She is not interested in any form of ostentation, and materialism bores her. 'I think that was a disappointment to Paul, that I didn't want jewellery and furs.' Her life is now devoted to Paul and the four children. 'Why have children if you don't want to be at home? I am a housewife. I was brought up old-fashioned. The husband works, the wife takes care of the family . . . '

This is OK. But when Linda McCartney tells you, 'All I've ever wanted is to be anonymous,' you have to bite back the obvious rebuke. The ordinariness theme is undoubtedly defensive. And it's true that every time she steps into the limelight, she is cut down. She put up with 'all that crap' of being married to a Beatle: 'You know, I was unfashionable, pushy, untalented, a divorcée. I chaperone him everywhere because everyone must want him. Well, they can have him. It's up to him. I don't screen his calls.'

She withstood all the flack of singing and playing in Paul's band, Wings: 'It was his idea and to begin with it was fun.' But then the critics got to her. 'I can see why they said what they said. I'm an unaccomplished musician.' But where does all this leave her? 'I am his wife,' she says. 'I never expected anything in life, never wanted anything except to live life.'

This is Linda McCartney at her most contemplative and beguiling. But there is another Linda, the one who forcefully maintains, 'Fuck what they say.' The one who admits that when she married Paul she lost all her old friends, forgot about them. 'I'm not a girlie person. I don't need many friends.' And for her, I think, the ordinariness is something else, an enhanced way of asserting difference. Playing at being ordinary is presumptuous and undermining. It says I'm so different from you that I'm not threatened by pretending to be like you. You can't touch me. And the veggie cause, for all its moral aspirations, is just a variation on this theme. Its underlying aim is nothing short of changing the world. And yet it seems a rather rarefied issue to place at the centre of a life.

Linda McCartney's life has not always been so different. She was the second child of four, three girls and one older boy, and her parents were Jewish immigrants. She was the dunce. They would sit around the table playing general knowledge quizzes: 'You know, who married who, what year so-and-so was born. Things my mind didn't want to take in.' And she would drift into her dream world of horses and rhythm and blues. 'I wanted to do what they wanted me to do but I couldn't be who they wanted me to be. So I felt guilty.'

Her father, Lee Eastman, was an upwardly mobile lawyer in New York City. Her mother, Louise, worried all the time about what people thought of her. 'I think that's where I learned, don't bother.' Something about the gentility of her background, the early bourgeois values, did, I think, alienate her. Perhaps she thought that she would never share it, that she could not aspire to such conspicuous success. She tells me proudly how her father became the personal lawyer to important artists like Willem de Kooning, Mark Rothko, Franz Kline, saying at one point, 'I grew up with Rothko, I knew him before his suicide, before he became depressed.' But there are no anecdotes forthcoming.

When she was 20, her mother was killed in a plane crash between New York and Los Angeles. She describes it like this: 'It was a bit of a shock, a bit of a tragedy for my father after 25 years. None of us is prepared for life. Do you think?

She gained her independence by marrying early, at 19, 'a nice man, a geologist, a Hemingway character', but it didn't work. They had a daughter, Heather, and he announced one day that he was going to Africa. She said, 'You check it out and if it's great, I'll come. But you know things aren't that good between us.'

Passivity and chance play a strong role in her story. So it was that she became a photographer. She was working as a receptionist at *Time and Life* magazine when an invitation arrived to a Rolling Stones bash. She turned up with her camera and of the hundred or so professional photographers waiting to get in, only Linda was chosen. 'What could it be? Blonde hair? Nice-looking girl?'

She was always a man's woman, was teased about it. Yen for Men, her friends inscribed in her college scrapbook. And so it goes on, brief little insights that you can never explore. She is a mistress of this, drawing you in and pushing you away until you feel like a yoyo, like the man on the stairs must feel, running up and down.

As I leave she's still talking. 'You can call me up, Sue. Anything you don't think I've done right, just tell me. We could have lunch, you could come over.'

Why, I ask her, couldn't we meet one to one, without the cronies? Like ordinary people. She gives me the elfin look, it's the one I like best. 'You didn't ask.'

Back in the car, I take it out on Geoff. One word, I say, and I'll murder you. At Waterloo he sheepishly asks, 'Are you still sulking?' What a job, I think. What a bloody job. The next day the phone rings. 'Allo, Sue, it's Geoff. Any problems, just call me.' As I say, I got to quite like Geoff.

21 February 1991: Judy Rumbold

Jeremy Beadle – saint?

To all you people who despise Jeremy Beadle, I say: reserve judgement until you've been round to his place for coffee. Then you might find it difficult to hate a man whose bird-table carries the inscription 'Let your conscience be your guide and feed the birds every day', and who then traipses out into deep snow with a box of Swoop. When I tell you he was wearing flimsy backless slippers at the time you will realise just what a selfless act this was.

How can you hate a man who says, about the christening of his daughters, that 'I wanted to bless them with the most beautiful thing I could think of' and named them Bonnie Valentine and Cassandra Venice Beadle?

Can you loathe an individual who says his sole purpose in life 'in these times of recession and war' is to make people laugh? 'My greatest pleasure has been picking those people in the audience who scream, "Me, me, me!" and giving them the opportunities I never got when I was young.'

Kind? Generous? Well-meaning? Let me tell you, if saints wore tracksuits . . .

Sure, there are things about Beadle that may get taken the wrong way; things that might make him sound a touch ridiculous. He has a cat called Turd ('She was one of the droppings of Poop'); he is a bottomless pit of sincerely delivered aphorisms like 'revenge is a soup best served cold', and 'Charity is the rent you pay on earth'; he has a vast library devoted to the filing and cataloguing of odd facts and figures ('my specialities are blood, sex and death – you want to know whether a murderer's breath smelt, whether a brothel keeper had three toes or four nipples'); and worst of all, he claims to know all the answers to all the questions in Trivial Pursuit. 'People hate a smart-arse,' he concludes.

People hate Beadle. He winds them up. So much so that Beadle-bashing has become great sport among members of the press. He is generous enough to acknowledge why he makes good copy. 'I mean, they're not going to write about a programme on Chinese embroidery, are they?'

But he longs for a fair character assessment. 'All I want is one – just one – intelligent article that examines what I do and why I do it.' Instead, journalists examine his facial hair and his motives; he gets called The Smiling Sadist, Prat Of The Year, The Smarmy Beard.

'I don't mind what they say about me,' he says, clearly minding enough to sue the *Independent*. 'What I object to is the things they say about my work, and what they say about the punters. They say they're loudmouthed and stupid.'

The audiences of *Game For A Laugh, Beadle's About* and *You've Been Framed* are neither of these, he says. 'No matter how fluent, eloquent or loquacious, when people are put into the situations I engineer, they're confused – we've attacked their sensibilities on so many different levels, from the serious bureaucratic threat to the absurd moment when they realise it's all a joke – that to expect them to come out with some smart line is unreasonable.'

They are willing participants, he says. They love the jokes, relish the pranks. Hell, they even like HIM. 'All these people who slag me off and say the public hate me are wrong. Because they don't hate me. The truth of the matter is that most of them like me. Not all of them, but then not everyone likes John Major and Elvis Presley.'

On *Right To Reply* last year, Robert Randall, the programme's producer, attempted to defend *Beadle's About* against accusations that it was cruel. 'It inflicts dreadful humiliation on those who take part. Why encourage people to laugh at others being wound up?' Randall's justification was that the programme ('the Rolls-Royce of practical joking, the Rolls-Royce of hidden camera stunts,' says Beadle) followed a great tradition of French comedy theatre, and didn't they know it was just good, healthy humour, an affectionate tease? Couldn't they see the fun in some poor sod's carefully tended front garden being turned into a graffiti area for kids? Couldn't they appreciate the humour in turning one man's beloved hard-earned caravan into housing for two homeless Hell's Angels?

No they couldn't. Nor can they understand the current popularity of *You've Been Framed*, the compelling home-video show that gets kicks from people falling out of boats, from boats capsizing on rivers, from rivers sweeping small children and old women off footbridges. Great fun. Hilarious. Beadle receives seven sackfuls of wobbly home-made hilarity every day. 'We're trying to hit a laugh every 17 seconds,' he says. He gets top Sunday-night ratings (18.5 million); he beats the pants off *Lovejoy* on the other side, 'and *Lovejoy*'s a bloody good programme'.

His detractors are, Beadle suspects, pompous, humourless bores, and dishonest with it. 'Show me a person who's never played a practical joke of one description or another, and I'll show you a liar.'

Beadle has played plenty. Here is a man who knows a thing or two about whoopee cushions. 'Everyone puts them under a seat. That's not what you do with a whoopee cushion. There are five other things you can do that are much funnier. People just don't think.'

He has hooked bicycles over lamp posts, filled fountain-pen lids with ink, often to get back at the people he most despises – bullies. 'But don't get me wrong. I'm not malicious. I'm not a vengeful person.'

No? He hints at darker uses for his larking. 'I've studied deception on a lot of different levels. Including the CIA KGB dirty tricks department. Fascinating. If I wanted to create destruction, create havoc, I could. But I prefer to use my skills to make people laugh.'

Beadle isn't stupid. He reads Maupassant and Flaubert, for God's sake. 'You say that to people and they think you're trying to be clever, but I'm not. They're just wonderful stories.' He talks about Flaubert like he was an old drinking pal. 'He wanted to get life down to 11 words and he claims to have got it down to 13. I do love him.'

Beadle has put this fascination with life's minutiae to good use. He was European editor of the *People's Almanack* in 1975, contributed ideas and scripts for TV, radio and advertising, worked on *Time Out* and wrote a book called *Today's The Day* – 'a chronicle of the curious'. Beadle identifies with rebels, mavericks, outsiders. 'People who have taken risks and been ridiculed for it.'

A lot of people would agree that they don't come much more riskily ridiculous than Beadle. 'You have to decide early on whether you're a comet or a satellite; whether you're going to orbit around convention or shoot off on your own.'

Make no mistake, Beadle is a comet. 'Routine is anathema to me. Routine is death, the ultimate hell. I've worked on factory floors, I've been there.'

He grew up on a rough housing estate in Hackney ('my mate said to me, " how did you survive with a name like Jeremy?" ') and got kicked out of his secondary modern in South London. 'I got no O-levels. I wasn't clever enough.' But it wasn't his fault, it was theirs. 'They never captured my imagination. As Winston Churchill said, "They never asked me anything I knew." '

Not only did he get kicked out of school, he practically got kicked off the globe. 'I got deported for vagrancy from everywhere I travelled as a teenager. I've slept standing up in telephone kiosks. I've had guns pointed at me.'

Now the telephone rings. It's the *News Of The World*, asking Beadle to comment on a home video of the Royal Family. 'It's a trap,' he says. 'Whatever I say they'll contort it. I think what the press do to the Royal Family is cruel and wicked, because I happen to be a convinced royalist.'

It wasn't always the case. 'I was an anarchist. I got sacked from every single job I did. Factory work, pub work, insurance salesman, cab driving, radio presenter on LBC, Capital, all of them.' He is proud to admit that he is 'unemployable – totally unemployable'.

Maybe it's something to do with his interview technique. When he went to see Tony Elliot, publisher of *Time Out*, for a job, Elliot recalls that he 'deliberately tripped down the stairs into the basement office'. That's the kind of guy he is.

But where faultless presentation techniques have failed him – 'he's not your Mr Slick Wheels Of Steel', says David Briggs, deputy programme controller at Capital – he makes up for it in other ways. 'He is a workaholic, a devoted entertainer.' Raw enthusiasm has got him very far indeed. 'He doesn't work as a star presenter, he works as a grafter,' says Briggs.

So to all you people who despise Jeremy Beadle, blame Willy Rushton. One fateful day, Rushton was unable to appear on the show written for him by Beadle, so Beadle had to step in. 'I was never meant to be on TV. I'm not a presenter. I'm not good looking, handsome or charming. I'm a programme-maker, and it just so happened they turned the camera on me.'

12 January 1991: Martin Wainwright

King of the crags

To find Harry Griffin, you must scramble over some of the *Guardian*'s most imposing furniture – leading articles, heavyweight features and columns of commentary on the world's political affairs.

In the middle of this dignified assembly, Harry opens the small window of the Country Diary every other Monday; and in blows a draught of pure, invigorating Lake District air.

Harry on skis. Harry on crags. Harry on foot. And Harry on the multiple threats to his beloved Lakes. Harry the eyes, ears and especially thick-socked, stout-booted legs of thousands of proxy climbers on Pillar Rock, Napes Needle or Dow Crag.

It was Dow Crag, brooding darkly beyond Coniston Old Man, which sowed the seeds of this particular record in British journalism; 40 years of unbroken filing, the 1041st column next Monday, well over 260,000 words.

Seventeen and fresh out of Barrow-in-Furness grammar school in 1927, Harry was a cub reporter on the *Barrow Guardian* and wanted to set about conquering other peaks. 'The Mayor of Barrow, George Basterfield, was one of the leading climbers of the day, and someone suggested I try him,' he recalls, getting ready to celebrate his 80th birthday this Tuesday at his Kendal flat. 'So down to the town hall I went and asked to see the great man.'

'Have you got an appointment?' said the commissionaire, a dignitary out of Stanley Holloway.

'No,' said Harry, feeling a bit like Private Samuel Small.

'Well, what's it about then?'

'Rock climbing.'

'Ah. He'll see you then. Come on in.'

A week later, Griffin was roped to the mayor on Dow Crag, zigzagging up Woodhouse's Route on B Buttress (leading the final pitch), down Easter Gulley, back up the arete, chimney and crack on A Buttress and finally down the Great Gulley, whacked. En route, Basterfield stopped, peered at bootnail marks in a patch of mud and observed: 'I see we've got Hargreaves and Clegg [A. T. Hargreaves and Billy Clegg, two other great cragsmen of the 1920s] out with us today.'

Harry's mother and father, who ran a Barrow decorating firm and only climbed ladders, were worried. But the mixture of terror, excitement and the climbers' close camaraderie immediately clicked with their son. He was soon one of the 'Coniston Tigers', a young band who bought a wooden garage in Barrow, re-erected it at Coniston Old Hall as a climbing hut and spent long days on the fells.

Above his bed, with its view over Kendal's slatey rooftops to Benson Knott and the crinkles of Whinfell, there still hangs a photo of him as a Tiger, albeit more of a plus-foured, pipe-clenching spider, pondering his next move up a hairline Dow crack. Downstairs, piped but not plus-foured, is Harry pictured last year, beetling up the Low Water slabs of Brim Fell.

As the young Griffin's technique developed, Basterfield, a man in his fifties, put him in touch with other leading climbers, on one occasion sending an invitation to Wasdale Head in an unusually illegible script. 'He didn't refer to it, but it turned out that he'd written with his left hand after an accident on Scafell,' says Harry. 'The leader fell. George, climbing second, held him. But as the rope tightened it took off his right thumb.'

Such awful anecdotes add adrenalin to Harry's diary, but he himself has survived more or less intact. Only painful, disabling foot problems which came to him in his seventies are a legacy of Tiger days.

'The idiots used to cram their feet into plimsolls a size too small for them to help get a grip on the rock,' says Violet, the new Mrs Griffin, a former Cumbria county councillor and pillar of good causes. 'She's got the MBE, DSO and bar, you name it,' says Harry, who told their wedding reception in November: 'This rumour in Kendal that we only got married because we had to is definitely not true.'

Violet is encouraging a Griffin book – the 13th – concentrating on the old Tiger days. Meanwhile all proceeds from his new, anniversary-celebrating volume, *A Lakeland Mountain Diary: From 40 years in the* Guardian – are going to St John's Hospice, Lancaster. Harry's first wife, Mollie, his companion for 50 happy years, was a leading supporter of the hospice where she died in 1987.

Books have come almost more easily for Harry than the fortnightly 300–400 words for the *Guardian*. He has never kept an ordinary 'Got up, had breakfast . . . ' diary; his dog-eared mountain notebooks are basically technical notes and lists of companions' names. His weekly 1,500 words for the *Lancashire Evening Post* (a 44-year run which ended last month) have come much more easily too; likewise his longer pieces for other *Guardian* sections.

These have ranged over the evils of Lake-touring motorists ('Droves of them, parking in laybys to read the *News of the World*') to a lovely obituary of the great Lakes photographer W. A. Poucher, who was also chief chemical analyst for Yardley's beauty products. 'He was so devoted an evangeliser for them,' remembers Harry, 'that he used to wear them, including lipstick and powder, on his travels in the fells.'

The Griffin lip is decorated only with a classic British colonel's moustache. Although he doesn't use the title, and deplores the thought of a Gulf war, Harry is actually Lt. Col. A. H. Griffin, Burma Star, ex-14th Army, staff officer to Lord Mountbatten and Slim.

More important for his diary technique was the mirroring of his military rise, from private to colonel, in journalism. He made a name on the *Daily Mail* in Manchester (the news editor appointed him after a chance meeting on Great Gable), refused offers from London (to stay near the mountains) and finally became the *Lancashire Evening Post*'s uncrowned king of the Lakes.

When the Attlee government sent a party of ministers to prospect the Pennine Way, he was their inevitable PR man and guide. ('I took them by mistake into an intake field with a bull in it. It spotted Barbara Castle's hair. Everyone was over the wall in a flash. That made all the nationals next morning.') And then the editor of the paper he had always hallowed telephoned.

'You can write about anything you like but for God's sake keep off birds. The others do enough of that,' said A. P. Wadsworth of the *Manchester Guardian*, appointing Harry to succeed George Muller as Lakeland diarist in January 1950. Lt. Col. Griffin, terror of *Daily Mail* stringers, king of the crags, accepted the instruction like a nervous novice and still has it engraved on his heart. 'When the golden eagles came back to the Lakes, I thought very hard about what Mr Wadsworth had said. Eventually, I thought, well, none of the other English diarists can really write about golden eagles unless they invent them. But I never mention the smaller birds – apart from the very occasional reference to a lark.'

Lakeland's sparrows and finches are set to remain in obscurity. Harry has a great many diaries in him yet. In sideways snow at the foot of Red Screes this week, he looked well-set for the next big anniversary – 50 years of Country Diaries, 90 years of Griffin, 2000 AD.

22 January 1991: A. H. Griffin

Mr Wainwright and his love letters

The Evangelist of Lakeland, Alfred Wainwright of Kendal, whose hand-written guides to pilgrims on the fells have sold more than a million copies, has died at the age of 84.

He amassed a fortune from his pedestrianism – guide-books to most of the mountain areas of Britain, mountain drawings, books of reminiscences, long-distance walks, Old Kendal, televised rambles – but he gave it all away to animal welfare. People sometimes said that he loved animals more than people, and perhaps he did. He described his writing as love letters – 'and you don't expect to get paid for them'.

Wainwright was a real connoisseur of hills, large or small. He loved them for their shape and beauty, and for their features – crags, cairns, walls, woodlands and wild life – but mostly it was their solitude he sought. Few people saw him at work; he took care of that. But he would have been sketching and photographing in the hills, exploring old routes up and discovering new ones, sketching waterfalls, bridges and cairns, working out distances and angles, and pottering about in old mine-workings or long-abandoned quarries.

Once or twice I accompanied him on his walks, perhaps the only one of his friends who ever did so. Hills, for him, were places where a man should be by himself, and he shunned the popular summits on crowded summer days, leaving their exploration to the winter time.

For years he refused to be photographed himself or interviewed; just one or two sketches of the broad back of a big white-haired man looking out at the view appeared in his guides. Recently, however, he had come out of his shell, blinking at the television camera and even talking for *Desert Island Discs*. The collected works – even statuettes – became a thriving Lakeland industry.

Mr Wainwright – previously, few people knew his Christian name – was a Blackburn man who, in his youth, was happiest when walking over Pendle Hill and Darwen moors. In his early twenties he took his first holiday to Lakeland and for a week together with a friend he roamed over many of the fells, beginning with the Scots' Rake from Troutbeck and on to Thornthwaite Crag. With typical singlemindedness he resolved, there and then, that when the opportunity occurred he would come north to live as near as possible to the hills.

The chance came some years later when he went to work in Kendal local government and eventually became the borough treasurer. It was during this period that he conceived the idea of a hand-printed series of guides to the Lakeland fells and these first seven volumes were completed during his term of office. He travelled into the hills each weekend by bus (he never drove a car) and worked on his guides every evening.

After his retirement, with much more time, he embarked on a detailed guide to the 250-mile Pennine Way, studies of the Howgill Fells and of the northern limestone country, and a series of Lakeland sketchbooks. In the early 1970s he prepared a book on a coast-to-coast walk from St Bees Head to Robin Hood's Bay, and later he dealt, in his thorough fashion, with the Scottish 'Munros' – drawing, but not climbing, them all.

No Lakeland guidebooks have ever carried the wealth of detail shown in Wainwright's in which even walls, trees and the smallest pools are all carefully delineated. As guidance for his remarkably lifelike drawings he took hundreds of photographs in the hills.

In the evenings he would settle down to printing and drawing his pages, every line finishing neatly with a full word, the maps especially drawn from the Ordnance Survey's two-and-a-half-inch sheets, and diagrammatic views of recommended ascents. On a good evening he would complete one page.

Some people complained that all this detail was taking away what little adventure still remained in the fells. To some extent this is true (Wainwright must have preserved countless tyros from finding themselves cragged in the mist). But walkers can keep their independence by using map and compass in the hills and studying the book on their return to see what they have missed.

Wainwright himself admitted he had never used a compass throughout his years of Lakeland exploration. This old-fashioned mountaineer, in his lightweight mackintosh, went quietly about the job in much the same way as the great M. J. B. Baddeley of the old red-backed *Thorough Guides* might have done: a bus to the foot of the mountain, old clothes for the ascent, and a six-inch map for the detail.

His first guide was dedicated to the men of the Ordnance Survey, and there were later dedications to lone walkers, the men who built Lakeland's dry stone walls (he would take long detours to avoid climbing them), the dogs of Lakeland, and the sheep.

In his later years he married a second time and now had a companion in the hills. He served on museum committees, held several exhibitions of his drawings at the Abbot Hall Art Gallery in Kendal and gave the proceeds from the sale of many of his drawings to several worthwhile outdoor causes. His remarkable achievement was modestly rewarded with an MBE – for services to the Lake District.

Wainwright was a quiet, retiring, privately generous man, capable of incredible patience, industry and exactitude. The pocket-sized books in anorak or rucksack will be his memorial for generations of walkers, and if his own popularity has unwittingly contributed to the erosion of over-populated paths in central Lakeland, he has revealed to thousands of others the 'untrodden ways' where he dwelt. Unobtrusively his ashes will be scattered on one of them (Haystacks, by his own published wish).

Alfred Wainwright, born 1906; died 20 January 1991.

26 January 1991: Letter

Fellows of the fells

I am a great admirer of Harry Griffin. I eagerly await his Lakeland Diary every other Monday and I belatedly wish him a happy 80th birthday. Long may his (solitary) tramping of the high fells of Lakeland continue.

However, I feel that he did less than justice to A. W. Wainwright in his obituary and particularly in his implied comment that the fell-walking guides have made it all too easy. I disagree. Those of us who are not fortunate enough to live in the Lake District and make a career writing articles and books on the subject very often have to make do with an annual visit at best, and one of the pleasures of the winter months is to thumb through the guides and to work out routes for the next visit. Wainwright may have introduced more people to the Lake District and fell-walking, but without Wainwright, how many of us would have found, for example, the Ullock Pike route up Skiddaw rather than the boring old tourist route? Maps are all very well, but they cannot bring a route to life in the way that Wainwright does.

I understand Mr Griffin's desire for peace and quiet, but you cannot keep the Lake District as a haven for people lucky enough to live there. Wainwright may have brought greater numbers to the Lake District but he has dispersed them to routes that they might never have discovered. Far better than everyone going up a few well-known routes. We townies have a great deal to thank A. W. for. More perhaps than the Harry Griffins of this world. I will always remember Wainwright and be grateful to him – particularly when I am climbing Haystacks.
Michael Walters.
Warlingham, Surrey.

8 September 1990: Leader

The voice for the people

It would be wrong to say that A. J. P. Taylor, whose death was announced yesterday, died loaded with honours. His orthodox honours were few. While others of lesser merit sped past on their way to professorships, he remained to the end plain A. J. P. No knighthood came his way, or seat in the Lords (though had any been offered, he would assuredly have refused, regarding such things as trumpery). His honours were of a different order, one he prized more greatly: the voracious and enduringly grateful attention of thousands of ordinary readers, some of whom would not have been reading history had they not acquired the taste for it purely through reading him. No historian of his age could sweep you along with the same exhilaration, could have you turning the pages with a sharper curiosity to see what would happen next. None was so ready to challenge the consensus; and none, above all, wrote so compellingly – and in prose so spare that in other hands it might have become austere. 'Imperial greatness was on the way out,' he wrote, taking leave of the reader at the end of 600 pages of his Oxford history of this century, 'the welfare state was on the way in. The British empire declined; the condition of the people improved. Few now sang "Land of Hope and Glory". Few even sang "England Arise". England had risen all the same.'

Some contemporaries found him vulgar. To be called the people's historian, as he often and rightly was, was no accolade in their eyes. Because he was never dull, some assumed he was never serious. Heads were shaken in common rooms, as they are nowadays over people like Norman Stone. He took to the television, commanding a huge new audience without notes, visual aids, faded sepia photographs, or clips from the Movietone News: a sombre, unsmiling figure against a fustian backdrop, holding viewers enthralled, week after week, through a whole hypnotic hour. On programmes like 'Free Speech' he argued hard and spikily for minority causes, especially CND. A son of Manchester non-conformity, who in earlier life taught at its university and wrote for its morning newspaper, he remained all along the champion of dissent. His favourite book, in large part a celebration of English provincial radicalism, was *The Troublemakers*: a group with whom he enlisted in early life, and whom he never deserted. His hero was Macaulay, the full five volumes of whom he re-read at 75. 'I am sometimes hailed as his successor,' he wrote. 'I only wish I were. In my opinion he was the best narrative historian there has ever been.' Where Taylor stands on the scale which Macaulay heads is a matter for endless argument. That he stood in his day unchallenged as a master of narrative history, as a man who made scholarship pleasure, is beyond dispute.

A. J. P. Taylor, born 25 March 1906; died 7 September 1990.

26 January 1991: Erlend Clouston

T. E. Lawrence's kid brother

The similarity is striking: slender, rectangular face, quizzical frost-blue eyes, shoehorn chin, blunt denunciation of establishment coteries.

'I regard all religion as vermin,' exclaims Arnold (A. W.) Lawrence, younger brother of T. E. and 'equally naughty', according to the suntanned lady archaeologist who keeps a watchful eye on him.

'The entire Arab revolt was an impious thing in the eyes of the Turks,' he growls, a spry figure in herring-bone slippers. 'Any wounded the Arabs couldn't take away with them after a train raid, the Turks threw on a bonfire.'

This all seems very far away from a cosy sixteenth-century cottage, Somewhere In Wiltshire. A. W. Lawrence, like T. E., has to go incognito – for fear of American literary scalphunters rather than Turkish assassins, 'They write these terrible letters,' shudders the lady archaeologist.

Gulf war drums have a particular resonance in the cottage's shadowy first-floor lounge. T. E. Lawrence –

Lawrence of Arabia – dreamed up the idea of an independent Iraq, and lobbied furiously for it in the teeth of opposition from the French and the India Office. 'Until he came on the scene in 1921,' said T. E.'s official biographer Jeremy Wilson last week, 'Iraq was destined to become a British colony.'

Now this exotic family heirloom endures a dreadful battering. Sitting bold upright in his scarlet armchair, 91-year-old A. W. contemplates the implications with reasonable equanimity.

'I should fairly confidently expect that the resultant Iraq would be a good deal better than it is now,' he growls again. 'The Falklands war was well worth it. How else would the Argentinians have got themselves free of that gang of generals?'

T. E. Lawrence was proud of – and relieved by – the creation of the new state. Many of the best men in his desert irregulars had enlisted from the territory once known as Mesopotamia. Persuading the government to steer towards independence, under Lawrence's co-guerrilla, Prince Faisal, seemed only fair.

'Iraq has had five years of peace out of us,' he wrote to Sir Hugh Trenchard, marshal of the Royal Air Force. 'If it went up in flames tomorrow, yet that five years would win forgiveness on doomsday for Winston and yourself, the sponsors of its scheme.

'Surely,' he adds, rather prematurely in the circumstances, 'my share in helping settle the Middle East atones for my misdeeds in war.'

Nonetheless, his proxy vote is given to Operation Desert Storm. 'All that T. E. achieved went when the Ba'ath party came into power by murdering everybody who had been in control,' sighs the youngest of the five Lawrence boys, who grew up to become professor of classical archaeology at Cambridge.

Would T. E. have balked at the price Iraq may have to pay for better government? The fierce white head shakes vigorously. 'No! No reasonable person would. You have to break eggs to make an omelette.'

Ironically, the Baghdad regime has recently adopted T. E.'s view of the strategic usefulness of the bloodily terminated Hashemite dynasty. As the son of the Sherif of Mecca, then the most notable figure in the Arab world, Faisal, Lawrence correctly gambled, would provide a potent rallying point for the infant Iraq.

Three decades after executing Faisal's grandson, the Ba'ath party has been busy resurrecting royalist statuary and discovering ties between Saddam Hussein and the family now acclaimed as early Arab nationalists.

'I once met Faisal,' A. W. reveals. 'He was impressive as a sort of Madame Tussauds figure. Educated in his own way, not, of course, in ours.' A. W., who spent seven years excavating in the Middle East, met Chamberlain too, with a plan for resolving the Palestine problem. 'But he knew what I didn't, that war was coming. So it was useless to try anything.'

On the sofa sat a thick green book. At an age when most people's ambitions don't stretch beyond the first shelf of the medicine cabinet, A. W. is updating his 1935 annotated version of Rawlinson's translation of Herodotus. 'It cost 30 guineas then. Probably be cheaper this time. They only had 700 copies printed. I was cut down in my fee.' T. E. helped him win the original commission. Hearing that the publisher David Garnett had the Herodotus project in mind, he scribbled a recommendation. 'I have been impressed with the verve and ruthlessness of my own brother – a younger brother – who calls himself A. W. Lawrence . . . He has dug in Mesopotamia, and travelled over the earth, and owns a good pen.'

Some of the ruthlessness survives. Striking woodcuts open Mr Rawlinson's chapters. They were rather nice, were they not? The herring-bone twitched scornfully. 'Beastly, I think.' A. W. has no time for second-raters. He tilts forward. 'Here's something T. E. told me. Hardy said to him: "Don't disparage the Iliad, young man; it's a very good poem, quite in the class of Marmion."' The fierce head chuckled with incredulity. 'Marmion!'

After six years in Cambridge, A. W. emigrated to the University of Ghana. There seemed something perverse about this. 'Well, I found Cambridge academics were not to my taste. The best thing that ever happened to me was when I got TB and went to a sanatorium in the Mendips where there were a couple of hundred ordinary people.'

'Like your brother joining the RAF?'

'I suppose so.'

The kindly lady archaeologist paused in her tea-pouring. 'They've so much in common; very naughty; not conformists; not in any way,' she said, as if we could expect T. E. to walk in the door at any minute wearing a frogman suit.

But that is the way with legends. Last month a sale of Lawrence of Arabia memorabilia fetched record prices at Christie's in New York. The recently formed T. E. Lawrence Society already has a paid-up membership of close to 500.

A. W., whose only memento of his brother is a Gilbert Spencer oil painting that dangles above the scarlet upholstery, hates all this. 'He was just a perfectly ordinary chap. The fact that he was ordinary can't be accepted by the newspapers.' A. W. dislikes the T. E. Lawrence Society almost as much as he dislikes the spasmodic sniping at his brother's reputation.

'It's been perfectly horrible for him,' sympathises the lady archaeologist.

'It's a nuisance,' agrees A. W. He blames Whitehall's jealous guarding of war secrets. 'Nobody could counter it by producing any evidence. I think it was extremely stupid of them not to release just enough papers to stop it.'

Lawrence the movie didn't help, either. 'A travesty,' says A. W. 'It made Allenby out to be a crook.' He was so scandalised by the private viewing that, at a cost to himself of £3,000, he cancelled director David Lean's right to the title *The Seven Pillars Of Wisdom*. 'I hoped that might have some effect on the press, but not a bit of it,' he grumbles.

The book of that name, T. E.'s extraordinary campaign history, is still in print after half a century. It tells how, 75 years ago, the Arabs chose to side with the British against the Ottoman Turks, despite the Caliph's call for a holy war.

Did A. W. not find this extremely ironic? The old man shrugged with the wisdom of many decades spent running two million years of life through his fingers.

'There's a sort of whirligig in history,' he mused, as he fiddled with his deaf aid. 'Over a generation very few people manage to preserve the same friends, or enemies.'

A. W. Lawrence died on 31 March 1991.

18 February 1991: Charles Nevin

Putting the skis under the royals

War is a great aid to proportion. Death and stupidity on such a scale throw a bright stark light on our institutions and habits. Questions are asked about relevance, purpose, importance. It is not a good time to be seen to be frivolous or uncertain. It is not a good time for the House of Windsor.

For the readiest, clearest understanding of this, look no further than the striking, seemingly unavoidable figure of the Duchess of York, Sarah Ferguson as was, 'Fergie' as is to all but the Court Circular.

It all started so well. Here was this jolly, boisterous, uncomplicated girl marrying the jolliest, most boisterous, most uncomplicated of the royal princes. She had a bit of a past, but then so did her future husband. Her father, jolly, boisterous Major Ron Ferguson, the Queen's polo manager, said in a *Daily Express* interview: 'Can you imagine not discovering anything about a young woman of 26? A lot of people would sneer "There must be something the matter with her", or assume she was terribly dull.'

The future Duchess was said to be 'a breath of fresh air', a chortling, rib-digging change from the sweet, iconic Princess of Wales and her painfully well-intentioned husband who were thought a bit dull. The Queen was said to be entranced by her and the Duke of Edinburgh was said to like her fruity jokes.

Fergie was in publishing, a girl of the world and of sub-Sloane Clapham, an enjoyer of Sloane pleasures, of riding and skiing. When someone stood on her train in Westminster Abbey, she let out 'a good swear word', according to Major Ron. They left Buckingham Palace for their honeymoon with an outsized teddy bear accompanying them.

As they left, we knew, courtesy of the *People*, that her hips measured 43 inches, not the advertised 38. We knew, courtesy of the *Daily Mirror*, that she had a five-inch scar above her knee from a childhood riding accident, that she wore Madame Rochas perfume and painted her toenails red. And we knew, courtesy of the same source, that Prince Andrew had a lavatory-roll holder which played 'God Save The Queen'. And if this was a little over familiar, or absolute bunkum, or completely made up, no one seemed to care very much. A new player in the soap opera, reminiscent of one of the female creations of the late Dick Emery, had been given her part and character; and besides, we knew, or would find out, that she was a great fan of *Dynasty*. Pick the irony out of that.

This rather odd state of affairs could probably trace its origins back to the 1950s and 1960s, and the criticism then current that the monarchy had become 'out of touch', outmoded. There were motions for glasnost from within the Court, despite the traditional view, as expounded by

Bagehot, the Victorian writer on the constitution, that mystique and distance were vital to the survival of the monarchy.

According to accounts, the Queen and Queen Mother were not eager for change; the Duke of Edinburgh, supported by Martin Charteris, then the Queen's assistant private secretary, urged the new informal approach that led to the famous 1969 TV documentary, *The Royal Family*, which stressed normality rather than majesty. 'Remember we're in the happiness game,' said Charteris.

The trick is to maintain a balance between the publicity needed to show the worth of the monarchy and the mystique needed to preserve it. This requires deference on the one side and decorum on the other. It is probably all right to reveal that the Duchess swore in the Abbey; something has gone wrong when a magazine like *Tatler* feels able to reveal that the Duchess said she was 'scared shitless' the first time she went to Windsor Castle.

Deference was the first casualty. Larry Lamb, editor of Rupert Murdoch's born-again *Sun*, saw great opportunities for stories and circulation in a more open approach to and from royalty. Prince Charles's search for a bride, ending with the perfect princess, proved him right. Everybody joined in: the stories became ever bolder.

Everything was up for grabs. Harold Evans, in *Good Times, Bad Times*, and Peter Chippindale and Chris Horrie, in their book on the *Sun*, *Stick It Up your Punter*, remarked upon Murdoch's impatience with the British monarchy, ' symbol of everything that was wrong with the Poms'. Lamb's successor, Kelvin MacKenzie, is quoted by Chippindale and Horrie demanding a front-page story on the royals with the rider 'Don't worry if it's not true – so long as there's not too much fuss about it afterwards.'

The death of deference demanded greater decorum, particularly from the younger and less obviously useful members of the family. Buckingham Palace's press office is a 'reactive' agency; it does not give advice on these matters, even if it seems to be needed. There was thus the embarrassment of Andrew's liaisons with Koo Stark, an actress of sorts, and Vicky Hodge, a model of sorts. Sarah Ferguson gained by comparison, but complacency was dangerous, despite Fleet Street's fawning before the marriage. She gave every appearance of enjoying the publicity, even of understanding it. But both she and her husband had failed to realise that the rules of engagement had changed and that it was now a matter of public relations, not noblesse oblige.

Within a year of the marriage, there was criticism of the large number of holidays the Duchess was taking – nine in nine months, shouted the tabloids – including one paid for by the government of Mauritius, and another free stay provided by Robert Sangster. Lord Hanson, meanwhile, was paying for her flying lessons as a wedding gift. The enticingly alliterative 'Freebie Fergie' made its debut.

Then Major Ron let the side down badly by being photographed leaving a massage parlour of dubious pedigree. Family matters continued to cause problems when the Duchess visited Australia leaving her very young first child, Princess Beatrice, behind. After an official 10-day tour, she twice extended her stay, following her husband's ship from port to port. The situation was so grave that it merited a reproof from Esther Rantzen. One Australian newspaper printed a picture of a baby with the caption: 'It's called a baby, Fergie.'

The mystique was over. Royalty was being told it must observe popular convention, not frame it or flout it, that privilege would be tolerated but up to a lesser point. The Duchess's extravagant holidaying had also drawn attention to a sensitive royal area: the weeks at Sandringham, Balmoral and elsewhere which jarred slightly with the saloon-bar wisdom that, say what you like, they work hard for Britain. Suddenly, royalty was expected to work a five-day week, like everybody else.

But the worst was that the Duchess was seen to be

greedy, a perennial pitfall for monarchy, and one particularly to be avoided during a hectic economic boom in which greed had become a political 'issue'. So there was a fuss over the Budgie books and the confusion as to where exactly the profits were going, and several other seized-upon incidents, like the apparent attempt to subsidise a holiday in South America by suggesting that she might re-start a round-the-world yacht race in return for free first class tickets.

Exclusive interviews make excellent PR opportunities, unless the interview arrangements make more news than the views expressed therein. In 1989, the Duchess gave an exclusive interview to the *Daily Express* in which she revealed that her husband was 'a great guy', 'a real man', that she occasionally cleaned out cupboards and that she resented critics of her holidays. 'I want them to just back off,' she said. 'After all, they can have as many holidays as they like within a year.' She also said that she was not pregnant; unfortunately, the interview appeared on the day it was announced she was pregnant. It then emerged that the *Daily Express*, understandably miffed, was paying only half the agreed fee for the interview, £126,000.

In 1990, the Duke and Duchess were interviewed by the magazine *Hello!*, which printed 48 pages of pictures of the Yorks and their children. *Hello!* denies any fee was paid to them, but no less loyal source than the *Daily Telegraph*'s Peterborough column claimed that much of the £240,000 payment found its way to the Duchess's mother, who had left Major Ron for an Argentinian polo player and was now widowed.

Then there is their new home, 'South York', a reputed £5 million worth of chintz, marble and mahogany in a style best described as Berkshire adobe. A gift from the Queen, it was warmed, we are told, with a £20,000 champagne reception attended by such members of the York circle as Elton John, Michael Caine, Billy Connolly and Pamela Stephenson. The bill for guarding the house was said to be £1 million a year; two months later 'a senior Thames Valley police officer' complained to the *People* that the Yorks were never there: 'They don't seem to be treating their new house as a proper home.' Vox custodis, vox populi.

This focusing of attention on finance is as unwise as it is on extended leisure opportunities. Nor is it sensible to complain about not being well-off when one's civil list payments are being doubled: the explanation that these payments are for official expenses and salaries loses its edge when another magazine claims the Queen earns £1.8 million a day, tax free.

That this is an exaggeration, that the Duchess works enthusiastically for good causes, is privately generous and probably very kind to animals, is beside the point. The Palace has lost control of its image and the people seem increasingly sympathetic to the view that royalty should pay its way and behave itself in a way that they, the people, think fitting.

But PR can't change the product. 'Why shouldn't I go skiing?' the Duchess is said to have said in the face of the politest of gentle remonstrations. 'Why shouldn't I have a new house?' she is said to have said in the face of the politest of suggestions that an existing grace and favour home might have been a sounder choice.

'Frankly, it's called lack of breeding,' says a 'royal watcher', wishing, in accordance with accepted practice, to be anonymous. 'Her father is the great-grandson of a duke (Buccleuch) but a lot can happen in a couple of generations,' says another. Arrogant, not prepared to take advice, is the view of both.

When there is image-polishing, it can be clumsy, like carrying out nine official engagements in 12 hours, or returning from a much-noticed skiing trip just in advance of war and almost immediately being photographed giving blood. Shortly after, she provided the impetus for the current criticism of unseemly frivolity by being over-rowdy in a West End restaurant. So rowdy, apparently, that an irritated fellow patron took revenge by calling the *Sun*.

This latest brouhaha is not an orchestrated bout of republicanism conducted by Rupert Murdoch, although it might be more comforting for royalty if it were. Murdoch did not know about Andrew Neil's editorial in the *Sunday Times* which set it off; *The Times* was loftily dismissive; the *Sun*, having started the hare with the Fergie story and a photograph of Lord Linley partying in lipstick taken in November, was breezily dismissive, and took a crack at Mr Neil's own well-documented nocturnal habits.

Nevertheless, a *Sun* poll had readers voting six to one that royalty was not doing its bit for the war effort, a finding reinforced by a Mori poll for the *Daily Mail* which showed 47 per cent of the sample dissatisfied with the present conduct of the Duchess and 53 per cent dissatisfied with Prince Edward.

It seems, too, that linkage has taken place. In an *Independent on Sunday* NMR poll, 80 per cent felt that the Royal Family should pay income tax, and 31 per cent thought them 'decadent and insensitive'. In the *Sunday Times*, a Mori poll showed that 42 per cent thought the Royals 'an expensive luxury the country could not afford', compared with 24 per cent in January last year.

Nigel Dempster, chronicler to the aristocracy, was in relaxed, if sombre, mood after completing his *Daily Mail* diary column. There was a PR problem, he said, there had always been a PR problem. But the Royal Family was not good at taking advice, or at noting changing times, or, in many cases, at choosing friends. For example, its members still rather expected people to provide them with perks and services in a way which might now seem to be greedy and unthinking, like the sponsorship of Prince Charles's polo, hardly needed.

As for the people, it was his view that there was an extraordinary ignorance, a lack of education, of a sense of history, which meant that nobody knew where the Royal Family came from, what it was for.

Bagehot wrote in 1867: 'The mystic reverence, the religious allegiance, which are essential to a true monarchy, are imaginative sentiments that no legislature can manufacture in any people.' Royal watcher Andrew Morton yesterday reported instances of charities and industry being unwilling to be associated with the Duchess of York. Dempster doesn't see the Monarchy surviving the present Queen: 'The jig is up.'

Any other business

30 August 1990: Fred Sedgwick, a headmaster in Ipswich

Heads you lose, tales you win

Stuart Murdoch had just been promoted to the job of youth coach at Watford Football Club. Before that, he was chief scout and youth development officer. Of course, every club in the country has a chief scout, and the advantage of links with the local community – as well as the untapped talent among local schoolboys – has led more and more clubs to have youth development officers. But the difference is that, until 1988, Stuart Murdoch was the headteacher of Chantry Junior School in Ipswich.

Lots of heads talk of getting out: increased paperwork, separation from staff and children, stress are all cited. When one ex-head announced his early retirement, his wife said, 'I wanted him at home . . . alive.'

The projects which heads dream up to make escape possible are varied, too; there are conventional ideas, like initial teacher education and in-service work, and less ordinary notions like personnel work in business. Others become insurance salesmen, or sub-post office managers. Some talk – vaguely, it must be admitted – about going back into the classroom.

Stuart and I used to sit in the back row of meetings, making satirical remarks about modern managerial clap-trap ('Before anything else' we both recall a colleague saying, 'you've got to get the infrastructure of your school right'). We also used to discuss ways of getting out and doing something that wasn't becoming more and more meaningless as bureaucratic nagging and the reform act began to bite. In the pub after one heads' meeting, we sat over pints – his an unpleasant-smelling, unpleasant-looking Guinness and blackcurrant – and talked about what next.

Stuart always had one possible exit: he was a part-time, expenses-paid scout with Graham Taylor's Aston Villa, spending most evenings and weekends on the common watching local youth sides, and telling the club about any finds. He'd played for Blackpool, his home town, at youth level.

One day he rang me at school to tell me the news: he had the chief's permission to leave immediately to go to Watford. The following summer he was awarded his FA coaching badge.

Now and then he breezes into our house at lunchtime on a Saturday, if Ipswich Town (our team) are playing a side Watford are meeting later on in the month. Stuart, the least shy man I have ever known, stands in the middle of our front room, making jokes, swapping football gossip, talking as fast as it's possible to talk, teasing our eight-year-old Town supporter son. His assemblies must have been unconventional.

The meaninglessness problem has become worse since

Stuart went: partly because legislation has chewed into teaching by making us financial managers, National Curriculum checklist operatives, testers, and PR officials instead of educationists, and also because Stuart isn't there with his jokes.

I asked him what satisfaction he got in his present job that he hadn't in headship: 'I suppose it's knowing that what I'm doing now, I'm not going to be doing until I'm 60. I moved from total security to total insecurity. This job could finish tomorrow, but it doesn't seem to worry me. I'm enjoying what I'm doing. And if I had to, I could go to Hertfordshire county council tomorrow and get work as a supply teacher to pay the mortgage until something came up, leisure management, America maybe – there's a lot of interest in football in the States again, lots of coaching opportunities, with the World Cup coming up.'

Most heads consider the security of headship as its one real benefit, now that autonomy and passable resources have gone. Stuart, I could tell when I used to meet him in the pub, found the safety suffocating. 'Insecurity is a driving factor – I had too much of the opposite at school. A typical day here has excitement for me.

'The summer holidays are the busiest time. I get in about 7.30am, travel round Watford in the yellow bus picking up lads in various places, then back to the ground to meet the youth team. I sort out the training, or maybe there's a match for the schoolboys. Yesterday I took two of them, Geordies, to Letchworth to watch Herts schoolboys against Cambridge, then I put them on the train. Then it's back to the ground to answer a few phone calls – clubs enquiring about players who might be available. Then there's probably an evening match to watch – non-league, or a reserve league fixture. I don't see much of the family some weeks.

'The thing that got me down about school was the change in role from teacher – children, the classroom – to social worker and administrator. At least now I work with young people, and I enjoy it. I'm not just training them, I'm educating them. I tell them, even if you don't stay with Watford, you'll be a better person for having been here.'

Stuart had not become a head to escape from children, as some heads had. He obviously likes young people: 'Of course you handle them differently, because they want to succeed if they come here, unlike school sometimes. But it's like school in other ways. You're working with individuals, you're trying to get the best out of them. Bawling at them isn't very productive. Not if you want to get the best out of them.'

I said I sometimes bawl at kids, though.

'Yeah, well, sometimes one drives you to it.'

But did football clubs limit boys' horizons by getting them into football too early? 'When I talk to schools, I often have to convince them that we're not just running a sausage factory. Like some teachers, I worry about kids being taken on too early and put on a pedestal. It's down to the club to keep boys level-headed.'

No job is perfect, of course. Thinking of my LMS computer printouts, and those parents last Wednesday accusing me of terrorising their children when all I was doing was investigating yet another petty theft, I asked Stuart what was the worst part of his week.

'Twenty-to-five on a Saturday afternoon, waiting to hear how they've got on. I'm rarely at the ground, I'll have been watching someone else. I dread hearing we've lost. When we were struggling to stay in the First Division, the first season I was here, I missed the result once at twenty-to-five and when I heard it at five, we'd won. So for a while I deliberately missed the result at twenty-to. It gets to you in odd ways like that.'

Stuart's one of those lucky people who don't worry about the next thing too much. There's plenty for him to do, and I doubt if he'll ever be on the teacher-starved supply register.

'I love football, I get on well with the lads. But the great thing is, I know for sure I won't be doing this job at 60.'

He ran off. It was coaching goalkeepers that afternoon. I felt sure that Stuart, career risks notwithstanding, had good positional sense, as well as a safe pair of hands.

22 May 1991: Catherine Bennett

If this is a good school . . .

Kelly! The teacher's tone was respectful, meek almost. She might have been trying to interest her pupil in a cup of tea, or a bun. Kelly ignored her. Kelly lay there playing dead, head slumped on her arms, arms slumped over her simple fractions. How many Oxo cubes are there in this box? What fraction is shaded?

Kelly! With infinite reluctance, Kelly raised her head.

'Wha?' Had Kelly done any of the sums on her sheet? *'No.'* With an air of having done her bit, Kelly replaced her head on her desk.

And Kevin? Kevin wouldn't stop talking. *Kevin!* Quietly, solicitously, Jenny Ward-Ure asked Kevin if he wouldn't mind moving. Kevin would. 'Outside, come on!' Kevin sauntered into the corridor, where he brushed aside a request to report to his head of year. Another child was dispatched to bring the head of year to Kevin.

Inside, two days before a mock GCSE, the class resumed independent study: ostentatiously reading comics, poking biro on each other's faces, drawing on their hands, examining themselves in mirrors, yawning, groaning, spinning protractors, catching up on the news. 'Sean? *Sean!*'

'Wha?'

'What computer you got?'

This, it should be emphasised, was the least able maths group at Thomas Tallis School in south-east London, a comprehensive of broad social composition, with a devoted PTA and the best GCSE results in the borough of Greenwich. Tallis has murals, and playing fields, and a school uniform, and outings, and a sculptor-in-residence, and parents with gites in Normandy. It even has an ambitious 'school ethos' to promote equal opportunities and mutual respect. Many of the Tallis pupils will get 10 or 11 GCSEs; they want to be architects, computer engineers, firemen, travel agents. They do *not* want to be teachers. 'Never,' said one child, speaking for all. 'It's too violent. And it's not my idea of earning money.'

Nor is it Jenny Ward-Ure's: 'Nobody does this for money.' No, she went into teaching because she *enjoys* explaining rudimentary mathematics to these gargantuan 15-year-olds, who are now considering the division of a gold bar into equal parts. 'If it was a gold bar,' one of her class objected, 'you'd nick it.' She drew a round cake on the blackboard. Then an oblong cake, adding for the purposes of differentiation, 'This is a ginger cake.'

'Is it one of them Jacobs cakes, miss?'

'No,' said the maths teacher. 'McVities.'

An emergency called Mrs Ward-Ure away. 'I've just got to make a phone call.' A girl looked up: 'Don't bother coming back.' 'Thank you, Sharon.' The bell rang, whereupon, with shrill cries and other banshee ejaculations, a mob of Tallis students thudded from classroom to corridor, mashing punier children against the wall, allowing swing doors to slam back into their teachers' faces. 'Lucky I wasn't wearing my glasses!' said an English teacher, brightly surviving a doorbutting.

It's not intimidating, the atmosphere at Thomas Tallis, which visiting teachers describe as a *good* school, a well-disciplined school, with little bullying or playground violence. Not threatening so much as charmless and lowering. But so, the teachers point out, are Lewisham bus queues and supermarkets, and football crowds, and the underground. So is London. 'That's how they think about behaving,' said Annie Corcoran, a history teacher. 'You'd say, "why don't you hold the door open?" and they just look at you. They don't have any *understanding*, I don't think. When I was at school the whole culture was to be hard working. Now they don't want to be seen to be cowed by authority, they don't want to be seen trying.'

The bell rang again, and a posse of trainers clumped into fourth-year science, where Margaret Young, a formidable woman with 25 years' experience, spent 20 minutes tranquillising her class into semi-attentiveness. 'It's society at large,' she said. 'Society has changed, and respect for their elders seems to have gone out of the window. They are not silent now because Miss says "be silent". You've got to earn respect. And I wouldn't want to earn respect just because I'm old and crabby.'

This noble aim is part of the Tallis ethos: children must be treated as 'real people, with rights and responsibilities'. And the children, being real people, exploit the ethos for what they can get, priding themselves on their exigence, their intransigence, on being difficult to teach. 'You don't respect people because of their jobs,' said a fourth-former. 'And they shouldn't patronise you. I think that adults forget how irritating it is to be patronised.' A fifth-year girl asserted that: 'It's quite healthy not to just accept everything you're told. I don't think you should automatically accept authority.'

So what do they accept? Not interference. 'Why do you keep asking *me?*' says a pupil, after two, courteously phrased questions. Not civility. Even the most popular, the most ingratiating teacher must expect to be ignored, or addressed as an inferior by children who shout out orders rather than requests, for paper, or attention. They instruct the teacher to get out of the way, to be quieter with the chalk: 'Miss, don't lean so hard on the board.'

Unwisely, perhaps, the staff have encouraged the pupils to assert themselves, to evaluate teachers by their eccentric, childish criteria. In English, 11-year-olds had been asked to draw a bad teacher and a good one. The bad teacher, according to one child, betrays himself through nerdy Kickers and a briefcase. A good teacher wears a bumbag, bright clothing and 'fashionable trainers'.

The fourth years' requirements were more exacting. The teachers should be humorous, they said, yet strict; teachers should tell jokes *and* bring back the cane because 'some of the kids here couldn't give a monkey's about work or nuffink'.

Nothing would induce a Tallis teacher to speak so harshly of 'less able' pupils, or children with 'concentration difficulties'. Emerging from her unruly, recalcitrant maths class, Jenny Ward-Ure criticised herself for inadequate preparation. 'It was too difficult. And I knew it, but I didn't have time to find another way round it . . . many of the children need more one-to-one teaching.'

And two years ago, some of them would have got it. Now, with cuts which amount, head teacher Colin Yardley claims, to 42 per cent of its 1989 budget, Thomas Tallis still prepares reports for remedial teaching, knowing it can no longer be guaranteed. 'I do feel sad because I used to enjoy it and now more and more I feel it's a waste of time, because I'm a manager, and I'm trying to manage resources which won't be there,' said Richard Stubbs, head of the special needs department. When he talks to some of the parents, he feels sadder still. 'I sometimes wonder whether good enough parenting goes on. Children seem far more left to fend for themselves these days. There's less of a sense that parents should tell children what to do. More children are left to make up their own minds . . . I think the parents could at least check their bags, and their homework.'

But many don't. It is left to the teachers to lecture their little victims on the importance of regular attendance, of reports, of education itself. In morning assembly last week, Stubbs attempted to introduce an insouciant fourth year to the concepts of homework, revision, pre-exam stress. 'You probably think stress is when you can't watch something on television . . . I'll tell you what revision means, because many of you have probably never met it before . . . ' He'd been teaching for 16 years, but it felt more like 9,000. 'I think the kids are far more them, than us, than they used to be,' he said. 'It's far more of a struggle to get the basics achieved. A struggle to make sure homework gets done, to make sure order ensues, to get them into school. It's all a struggle now, and we are in a *good* school. I'm sure if I were in a bad school, I'd give up.'

But even in this good school, some have had enough. 'You think, you could have a nice little job,' said one teacher, 'with nice people who smiled and said please and thank you, and who don't have to put up with this kind of aggression.'

There are, however, more pressing reasons why this woman, an energetic and popular teacher (who did not want to be named) has decided, after eight years in education, that it's not worth the effort. The wages have dwindled. The hours have multiplied. Budget cuts, after the borough of Greenwich took over from Ilea, led to staff cuts, then bigger classes, more lessons, more marking, more preparation. 'On average, I put in an extra two hours a night . . . and it's a workload where I'm not sure the value lies. Society doesn't value us. The government doesn't value us, and increasingly, you see parents who don't seem to care about education.'

And even the middle-class parents, the ones who *do* care about education, do not necessarily care about the teachers. They want their children to come top in everything. 'At Tallis,' says the same woman, 'they are always telling you what they want. They want another language, or different kinds of reports, so we have to do them all over again . . . Perhaps *they'd* like to do the job and come and be paid £16,000 a year? I sometimes think, "I've got the same qualifications as you and you treat me like shit." '

Last year seven teachers left; one to train as a solicitor, another to become an accountant, others to go into industry, the police force. 'They *all* say, look I've got nothing against the school,' says Yardley. 'They see no future in public education, they want to earn more money and, they *always* add, they want less aggravation, stress, strain and long hours.'

Not yet half-way through the summer term, many of Mr Yardley's staff look exhausted and dejected. 'This is all taking a personal toll, you can see it in their faces,' said Margery Nzerem, the chairman of the governors, who has two children at Tallis. Her unpaid involvement she describes as 'a debt of gratitude' to 'this wonderful school'. Last week, few of the teachers showed much appreciation. Mrs Nzerem and her fellow governors had just voted for a new, improved curriculum, offering a second modern language. It would require longer hours from everybody. Some objected on principle: 'The pressure comes from middle-class parents for results,' said Tim Joyce, head of year. 'We need their support, but if we keep going that way, we begin to isolate the less able pupils.' Others resented the hours. 'It's a way of saving money,' said Brian Jones, a geography teacher. 'But already the workload is intolerable, because teachers are preparing for the national curriculum, and now they are being loaded up with more. The management were pushing for it because they want the school to be an attractive proposition to parents but teachers are not very happy about it all. It's just a further worsening of the conditions of service, with all the resentment that can go along with it, and undermining of morale.'

But Thomas Tallis is still a good school. Undermined morale has not yet surfaced in the classrooms, where children are still obliged to learn the Factories Acts, read *Romeo and Juliet,* burn minerals in bunsen burners. Only in the staffroom, its stained breeze block and torn carpets a dismal replica of prison visiting arrangements, do the teachers slump on grimy plastic chairs, and say it can't go on indefinitely. Or not in the same way. 'I used to stay behind every night, developing materials,' Jones said. 'But when you feel under so much pressure, you just want to get away from the place. It's day in, day out, irrespective of your mood, or how tired you are. You can burden teachers with so much, and there comes a point where you think I'm going to treat it as a nine-to-four job, and get out of there.'

But so what? The school does well, and on less money. Acts of Christian worship have yet to be scheduled, but in every other respect the school is obediently preparing for the national curriculum. The flat roof may leak, the science department may have run out of paper, chalk and exercise books, but there are 79 children on the waiting list, 69 from band A, the top ability band.

'In the eyes of the government, I see your point,' said Colin Yardley. 'There's nothing the matter. However, we are living on the fat of yesteryear. The textbooks are tattier . . . It used not to be the case where staff and pupils bought their own stationery, and that I had to spend 25 per cent of my time on activities related to money raising. Teachers are under more strain, and although extra-curricular activities survive here, I don't know how long we can sustain that.'

Then why not opt out? There would be more money, more staff, more middle-class parents, more fund-raising. 'It would be purely opportunistic,' said Yardley. His staff agree. 'If they opted out, I'd leave,' said one. Nor will they abandon the exhausting, messy business of mixed-ability teaching. It's part of the ethos. 'If you stream, what sort of messages are you giving to the less able kids?' Annie Corcoran said. 'Mixed ability *has* to be the aim.' But the outside world is streamed, isn't it? 'If education isn't idealism, then there is *no* idealism,' Corcoran said, with enthusiasm. 'Perhaps that idealism can't be sustained outside school, but without it we are nothing really, are we?' So she'd recommend the job to her pupils? No, she wouldn't. 'Why recommend somebody to do something very difficult?' Even in a good school. As Richard Stubbs said, 'If we are feeling this, God knows what the others are feeling.'

2 October 1990: Kevin Sullivan

University the Japan-easy way

Final-year students at Japanese universities return to their studies this month faced with an agreeable prospect. Ahead lie six months of mild intellectual exertion followed by some of the world's least demanding final exams. None of this year's examinees will be troubled by the uncertainty of job-hunting after graduation – companies have been courting the class of 1991 since early this spring. Short of joining an urban guerrilla active service unit or an order of Buddhist monks it is almost impossible for a Japanese university graduate to reach the end of term without an employment contract.

There are more than three job openings for each of this year's graduates. Industrial conglomerates, international trading houses, financial institutions – the sort of companies which used to limit their graduate intake to a privileged elite – now plead with prospective employees to join the payroll.

Undergraduate life in Japan is blissful largely because school life is not. The Ministry of Education revealed on 27 September that private high schools are still setting entrance exam questions on subjects which are not covered by the state primary school curriculum – to get into a good school, you have to be ahead of the pack by the age of 11. Good schools offer a direct route to university. Consequently, the students who will be sailing blithely through their final university term this winter spent most of their youth at evening crammers, doing hours and hours of homework and negotiating an inflexible syllabus, characterised by an endless succession of exams. By the time you gain admission to university you have all the basic education a Japanese corporation requires.

By one of the world's strangest national compacts, no one is expected to do very much at university except recover from the rigours of school and prepare for the rigours of corporate life. One 1987 poll found that the average Japanese university student spends 30 minutes every day reading comics, another 26 minutes reading newspapers, and just 49 minutes reading books. Around half of those polled spent less than half an hour reading books every day, and a full 17 per cent came out with the astonishing admission that they hardly ever read at all.

Corporate Japan has apparently just one objection to an academic regime which even students admit errs on the side of indulgence – it takes up too much time. Companies are trying to persuade the Ministry of Education to shorten four-year degree courses by a year.

Japanese companies routinely train graduate recruits for up to six years and operate on the assumption that anyone bright enough to get into university is bright enough to respond positively to on-the-job training. How well you did at university is less important than the fact that you went to university in the first place. The Japanese milk round consequently resembles an unseemly scramble for bodies. According to the terms of a gentleman's agreement, brokered by the Ministry of Education, recruiting starts on 1 August each year. Japanese companies, however, are anything but gentlemanly, and by 1 August only the urban guerrillas and Buddhist novices remain unspoken for. The pre-August recruitment process is in itself an introduction to corporate ethics. Everyone adheres to the fiction that recruiting has not actually begun, and deals between companies and undergraduates are as secret as they are binding.

At the very minimum, companies will send out glossy, well-designed publicity kits – no self-respecting job-hunter would consider a corporation represented by a photocopied hand-out. Students recommended by professors and career counsellors are approached directly. In order to save students the chore of reading through publicity material, some companies send their recruitment information on video. (The poll cited above found that Japanese undergraduates watch TV or video for an average of 105 minutes every day – exactly the time they spend on comics, newspapers and books combined.)

Nippon Steel Corporation, once considered Japan's most prestigious employer, has become less popular in recent years because of the financial services boom, so the company recruited American actress Sigourney Weaver last year to star in a commercial touting the joys of making girders and the general cachet of a career with the world's biggest steel producer.

Hitachi, the electronics giant, tried to lure graduates by opening, with a huge fanfare, a company dormitory to end all company dormitories. Large Japanese companies provide subsidised accommodation for as many as half their junior staff. At Hitachi's 10-storey deluxe dormitory occupants are allocated single, air-conditioned rooms, with television and private phone. The monthly rent is £25. Commercial rates for the same rooms in Tokyo are in the region of £400.

Nippon Steel and Kawasaki Steel, one of its main competitors, have both announced impressive company accommodation programmes aimed at attracting graduate recruits. Kobe Steel, appealing to undergraduate intellect rather than nascent nest-building instincts, presents its recruitment package in the form of an 80-page comic book.

James White, managing director of JDW Associates, a consulting company in Tokyo, says the Japanese preference for generalists is the key to recruitment. 'For a company involved in an area of general business the system works because no Japanese executive believes that anyone who comes into a company fresh knows anything about the company or about business in general, so they go through intensive training, normally six years. In terms of building a corporate soldier, it's very good.' White adds that among recruits a company's status is more important than the starting salary it offers.

Julian Burnett, chief executive in Japan of PA Consulting Group, explains that different attitudes to recruitment and training are the result of different career patterns. 'Most British students are impatient to get on with the job. Japanese settle down for the long haul. In the UK the vast majority of graduates will change jobs within five years. That's not the case in Japan.'

As Japan's class of '91 finish their sojourn in academic life they can look back on four years of blissful ease. After entering the labour force, however, they face years of rigorous training, with low pay and little immediate job satisfaction. That is a prospect which may cause them to envy their studious British counterparts.

3 July 1990: Michael White

Where the student is always right

The earnest young student who showed me round a hall

of residence at Birmingham Southern College in Alabama rapidly explained why life seemed so tranquil on his campus.

I had been puzzled by the absence of turbulence during two weeks as a grandly-titled Woodrow Wilson visiting lecturer at BSC and – 800 miles across the Mississippi Delta – at Tulsa University (TU), another liberal-arts college in Oklahoma. Nice healthy kids in both cities, sitting around chatting in their Bermuda shorts, spring tans and neat, white teeth. No hint of anger, social or political, no sign of dope, drink or subversive music. They were calling me 'Sir' and asking respectful questions about 1992 and Premier Thatcher's poll tax problems: 'That Labor woman who won the election in Mid-Stratfordshire talked about a revolution, Sir. Was she in the Militant Tendency?'

BSC, the South's top regional college according to one recent survey, has 1,200 students, most of them living two-to-a-room with TV, fridge, microwave (toasters are a fire hazard) and, of course, own telephone. Outside there is probably a Honda Accord, a small Chevy or a VW Rabbit, so many of them that parking is one of the few problems constantly impinging upon this middle-class idyll. With difficulties like this, life is bearable. Even the ratio between the sexes is 50-50. What about girls? I asked my student guide. 'Your parents sign up for Option 1, 2, 3 or 4, Sir.'

Option 1 means no mixed visiting at all at BSC. Option 2 means leaving at 11pm (1am at weekends), Option 3 is midnight and 2am, while Option 4 gives the offspring a free hand, subject to college rules. 'No co-habitation, Sir. You are considered to be co-habiting if you bring a toothbrush.'

And how is this enforced? By the Honor Code. Caught leaving a dorm after hours and the security guard posted outside can fine you $25. Do it three times in a term and your wayward student is up before the 16-person Student Judiciary who can impose larger fines. Drugs may be a matter for the police, but cheating in tests, excessive noise or drunkenness go to trial by peers.

As a brief visitor I hesitate to pass judgement on educational attainment. Neurosis about standards in American higher education is even more acute than in our own. But at least it delivers the *quantity* that eludes us: over 50 per cent of 18-year-olds go to college. Adults go back.

Did somebody mention money? Yes, almost everyone does. 'It's easier to attract Faculty (staff) than students, so the customer is always right,' murmurs one sceptic. 'We're in the education industry.' The need to raise money in order to fund capital projects and attract students via scholarships is pervasive, even for TU whose oil legacies have made its $270 million worth of endowed assets 42nd richest in the nation. It is, admittedly, a long way behind Harvard ($4.4 billion) and oil-glutted University of Texas ($3 billion). Princeton comes third at $2.4 billion.

Contrary to previous impressions I had of parental bankruptcy and three-job students there were few I met who didn't get some help from the labyrinthine network of federal, state and college grants, scholarships, loans. Plus something called 'work study' which means you work on campus for 12-15 hours a week in the library, the dean's office or housing management, usually at the minimum wage (now raised to $3.85, around £2.30), up to $10 for a skilled research task.

But work study's availability is subject to family means-testing. And since it is a federally-funded programme, nominally study-related, colleges sometimes use it casually as a cheap labour pool. 'It's a scam,' explains one student. 'A racket.'

In addition undergraduates can borrow up to $13,000 over a four-year course, state guaranteed at the bank of their choice. But remember, the customer is always right in this industry. So a bright student (or promising athlete) may get a full tuition scholarship – not always means-tested – which would lop $8,200 dollars off the $12,065 cost of the average BSC course in 1989-90, fairly typical for US private colleges (TU's tuition costs $7,450).

Dormitory costs come cheap at around $1,300 a year; meals $1,980 on the '14 meal plan' at BSC – five times the estimated cost of books. And there's the $5 automobile registration charge.

Missy, a 21-year-old maths graduate from Mobile, who is getting married in June and going to study law at Vanderbilt in Nashville, has supported herself with a part-time job and has a $400-a-week summer job lined up in a law firm. Her parents gave her a Ford Taurus as a graduating present. Her fiancé, however, has borrowed $35,000 to get through medical school.

Loans are interest-free and not repayable until six months after graduation. Then interest rises steadily. Those who choose to teach get them written off by some states. But the default rate is huge enough to put the system into crisis. Local papers routinely print lists of defaulters. Goods can be seized, pay docked at source.

Gene, who took me to the pool room where the Vietnam vets hang out, prefers to work for $2.19 an hour doing valet parking at a swanky Birmingham restaurant because he can average $75 a night in tips and once made $140 – in a country where the average family makes a little over $500 a week and $1,000 is comfortable middle-class.

Kay, 21, works nights at a Tulsa newspaper. She fled to TU from ORU, TV-evangelist Oral Robert's university down the road. 'My parents were trying to straighten me out as a missionary . . . a pretty uptight place. They made me wear skirts to class.'

These students are lovely people, open and hospitable, but raised in a money-driven system where even primary school children can buy shares in the tuck shop to teach 'em how. Bright students doing a course on Western Civilisation asked me bright questions about Mr Gorbachev, Jacques Delors and Rupert Murdoch. But their own civic horizons seem set on bottle banks, saving trees and good works in what are euphemistically called 'bad neighbourhoods.'

And when I insisted on walking the nightly quarter of a mile down a main road to my hotel, folk were genuinely worried. 'You might get mugged, Sir.'

13 October 1990: Martin Walker

Votes on ice

We knew that Americans take their democracy seriously, and insist on voting on everyone from their judges to their sheriffs and their dog-catchers. We had not expected the process to begin quite so young.

The house is in a flurry of campaigning. There are campaign posters all over the kitchen, and upstairs the candidate is rehearsing her speech in the bathroom. When the phone rings, it is probably the campaign manager with the latest polling report, just gathered in the local pizza parlour.

Kate is running for president. Polling day is Tuesday. We are the insurgents, coming from behind in a tight race against entrenched incumbents. Much hangs on the outcome. This is the most extraordinary fun.

Kate, who is eight years old, is campaigning for the presidency of her School Council. This used to be considered a largely honorary post until last year, when a determined campaign persuaded the teachers and the local school board that ice cream should indeed be added to the lunch menu. The voters, whose ages range from five to 10, were deeply impressed by this evidence of the power of their elected representatives. There is now keen competition for the posts of president, vice-president and secretary and from a school population of about 400 there are 21 candidates.

This is serious stuff. As well as the campaign speech, delivered before the entire school, we also have the campaign video. Our local primary school has its own TV studio, so Kate and all the other candidates have been studying the art of media manipulation. Some real political professionals are at work here. One candidate of Hispanic ancestry has come up with the most formidable slogan: 'Don't be a weirdo, Vote for Izquierdo.'

There are two main planks to Kate's campaign platform. The first is that the presidency has for too long been in the grip of the deadbeats in the fifth grade, who can be as ancient as 10 years old. It is time to hand the torch to a new generation, a fourth-grader who can speak for the entire school and remembers her roots in the younger grades.

The second campaign issue is that the ice-cream battle is only half won. Sure we get ice cream, but only vanilla or strawberry, and it is yuck. This being America, where anything is possible, Kate's campaign pledge is to negotiate a deal with the manager of the local ice-cream parlour to start supplying the school canteen for the same money the kids pay now. Since he serves about 60 astonishing flavours, which include bubble-gum and peanut butter, this is thought to be a certain vote winner.

The entire family has been recruited into the election process. Younger sister, who is five, is campaign manager for the kindergarten, which also gets to vote. This is the key to Kate's campaign. Nobody else is really working the five-year-olds, so if Fanny can deliver her class as a block vote, Kate is in with a serious chance.

The election slogan pretty much wrote itself – 'Kate is great, Vote for Kate'. It is the kind of catchy, rhythmic chant that unfortunately gets Fanny stomping about the house beating her drum. Still, if she can use the chant to get 36 five-year-olds marching into the polling booths, it will be worth it.

I was in charge of getting 50 photocopies of the campaign poster, a blown-up holiday snapshot of the candidate, on which she then lettered 'Vote Kate' in a bold hand, and stuck up all over the school. The candidate also did me the honour of practising The Speech on me a few times, which is how I know that bit about the dead hand of the old fogeys in the fifth grade and the torch being passed to a new generation.

'You lifted that line from President Kennedy's inaugural speech,' I told her. Kennedy is Kate's political hero. Children's libraries here are full of hagiographies about the charismatic young president. 'It's a good line. It worked for Kennedy,' she said, irrefutably.

My wife is the campaign's transport and communications manager, in charge of motorcades, the candidate's car pool, and taking phone messages from the campaign staff. There are cryptic notes scattered near the phone, saying that Grade 3 is nine pledges and six maybes, and that while the soccer team is solid, the gym class is weak. All across our neighbourhood, and indeed all across America, other mothers are performing similar tasks. Year after year, the habits of democracy are inculcated into successive generations of schoolchildren.

There are elections for class president, for school president, for editor of the High School Yearbook. For the grown-ups, there are elections in the Parent Teachers Association, which actually runs the schools throughout America, and elections to the school board, which governs the education system.

Voting and campaigning come so naturally here that I cannot fathom why so few of the adults bother to turn out on the real polling day. In the last presidential elections, barely half of the eligible electorate went to the polls. The turnout in the average primary is around 20 per cent, and the average state or Congressional race gets about one voter in three.

Maybe they just get sick of all the voting. Or maybe it is a deeper problem of disillusion with a political process that has candidates saying 'Read my lips – No New Taxes' or running despicable 'attack videos' against each other. The gap between the glorious myth of American democracy in which Kate is now being raised and the reality of the modern power struggle is sickeningly wide.

From upstairs, I hear the voice of the hopeful new generation. It sounds uncannily like the old.

'Ask not what Bradley Hills primary school can do for you. Ask what you can do for Bradley Hills.'

As she says, it worked for him.

22 February 1991: Alan Rusbridger

Hands off, Donald, they're ma troosers

A couple of weeks ago I purchased a pair of trousers. They appeared unremarkable trousers at the time. They were plain grey corduroy, and they were half-price. The half-price clinched it.

I have worn them to work more or less every day since, to widespread indifference. There is only so much excitement a fresh pair of grey corduroys can arouse in an office. Indifferent was how I felt until my eye happened to fall upon the March issue of the *Face* which, for reasons that escape me now, was lying on my desk.

The main feature of the issue – stretching over 14 pages – concerned my trousers. Well, not my actual trousers, but the phenomenon of my trousers. For, as I dimly remembered leafing through the style-setting pages of the *Face*, my trousers were made by a French firm named Chipie. And here were 14 pages devoted to just this: the 'Chipie Phenomenon'.

Indifference was replaced by quiet satisfaction. Over the hill? What, when one is clearly in the 'forefront of the new casual culture'? When 'everyone agrees that if you wear Chipie . . . you look the part, you earn "respect" '? My only mistake had been to wear my belt over the Chipie label. As Pablo, a 17-year-old south Londoner, who acts as unofficial style consultant to the manufacturers, explained: 'It's important for people to see the label – if it's hidden by a belt, you move the label.' Some Chipie wearers are apparently given to unstitching the label and reattaching it in more eye-catching positions: on the flies, for example. I resolved to move my belt.

By page nine, quiet satisfaction was giving way to an inner glow. 'You dress in Chipie,' one Tai-Ann, 18-year-old president of the South London College Student union, told the magazine, "cos everybody looks at you. You buy it to show off, to show that you've got money.'

But mention of price brought a darker tone into the article. There are those Chipie wearers, like Pablo, who put down deposits and pay for their trousers by instalments. Other are less patient. 'Everyone I spoke to knew someone who had been mugged for their clothes,' wrote the author, John Godfrey. 'Some had been the victims and other made no bones about the fact that they'd done it themselves. Whereas in the past people used to damage each other's clothes (paint throwing on the terraces or a quick flick of a Stanley knife in a suburban discotheque) the risk factor in looking good today involves being able to hold on to your "garms".' And Mr Godfrey quoted a 16-year-old from Wandsworth: 'You have to be ready to fight for your clothes.'

This, I admit, put my new purchase in an altogether different light. No sooner was I ready to bask in the kudos of making a big fashion – and, let's face it, financial – statement with my garms than I was faced with the prospect of fighting off attempts at debagging on my way to work each morning. The accompanying fashion shot of a young Chipie wearer bearing a lethal knife in each hand was not reassuring.

Chipie is said to be reluctant to comment on this marginal drawback to wearing its label with pride. But according to Mr Godfrey, security has been beefed up in the company's own shops after a spate of mass invasions by would-be Chipie wearers reluctant to part with anything as mundane as cash. Chipie robbers are said to have responded by lying in wait outside Chipie shops and assaulting unsuspecting trouser wearers on their way out.

One knew that this sort of thing went on in New York with trainers and sweat shirts. But somehow one never suspected that picking up a bargain pair of cords on a quiet Saturday afternoon in north London could lead one to become a fashion victim in the richest sense.

Mr Godfrey elaborates: 'Unlike New York, where violence is operating on its own irrational plane, on the streets of London there are only two reasons for trouble: your "garms" or your area.' The most recent bout of gang warfare was apparently between the Untouchables (Brixton), who dressed in green puffa jackets, and The 28s (Tulse Hill), who wore bandanas and Chipie jeans. Since then the style wars have spread: Peckham v. Hackney, Ladbroke Grove v. Harlesden's Stonebridge, and the Clapham Junction Boys v. Anyone.

'Peer pressure,' writes Mr Godfrey, 'might fuel the kinetics of the fashion, but the bottom line is that there is a thin divide between competition and conflict, and if you're going to cross it, you'd better make sure you're not alone.'

I confess I am out of my depth. It is only a modest walk from the car park to the office each morning, but I suspect it would seem rather longer if clad only in boxer shorts. It strikes me that a trouser donor card may be one solution. Have my Chipies, but spare my life. No disrespect to my garms, but I have a wife and family to think of.

In fact, Mr Godfrey's article concludes with the perfect let-out. He reveals that Tai-Ann is already contemplating abandoning the label: 'I don't like to wear Chipie as much now 'cos I don't like to see 12- or 13-year-olds kids in the same clothes as me.'

Me neither. Anyone interested in a pair of grey corduroy trousers, only slightly used?

3 September 1990: Joanna Coles

The bottom line

'What an incredible bottom. Just look at that, it's a full circle,' Morag Iona Young, image consultant, told the group of businesswomen stripped down to bra and briefs.

She was pointing at Jennifer; the others murmured enviously. They were learning how to Dress for Success.

'By 3pm you may find you're depressed,' Ms Young warned at the start of the £75 session designed to improve personal image. It would, however, pass. By 6pm everyone would have established their own clothing personalities and would never enter a social situation dressed incorrectly again.

'Look at what I'm wearing,' she said, stroking the shoulder pads on her elegant black and white jacket. 'I could go to a wedding in this.' She could also have appeared on Dallas, married to JR.

Radiating glamour, Ms Young is convinced many British women are sabotaging their chances of success in the workplace because they look a mess. That was why she set up Britain's first image consultancy six months ago, and has been inundated ever since.

Looking good, she says, is all about knowing who you are and what you want. 'If you married a millionaire what would you take with you? Think about it. It might happen.'

To establish clothing identities clients are subjected to a personality test. 'Is everyone familiar with Yin and Yang? It's like Jerry and Tom . . . '

Sitting round a table the two estate agents, a designer and a soon-to-be-divorced wife discussed whether they were artistic or businesslike, angular or soft, lacked interest in underwear or loved shoes and food.

Then it was on to body and face shape. 'Oblong bottom, square top . . . round bottom, rectangular top . . . Annie you have a triangle-shaped face, did you know that?'

'No.'

'Oh, yes. I can see you sitting on a toadstool.'

Most British women did not look good because they did not spend enough, she said. 'I'm talking blouse no less than £50, skirt £65, dress £100, belt £35, jewellery between £40 – £100, handbag £55.

'The bottom rung on the ladder to success is Jaeger.' Someone gasped. 'If you don't get into designer clothing, you won't learn discernment,' she scolded. 'To say clothes are not important is a fallacy. It's mind over money.'

Another thing which worries her is the British woman's tendency to lurch between Tart and Victim.

'Never wear cardigans in the office, that's really victim,' she said. 'Never use a carrier bag for work, no flat shoes, very unprofessional, no tatty shoes and no tarty shoes. Do not wear ankle bracelets and no bare legs please. Bare legs are about sex.'

At the end of the session people bring their own outfits to try on for Ms Young's approval. No doubt used to the absurd, she has developed a disarming line in candour. 'That orange is appalling on you . . . that makes you look tarty . . . well, maybe with a glittery brooch . . . I'm sorry I can't say this any other way, that makes you look cheap.'

9 February 1991: Carla Lane's diary

Doves in the midst of war

Monday

I wake as always at 6.30 to the sound of the doves in the conservatory. Manage to fall out of bed at 7.00, mainly because one lurcher puppy and seven cats insist. Climb into baggy clothes and, with eyes still closed, feed dog, cats, fish, rabbits, tortoise, guinea pigs, rescued pigeons and 72 other birds.

9.00: Coffee, bran biscuits and honey, and the ever-growing pile of mail. My lady arrives to put the house back in order.

11.15: I am walking through Chiswick Park with my lunatic dog. He is harassing everybody and everything; my mind is on my scripts. My brain is reaching out for a beginning but my mind is busy thinking how wonderful the trees are; it rises and falls between the glory of Nature and the doom-laden knowledge that man is slowly torturing the planet to death. The only thing I know when I leave the park is that in my next script, one of my characters is going to say, 'Man is slowly torturing the planet to death.'

1.00: Cleaning windows that overlook the river – cannot bear them to be dirty. Going to start script in a moment, but one of my rescued pigeons has pecked a small finch and I have to keep vigil on the victim.

1.45: In the conservatory putting barriers up between the mighty and the small. Think my Dutch rabbit is pregnant – she is gathering newspapers and mugging everybody. I can see through the glass doors that my lurcher has taken a plant out of its pot and is towing it around the house. Will start script when I have cleaned up.

2.15: Gulf war is on my mind; I can see the faces of young soldiers, weeping wives, and a little bird sinking in the oil. My imagination races – how do they feel? Suddenly I am

feeling for all of them. Must get out.
3.00: Whizzing round town in the Range-Rover. I have bought several things I don't need and am looking for a health food shop for yoghurt, organic tea, vegetarian cheese and cereal for the rabbit.
4.30: Dark and the creatures are all hungry again. The blind birds need placing in their sleeping nests and the flightless pigeons need to be put on their night-time branches. Will start script when I have covered the parrot.
5.30: All quiet. Cats in summer room, phone calls made, pen in hand. Remember the mail. Someone wanted me to write a film. I put my pen down and re-read the offer. Cannot do it – too busy – but spend half-hour thinking out a scenario, out of habit.
8.00: Watching the news. There is no escape from it. On one side there is a documentary about people with cancer, on the other a foxhunt, on the third the war again. I have written on one page: 'Bread, Number 6, by Carla Lane.' Too late now – can't work after dark, and my dog has arrived with his toy bear.
9.00: In bed. TV is on and the entire world is phoning me. Fall asleep in the middle of *Golden Girls,* and my last thought was a good idea for the first sentence of the script.
Midnight: Wake to switch off TV. Good idea is back in my mind, dialogue starts to flow, great creative forces charge through my brain, but my body won't move. Start to think about slaughter-houses, laboratories, factory-farming, oil-slicks. Sit up in bed and wonder why I am so afflicted. Reach for the radio – somebody is phoning in about their favourite comedy programmes. None of mine are among them. Go to sleep wondering why the hell I'm doing it.

Tuesday

The dove started even earlier this morning. In the conservatory there are two new ones, pale grey powder-puffs with bright pink eyes. Combine eating my breakfast with dashing in to look at these tiny miracles.
9.30: Driver calls to take me to Television Centre. Climb

into the car with bird droppings and hay in my hair, and between Chiswick and White City, try to convert the driver into becoming a vegetarian. Delivered to make-up where little silk brushes magic away shadows and imperfections. Stopped in the corridor by three youngsters who want my autograph. They thought I was Susan Hampshire.

10.30: Usual interview with the same questions I was being asked 20 years ago. Can feel myself being deliberately mysterious and taking long enigmatic pauses before answering each question, only because I don't know where I get my ideas from and I don't know what I am going to do next.

1.00: Posh restaurant, Holland Park, posh magazine and posh journalist. She ordered our food and placed her little black tape-recorder in front of me. In between mouthfuls of salad and cottage cheese, I tell my views on life, pollution, the war, the planet, the creatures, government spokesmen, men, women and sex. A curious light visited her eyes when we got to the last subject. At last she was going to prise my private life out of its closet. 'Do you live alone?' she cooed. 'No,' I said. The eyes glistened. 'Are we allowed to ask names?' 'Well,' I said, 'there's Wolfgang, the ginger one, and Danielle, the tabby . . . Egor, the lurcher.'

2.00: At home. Time to write now. The house is quiet, the river full, so I take some photographs of it and of a cormorant fishing and an old man who has stopped to gaze up at the house.

3.00: Jeff Frances rings. 'We're looking for a home for a pig,' he said. 'They're going to slaughter it.' I ring my very dear friend Linda. 'We're looking for a home for a pig,' I said.

4.30: The press have been harassing me. One of the cast is leaving – they want to know what I think. I am wilfully rude to them, remembering when Peter Howitt left and my comment was: 'Why shouldn't he, he's a young actor, he must move on.' Next day the headlines were: 'Furious Carla hits out.'

6.30: Sit in the chair watching the news again. The dog is eating my trainers. Great waves of despair wash over me as I see young soldiers surrounded by their high-tech weapons, with fear on the faces. I phone my sons.
7.00: Time to get ready for dinner. A good and true friend is coming; he will put me right, and over a bottle of wine we will sort out the dilemma of the Universe.
Midnight: My good and true friend is drunk in the living room. I have covered him gently and gone to bed. I have looked in the aviary, and all is well. The phone rings. It is Linda. She and Paul have had a talk and they will take the pig. It has been a good day and I will start the script tomorrow.

30 August 1990: Sarah Johnson

The other woman bites back

I am the 'dalliance' referred to in *Today*'s story on Leo and Jilly Cooper's marriage (though I don't see how the word can cover an eight-year relationship). As *Guardian* readers are unlikely to have seen it, suffice it to say the double-page feature was only the latest in which Mrs Cooper has talked about my love affair with Leo, claiming I was 'energetically pursuing' her husband. As she seems intent on prolonging my pain, I feel I can no longer remain silent.

Tales abound in the tabloids of newsworthy husbands' infidelities and in most cases the erring husband and his long-suffering and forgiving wife present a united front, belittling the affair and the 'other woman' involved. But what of her, this third person in an often complex situation, who has little redress when everything falls apart?

How does she cope? Should she decide to enter the fray and publicly defend herself, it will be seen as either an act of revenge (hell hath no fury) or a bid for financial gain. Much better that she creeps quietly away into a corner, licks her wounds and keeps her mouth shut.

Of course the knowledge of her husband's infidelity will be painful to the wife, but her husband's presence and public support will surely be some compensation, while what is the mistress left with? Most likely she will have made her lover her whole life. Such a situation would have demanded it.

I am such a mistress and my desperate attempts to come to terms with a life without Leo, after eight years, are continually being sabotaged by articles in the press about his marriage. For this reason, and on behalf of those thousands of ill-used and discarded mistresses without redress, I would like to tell my story.

I first came across Leo at the top of a publishing house staircase (which, as he later admitted, was the moment he set me in his sights) as I motioned him upwards for an appointment with my boss. He made very little impression on me initially, but then began a relentless campaign (Leo is a military publisher) to persuade me to embark upon an affair with him, being very attentive whenever we met in the office, insisting on coming to my house in the presence of my children and boyfriend, begging me to have dinner with him.

He was so persistent that I eventually agreed to the occasional dinner or opera, always, despite his passionate entreaties, keeping him at arm's length and being adamant that I would not become involved.

He kept up his campaign for two years, using all the force of his extremely strong personality. He is wonderfully adroit with words, often poetic, and above all full of wit and humour. I began to be convinced by his desperation – he was lonely, it was difficult being married to

Jilly, always taking second place to her stardom – together with the flatteries and persuasive ways of a man determined to have his way.

I eventually gave in. We began to see more of each other and he assumed more and more importance in my thoughts until I became deeply attached to him. I had had a fairly difficult life, bringing up three children as a single parent, and this sudden gift of such incredible happiness from someone so reassuringly strong, protective and loving was a balm.

I don't want to make public the intimate details of a gloriously passionate relationship; suffice it to say that he became my life and we gave each other extraordinary happiness, joy and love. He was divine to my children and we managed a very full life – dinners, the opera, his professional functions, my friends.

This continued for six years, Leo often under the extreme pressure of his double life and my weekends alone made bearable by his frequent reassuring calls, often made with hilarious ingenuity, sometimes from his home and surrounding telephone boxes. He took enormous risks all the time, often running into people he knew, but somehow passing me off.

As my dependence on Leo grew, it got more and more difficult to be engulfed by him during the week and abandoned for another at weekends, plus having to cope with the many articles about their idyllic marriage. After one particularly difficult article, I broke and went down to their house, naively but honestly believing that if we all sat down and discussed it, something could be worked out. Of course everyone was very upset, particularly Jilly who was in a state of shock, but she was extremely nice to me and we all did a lot of talking.

Next morning I was bundled unceremoniously, quite understandably, back on the train and I retreated from work to bed for two weeks, unable to eat or sleep. Leo paid me a visit, reassuringly telling me that all would be back to normal once the dust had settled. A week later we had dinner, after which there were further dramas involving us all, bringing about what seemed a complete abandonment by Leo.

A friend sent me to recover at a health farm where Leo rang me, asking for a meeting on my return. He wanted everything to go on but under conditions of the utmost discretion since Jilly would be highly suspicious. Loving him so desperately, I had no choice. It was as though my life had been given back to me. He told me that, no matter what, he would never leave me, always look after me. I believed him.

Things continued much as before for about nine months, at which point we were seen at the theatre and Leo, on being accused by his eldest daughter of still seeing me, came and asked me what he should do; would I save him and his marriage? Several nightmarish weeks followed; our families were badly affected and there were emotional meetings, threats, entreaties. We were all in a desperate state.

I continued to see him occasionally for a drink when he said he loved me and that he would look after me. But then he decided that his best interests lay with Jilly; he loved her and they had been married for so long.

So he took the necessary steps to prove to her that it was all over, calling the police in front of his secretary to escort me from his office where I had gone to beg him not to abandon me after so much and so long. I was made to attend a meeting with his friend and eldest daughter where I said that I accepted that it was over but asked to be treated with kindness and consideration. I could not cope with the loss coupled with what seemed such extreme and selfish cruelty when it seemed to me that my only sin was loving him.

However, the next thing was a lawyer's letter threatening me with an injunction if I did not completely let go. I was forced to take legal advice and advised to write saying I would have no further contact.

Several months later we met (those months had been so lonely) and we have had many meetings since, but I love him so much and not being able to show him has made me behave badly at these meetings and he has again cut himself off.

They say time heals everything but I don't believe it. The intensity of my love for Leo is as great as ever, and the pain of life without him insurmountable. I have spent money I don't have on psychiatrists, pills, psychologists, all to no avail.

Nothing seems to alter one's mood of total despair and hopelessness, and the feeling that the price is unjustly high for simply having loved a man at his behest. There are no distractions in a life that had become necessarily empty during the years with Leo. My mistake was that I took everything he told me at face value – that he would always look after me, never leave me. And even the knowledge that this is not the case does not stop my love.

Perhaps Leo feels guilt for the suffering he has caused two women. Then again, perhaps he is enjoying being in the limelight on his own account for once and can assuage that guilt by basking in the knowledge that he's once again faithful and true.

I feel, in all honesty, that my suffering has been and will be the greatest, but that it's of little importance to anyone. I do object, though, to Mrs Cooper continuing to rub salt in the wound by her everlasting undressing in public.

So how do other women in similar situations cope? Are they made of sterner stuff, more intelligent and realistic about the situation? Do they find it within themselves to forgive and forget? Am I bitter, self-pitying, weak and obsessed? Perhaps so, but I don't know how to come to terms with this. Does anyone else?

4 September 1990: Matthew Fort

Sperm wail

The telephone rang in the boardroom. 'Matthew, it's for you.' I frowned. I was trying to work up the necessary concentration for my part of the advertising pitch.

'Yes?'

'Your wife rang.' The dulcet tones of Cheryl the telephone lady fluttered in my ear. 'She says can you deliver the goods, please. I told her you were in a presentation, but she said it was very important.'

'Deliver the goods?' What, now? Oh, hell's teeth.

'Cheryl, be so kind as to summon a motorcycle messenger. Right now.'

I extracted a small plastic bottle and excused myself from the presentation. I went down to the men's lavatory on the first floor, locked myself in a cubicle and masturbated into the plastic container with as much gusto as I could manage.

I squeezed the top on to the container and popped it into a Jiffy bag, sealed it and made my way down to reception. A colossal figure, like a primitive spaceman, was already standing there. I couldn't see his face through the visor of his helmet. I handed him the Jiffy bag.

'Ride like hell for Harley Street,' I cried. And then I had a vision of him skidding off round Hyde Park Corner and my personal sperm bank hurtling into the gutter for all to see. 'But be very careful. This is a precious package. It could be a matter of life or death.'

'Mmmmhmmmmah,' mumbled the Colossus and, stiff-limbed, clomped out.

A touch drained, I made my way back to the presentation.

'Ah, Matthew. You're back. Perhaps you could tell us about the creative strategy . . . '

The idea that there is any connection between romance and conception, or even between sex and conception, is a laughable one for couples who experience difficulty in having children. Why is it that all your friends seem to be able to get pregnant by exchanging looks, while you, with all the aids that medical science has to offer, have to cope with month after month of disappointment and despair? We tried it drunk. We tried it sober. We tried it spontaneous. We tried it calculated to the last millisecond.

One morning we tried it just as I was about to leave for work. At this stage of the game we were giving the primitive but still complicated business of the douche a go, to try to reduce excess acidity in the vagina. It involved filling a bladder-like bag with water and bicarbonate of soda, then hosing the mixture into my wife.

After this intense foreplay, I had to plunge in right away, while the water-bicarb was working its wonders. It is not a process conducive to romance, passion and prolonged sexual ecstasy. In fact, being slightly anxious about getting to work, I slipped my lower garments off, but kept on my shirt, tie and waistcoat during the management session.

By some quite extraordinary circumstances, my wife became pregnant after this episode. It didn't last. She miscarried in the seventh week. But for some time after that I was convinced that my waistcoat played an important part in this magical process and would insist on wearing it whenever we got down to some serious management.

It was no more or less effective than the nostrums put forward by the medical profession. The fertility experts are plausible, persuasive, technical on all points except that which really matters – the chances of success. Then they shift uneasily in their seats and fall back into a blizzard of numbers and the pitying look that asks how you could trouble your mind with things like that.

The fact of the matter is that even if you are 25 and fairly near the floodtide of sexual potency, it still takes on average four months' heavy activity to get pregnant, i.e. you've got a 25 per cent chance per cycle. Your chances diminish the older you get. By the time you are in your mid-thirties your chances are depressingly low. But still you are prepared to go through the probings and proddings, drug regimes, great and petty humiliations, are prepared to part with anything up to £1,500 a shot under IVF in order to conceive with so little chance of success. In May 1988 *The Lancet* published a study of 1071 cases involving the Gift procedure, a kind of souped-up in vitro fertilisation technique. Of the women, 193 were over 40, and 37 of them conceived. In other words, 156 of them did not. Of the 37, roughly half miscarried. So of the original 193, 19 women actually gave birth.

We started with one of the great names among fertility doctors. His reputation is worldwide. So, consequently, is his practice. He sees dozens of childless women a day. Some get about 10 minutes every two months, usually – and invariably, in my wife's case – two hours late. It was like a processing factory. I don't think they even tested my sperm count properly – and after all the trouble I had gone to.

This was the first of my love affairs with small plastic containers and, like a lot of first love affairs, it was a painful business. This was because there was a tiny plastic shard attached to the rim of the container, where the two halves joined. I did not notice this booby trap until I was trying to direct my ejaculation into the neck of the bottle. In my excitement, the little shard nicked the end of my penis, causing a momentary halt in the proceedings. Have you ever gone to work with the end of your penis wrapped in cotton wool and elastoplast? Thank heavens the sample itself was unsullied. What would the lab technicians have made of pink semen?

They probably didn't think much of it anyway. The first blow to your image of manhood comes from the pathetically small amount of semen all this huffing and puffing seems to produce. There is this tiny container with what appears to be a slight milky precipitation in the bottom. Is this all the future of the Forts adds up to?

And then there's the reluctance of the individual spermatozoa to do what they are supposed to do. As one of the subsequent specialists observed, 'Not very many of what I call "streakers", Mr Fort.' It was true. My spermatozoa had a habit of going round in circles for a while then, obviously deciding this was getting them nowhere, downing tools and sitting around doing nothing.

We ended up at the Wellington Hospital, in the hands of Dr Craft and his team, and with Professor Brinsden in particular. The organisation was excellent; the way in which we were treated mixed professionalism and personal interest. Both Brinsden and the nurses seemed to recognise that the people who came to them were human beings with very particular emotional vulnerabilities which needed to be handled with delicacy and tact. Nor did they in any way disguise our slim chances of success.

Mind you, they did devise yet another variation for Matthew Fort's Masturbation Manual. The sperm in your first spurt are, so I am told, more concentrated or of better quality than those of subsequent ejaculations. Not many people know this. Certainly I did not, so I was rather surprised when the nurse handed me a double-barrelled receptacle, two plastic containers taped together.

'The first spurt in the left-hand container, Mr Fort,' she said briskly, 'and the rest in the other.'

'I beg your pardon?'

She didn't even bother to look at me.

Struck dumb by this latest demand on my technical skills, I sloped off to the appointed wankatorium, a small grey room. There wasn't even a pornographic magazine, which I have heard that other clinics thoughtfully provide, to help. However, somehow I managed to get up sufficient head of steam but let me tell you, attempting to follow instructions caused beads of sweat to burst from my forehead. It is extremely difficult to remember exact instructions at the moment of even so artificial a climax, let alone coordinate hand, penis, eye and receptacle.

I was reminded of a friend of mine with whom I was discussing the technicalities of this business one day. Her husband had been called upon to provide a sample. 'What?' I exclaimed. 'You gave him a hand?'

'Certainly,' she replied. 'I wouldn't trust Mark to run a bath for himself. As it was, most of it ended up on my skirt.'

27 December 1990: Mark Morreau

Aerial tactics

'John Major, son of a trapeze artist . . .' came leaping out of the page at me. I suppose that I knew that somewhere in the recesses of my memory, but it set me to thinking. We trapeze artists are the stars of the show, sure, hanging high in the air, defying death night after night, but scaling those dizzy heights requires hard work akin to masochism. I wonder, would I encourage any child of mine into this aerial profession?

Every day starts with an inventory of my body, assessing the latest damage. Any more pulled muscles? Rope burns? Bruises? Are my hands in any fit state to work today? Every morning I wish for a live-in masseur/osteopath/physiotherapist. At 30 years, am I too old for this already?

Hands suffer most: one needs to be disciplined about hand care, trimming off callouses with a razor blade before they get too big and rip off, using moisturiser to keep them supple, to stop the skin from cracking. Pissing on your hands hardens them up and keeps the small cuts and cracks from getting infected. Arnica for bruises, calendula for cuts, comfrey for sprains. The herbalists are making a fortune out of me. Every weekday I meet my partner, Juliette, at Circus Space in Islington. An abandoned warehouse converted into a training area, populated in equal number by circus performers and pigeons. It takes several cups of coffee before we feel ready to face our day's training. Stiff bodies stretch slowly into suppleness as we try to warm up on the cold mats. We have desultory discussions about what we're going to tackle. (It depends on what injuries we have.)

Front balance to half angel drop? No, Juliette is too bruised from doing that yesterday. Feet to feet hangs? No again, my feet are too scabby from rope burns. Eventually we'll find something to practise, a new trick to work out, to add to our routine. Having seen ourselves on video, we'll go through our doubles trapeze routine once or twice, paying special attention to sections which looked sloppy, or which could be improved upon. It's hard work, and it hurts but we daren't stop for too long for fear of getting cold and seizing up. Two hours of this is as much as we can take. Over coffee and cigarettes (for me) and chocolate (for Juliette) we talk about ways of getting more work to pay for our publicity and our promotional video. We've had a well-paid offer from a traditional circus for three weeks' work over Christmas, but we won't compromise our principles and work with animals. We're both relieved to have made that decision. We may be broke, but we're not desperate.

On Thursday nights we make £50 each by doing a couple of spots at the Hippodrome, the self-styled 'World's Greatest Discotheque'. Of all the work we do this is the most depressing. Tracey and Sharon dance around their handbags as we go through the motions above their heads. We come down, panting and sweating, and we call it a good night if we get a smattering of applause. We push our way back to the dressing room and agree that there must be more to life than this.

Mr Major senior must have felt the same way. But I wouldn't change places with his son, even if he has become Prime Minister. Despite the pain and the (relative) poverty I love what I do. Nothing on earth can match the buzz I get from doing a good show: the danger-induced adrenalin, the trust between us, the sharp gasps of breath from the punters, the applause and the acclaim, the satisfying exhaustion at the end of the act. These are the things I live for. The roar of greasepaint and the smell of the crowd. I'll leave running the country to someone else, thanks.

23 March 1991: Alan Mitchell

Dove tales and cherry mysteries

Several trees well known in our gardens came to us in curious ways. One is the Dove tree; or rather two are the Dove trees, for there are two different forms, with differing origins but somewhat mixed up histories. The Dove tree can be called a Ghost tree, without great offence, or the Davidia, but absolutely not the trivial name so often used, which is too awful to repeat here.

The Dove tree was discovered by a Basque Lazarist monk, Jean-Pierre Armand David, who was sent to Peking in 1862 and became devoted to all branches of natural history. He collected insects, animals, birds and plants and sent a stream of specimens to the museum in Paris. The museum director was so impressed that he asked the Lazarist Superior General to allow the Abbé David to make three extensive expeditions. On the second of these in 1868, David sailed to Shanghai and up the Yangtse into Sichuan, then overland to Mupin, near Tibet. In this region he found the Giant Panda, and a Davidia tree. He contrived to transport the panda live to Shanghai and so to

Paris, together with flower and foliage specimens of the tree.

The next tree of Davidia was found a thousand miles to the east of Mupin in May 1888 by Augustine Henry, a doctor specialising in herbs in the customs service and, like David, given permission after a plea from Kew to botanise far afield. He was based at Ichang and made one trip to the north of the Yangtse and one to the south. They resulted in herbarium specimens of over 500 new species and, from the second trip, of Davidia. It was eventually decided at Kew that a man should be trained and sent out to collect seeds, and Ernest Wilson was on his way by April 1899.

David had long been back in Peking and his tree was too remote. Henry had been moved to Simao in Yunnan, and Wilson left his gear in Hong Kong and set out on the 1,000-mile journey to meet him; it took four months. Henry gave Wilson a postcard sketch map, with the Yangtse, three paths and three villages scribbled on it, plus the word Davidia but no apparent dot to place it. The area covered was the size of France.

Wilson retraced the 1,000 miles to Shanghai, went on to Hong Kong for his gear, then back to Shanghai and 500 miles up the Yangtse to Ichang and 100 miles beyond to a mission where Henry had stayed, and in April 1990, he found the tiny village nearest the tree. Some people there remembered Henry and his tree and took him to the spot. There was a 'rather new house' and a tree stump. The Davidia was in the rafters.

Wilson set out to comb 100 square miles of forest. While collecting generally, he found a 50ft Davidia on 19 May and then 10 more within his set area. When their fruit was ripe, he sent great quantities to Veitch's to be sown in the spring of 1901. None had germinated when Wilson returned in April, 1902, to see them in the Coombe Wood nursery. But by May, he had helped to pot up 13,000.

He then discovered that his were not the first. In 1897,

Vilmorin's nurseries outside Paris had received 34 seeds of Davidia from a French Jesuit missionary, Paul Farges. One germinated and was soon being reproduced by layers and cuttings. But these are distinguishable as var. *vilmoriniana,* with leaves which are smooth underneath and short stems to the fruit. The David form has silky white hairs beneath the leaf and flower stalks twice as long. It also colours orange and crimson in autumn. The Vilmorin form grows faster, and is much commoner in our gardens.

The first coast redwoods in Britain came from Russia, not California. The tree had been taken to Portugal by missionaries around 1770 but was not known to botanists until Archibald Menzies sent a specimen to Kew in 1796. David Douglas had evidently seen tall stands of it without knowing what to call it; he classed it as a Swamp cypress, but if he collected any seeds, they and the record were lost.

The Russians, however, had a colony at Fort Ross, 60 miles north of San Francisco, until 1850. Seeds had been taken from there to Russia and trees raised in the Crimea. Dr Fischer, botanist at Leningrad, thought that the country of Menzies and Douglas ought not to be without such an important tree and in 1843 sent seed to Knight and Perry, nurserymen in London. Since no other seed is known to have come to Britain before William Lobb's supply in 1851, all the earlier trees are of Russian origin, derived from Fort Ross. The oldest specimens in Britain date from 1844–5.

Another unexpected origin, the most remarkable of all, is that of the lovely Tai-haku cherry, now seen everywhere. It has the biggest flowers of any cherry: single, white from pink buds, opening among the deep red unfolding leaves, among the earliest of the Japanese cherries.

Captain Collingwood Ingram was responsible for giving this tree to the gardens of the world. He had been studying flowering cherries for many years when he went to Japan in 1922 to see the source of so many of the best. He was shown round by a professor of botany who had made a life study of them. At the end of the tour, the professor said that Ingram had seen all there were in Japan and therefore all the best in the world, but he could not be shown the most glorious of them all because it was extinct, and his own lifetime of travel had not re-discovered it.

The professor then unrolled a silken embroidery made in about 1750 showing huge, single white flowers among the red leaves. Collingwood 'Cherry' Ingram thanked him, adding, 'I can now put its label on the tree in my garden in Kent.' The old man, politely, disbelieved him. Back in England in 1926 'Cherry' sent opening buds to Japan by air. The professor had died but his successor opened the flowers, and they matched the embroidery.

When he had been judging at a show in Sussex, 'Cherry' was approached by a woman with some shoots of a cherry. She asked if he could propagate them; it was a wonderful tree but was dying and these were the last good shoots. She had acquired the tree in 1900, with five others, in a job lot advertised in a local paper as trees from Japan. The other five were well known Japanese cherries, but this one was new to her. 'Cherry' made successful grafts and soon spread the tree everywhere, but no one has any idea how Tai-Haku came to get in that lot, nor where it had been for perhaps 150 years.

3 June 1991: Geoffrey Taylor

Arguably the worst dish in the world

Perhaps the most unwelcome side-effect of the food

revolution has been the huge increase in ratatouille consumption. As recently as the late 1960s ratatouille was virtually confined to a few small areas of London, north of the Thames. It has gradually taken hold as far afield as Matlock, Workington, Gateshead and the eastern counties of the Irish Republic. By the end of summer many more people are likely to have come into contact with it.

Elizabeth David wrote of ratatouille that it was 'a dish which takes kindly to reheating'. No doubt it does, but in appearing to praise or at least condone the mixture and the many variants derived from similar ingredients, Miss David took no account of the high blood pressure, feelings of nausea and stress and loss of appetite which the smell of simmering ratatouille can induce. If it isn't used up at a sitting (without prejudice to the undesirability of serving it in the first place) a less antisocial use for it is to dry it out thoroughly and mould it into blocks for use in the construction industry.

One of the *Guardian*'s former cookery writers, either Harold Wilshaw or Ambrose Heath, renamed ratatouille as Yuk Provençal and I doubt whether a better term has been found. Unfortunately that part of France has much to answer for. It is also one main source of a mutant vegetable which has taken over the ecological niche formerly occupied by broccoli, even to the extent of pirating the name.

I have never had more sympathy with George Bush than when his wife said, 'There's no way you are going to get the President of the United States to eat broccoli.' The old vegetable gardeners, notably E. R. Janes, who was published in Penguin in 1954, regarded broccoli as a continuation of cauliflower by other means. It looked very similar. Its slightly more conical head, which originally was a dirty yellow, was improved by breeders until it had almost the ivory colour of cauliflower itself. Roscoff Extra Early and Superb Early White are varieties to be sought out. What passes for broccoli today is a form of the Italian white-sprouting calabrese, which I think is probably a type of broccoli whose genetic code has been cracked by a deadly virus, possibly one of Fred Hoyle's from the tail of a comet.

Whatever its provenance, the result is flavourless greenery, often found wrapped in clingfilm. This mutant strain can easily be recognised in cooking because when one end of the sprig is tender, the other is still hard, and if the hard end is cooked for longer the other end is soggy. Sogginess is the hallmark of this nouvelle cuisine. The only saving grace of ratatouille is that when politeness requires it to be eaten it can be gently eased down the throat without tasting it.

My view, though it is probably old-fashioned by now, is that in a liberal democracy people should be allowed to eat ratatouille if they wish, just as they should be allowed to smoke or listen to heavy rock. But out of concern for the feelings of other people who find the fumes offensive, they should do it in private. I would never go so far as to put up one of those prissy notices saying 'This is a non-ratatouille household. Please observe our wishes and go outside', but I would be in favour of designating areas of restaurants where certain foods may not be eaten. Aubergines would be top of the list, followed by any combination of red or green peppers cooked with tomatoes or olive oil. I can't pretend that that alone will crack the problem, but it will be a start.

What form, then, will the next revolution, or counter-revolution, take? The pendulum never swings back to its original position, so it is unlikely we shall be eating crumpets, muffins and pikelets for afternoon tea, with roast beef on Sundays and goose now and then, followed by cassoulet next day. Some hint of what is to come can be derived from Derek Cooper's *Food Programme* on Radio Four.

There was a time not long ago when it seemed that Mr Cooper liked nothing more than a good meal. It might be a traditional English dish well prepared from fresh produce, the majestic offering of a Burgundian restaurant with three Michelin stars, or an authentic curry. A subtle change has occurred in recent years so that instead of whether food is enjoyable or not the programme is more concerned with the politics of food. When I say politics, I should perhaps say ethics: whether it is not morally wrong to eat at all.

This way, then, lies the next stage in our culinary culture. Instead of 'a little recipe we picked up in Perigeux' or 'I hope you like this: it's adapted from a dish they eat in Finland' we shall probably hear: 'I'm sorry about this but as you're here we thought perhaps you might agree to have a bite with us. It's only ship's biscuits with some sorrel which was going to seed – oh yes, and a touch of asafoetida.'

We are still, however, at the half-way stage and have not yet come fully to terms with the ratatouille and broccoli syndrome. As far as the former is concerned one can always hope that aubergines will be found to cause serious disorders of the urinary tract and that an enzyme present in courgettes leads to premature baldness.

Broccoli can be dealt with by different methods. All over the country, people are being sponsored to do what they like doing anyway. Our local cricket match is sponsored by a local greengrocer and the snooker league by a firm of builders' merchants. Would it not make more sense to sponsor people for doing what they don't like? At one pound a sprig from several sponsors I'd be prepared to eat several sprigs of steamed broccoli, which is arguably the worst dish in the world. Not only would charities benefit. One would be doing one's bit towards the anti-food regime which the new order brings in train.

15 June 1991: Charles Nevin

Very Manchester

Now it's drugs, guns and machetes: Manchester always did have an image problem. Too big, too much: Liberals and radicals, Cobden and Bright. Mills and merchants, soot, profit and slums. Cottonopolis. Irish, Germans, Jews. The Shock City of the nineteenth century, where Dickens and Disraeli came to wonder and worry. Peterloo and Engels: this is where the revolution starts. Made in Manchester. Manchester made Marx. The Anti Corn Law League, Free Trade: Manchester won, the Gentry lost. Manchester looked London right in the eye. What Manchester thought today, the world thought tomorrow. The International City. Not a bad newspaper, either.

Then High Victorian certainty gave way to a slow decline. Manchester faded, like cotton; it seemed tired, with new, less real, less substantial images, *Coronation Street,* and that echo of the old internationalism, the old specialness, Manchester United, the most famous, glamorous football club in the world. Manchester suffered grievously in the job-killing early Eighties. But while Liverpool was getting angry, Manchester was trying to get even, attracting service industries, building on its position as a financial centre. Manchester got bold again, image-conscious again, refound a bit of a swagger; and made a bid for the 1996 Olympics. The South-east smiled indulgently, particularly when Atlanta won, but stopped when Manchester beat off London's challenge for Britain's bid in 2000.

And then there was Madchester. Suddenly, in 1988, everyone began to notice that Manchester music and Manchester clubs were rather more interesting than music and clubs anywhere else. They had been for several years; enthusiasm for northern soul had turned naturally to enthusiasm for house music. And there were the guitar bands, the Happy Mondays, the Stone Roses, New Order, a Manchester sound united, as is usual, by not much more than coming from Manchester. Youth pundits pondered the significance of flared jeans and the importance of Ecstasy. Madchester made the cover of *Newsweek*. Another year, another image.

Now it's drugs, guns and machetes. Now Manchester is Violence City UK, Moss Side is Britain's Bronx, and *Newsweek* is back. One man shot dead, two others shot and injured in one Moss Side weekend; 19 serious woundings this year, six drugs and feuds killings in four years, five shot. Shotguns and handguns, rumours of Uzis and Yardies, police body armour on issue, police buying their own bullet-proof vests, crack as well as heroin and softer. Moss Side, dangerous, exciting, gang war; let's run with this one, this is good stuff.

Some context: the murder rate in the United States was nine per 100,000 of population in 1990; in Greater Manchester it was under one. There were 2,500 murders in New York City last year, 23 in Greater Manchester. But in 1957, there were three murders within three months in Moss Side. But in 1964, Manchester was 'rife' with teenage gangs and knife fights, and a youth of 17 died from a mixture of heroin and cocaine. Anthony Burgess's stepmother kept order in her Manchester pub in the Twenties with the aid of two service revolvers. Manchester has always been as rough as the more notorious Liverpool, if not rougher.

But there is a special quality to the latest Moss Side shootings. Shotguns are fired from passing cars, on one occasion into a group of children, blinding a 12-year-old boy; a restaurant is 'peppered' with gunfire; guns are loosed off in a crowded night club; a man is shot dead in a pub in an argument over a girl and drugs. There has been a similar pattern in London over the last two years: guns being used in a regular, almost casual way, to settle squabbles. Guns, it seems, are no longer special.

In Moss Side, the police will tell you, a small war has been going on between less than 50 young drugs dealers. Charges have now been brought for the latest murder, a 17-year-old hacked to death with a machete, and the area has assumed a calm which may or may not be temporary. The police will deny, despite accusations to the contrary, that they have let things get out of hand, that they have been operating hands-off policing since the riots here in 1981. They will tell you there are no 'no-go' areas in Manchester, that it is safe to walk the streets of Moss Side, day or night.

Anthony Burgess, using his occasional bluntness for effect, has described Moss Side, where he was brought up, as a Caribbean slum. In fact, more than 60 per cent of its 14,500 people are white. Another problem for easy answers is that the battle-ground, the Alexandra Park estate, is a carefully planned 1970s low-rise estate, all discreet closes, angles and grass, which borders on the green and pleasant Alexandra Park.

Gooch Close is the centre of operations for one of the groups of dealers; the police do not like to call them 'gangs', this being rather too glamorous and Chicago. Gooch Close is not glamorous; nor is it particularly dire. Taxis arrive and depart, meetings take place down alleyways. 'All the best, Saddam,' reads one piece of graffito; this is less likely to be the work of unpatriotic dealers than of the hand which has also written, 'Kill the rich, not the kids'.

Anthony, as we shall call him, is working on his car, a gleaming Alfasud of fair vintage. Other, newer, cars – BMWs and the like – are to be seen around, though not in the expected profusion, as are children on mountain bikes, said by the police to be lookouts for the dealers. Anthony says most of the dealers are young, in their teens. He is 28 and not working. 'My personal opinion is entirely with the kids. You go to school for x number of years, you come out with all these qualifications they've told you to get, and there are no jobs.'

Male unemployment on Moss Side runs at about 30 per cent. When the local Scottish & Newcastle brewery advertised 50 jobs, it received 9,000 applications. Robert Key, the junior environment minister, has just announced £1.4 million for projects aimed at training 300 people a year; some £10 million in all is going into the area over the next two years. But Anthony has no time for government schemes. 'Who wants to work for £50 a week?' Drug dealing has its attractions. 'You can double a £100 outlay in less than a day.' Earlier this year, Greater Manchester police arrested a dealer who proved to have £40,000 in cash.

The shootings are 'well overboard' says Anthony, 'but the kids aren't being shown anything else. A lot of the mums and dads know what they're up to, but they're being given the odd £200 a day so they're not doing anything. It's a bit topsy-turvy really. A lot of things need sorting out, starting with work.'

Anthony says there are plenty of guns around: 'You can get anything you want.' Uzis? Well, there's this rumour that they have one of those things that can bring down a police helicopter, and he wouldn't be too surprised, no. Grenades, too, they say. Police have seized about 50 weapons in raids on Moss Side. Pistols are fashionable, easily obtainable in Europe, apparently. The going rate is £150. (It was £50 in Colchester and Aldershot after the Falklands, it is said.)

Community workers? Anthony is not keen. Community meetings? 'Suck it,' says Anthony. Richard, as we shall call him, lives in Gooch Close, is unemployed and black, like Anthony. 'It's a joke round here, a joke. You can hear someone being shot, see someone getting smashed in by a machete, and you think, that's life, *c'est la vie.* The area's so small. We were all at school together.

'It's crazy. It's a joke. They've got Moss Side on the

television in London. These people are out of touch with reality. They say, I do bird when I'm 18, I'll do 10 years, I'll do bird, I'll be 28 when I come out. You get picked up, there's ten grand under the bed and you're out in six months' time. A lot of these kids have got A-levels but they can't get jobs. We don't want catering jobs, brewery jobs, we want professional jobs.'

Richard considers, and delivers: 'You're living in Manchester and you're having a good time. It's not true. It's just another nigger day. *Carpe Diem,* seize the day, go and sell some drugs. It's a video world, netherworld.' Well, yes, except that you *can* walk around the Alexandra Park estate by day and night, and there are no guns on the bar of the rival headquarters, the Pepperhill, and most people in Moss Side seem intent on continuing the unequal struggle with the real world.

It's Saturday night in Piccadilly, Manchester Piccadilly. A.J.P. Taylor thought the name was a deliberate snook at London, part of Manchester cheek and Manchester pride. He also thought Manchester irredeemably ugly, which is unfair; nowhere can be so considered which contains, for one example, the old Refuge Assurance building, the essence of the Manchester marriage between brass and grandeur, with a bit of romance thrown in, an impossibly Italianate tower above massively solid red brick.

The Refuge has taken refuge near leafy Wilmslow now, like so many grandees before, leaving a new-old hotel behind amid the tiles and pillars where the clerks toiled. (Wilmslow, well-heeled, at least 20 shoe shops, is Cheshire, the detached home county: very posh and barboured, Duke of Westminster, bows to no one.)

These days, though, central Manchester has a ravaged air: great works are afoot, another bold enterprise. After 40 years, the trams are coming back; a public and private £130 million light transit railway leaving the track to run on rails through the centre. Roads are up and blocked off, giving a slightly post-imperial, Third World effect. Inevitably, rail laying has been affected by the famous local humidity, but the first stage is due to open in November.

In Piccadilly Plaza, a group of girls chatter by. 'I tell you what, I'm glad I had that bottle of Babycham before we came out.' Old habits die hard. A group of lads are debating about going into the posh club, Piccadilly 21. But we are not going there. We are going to the Hacienda: the Hassie, the cradle of Madchester, an old warehouse with a sound system like no other which holds 1,200 people and where the walls run wet with a new Manchester humidity. The Hacienda closed in January. Inner City drug dealers from Moss Side and Cheetham Hill had moved in, were not averse to protecting themselves, or offering to protect others. There were hassles on the door, police complaints, a death from Ecstasy, capital E.

Now it has reopened, with a new team on the door, and a metal detector similar to the one in that other hot club, the House of Commons. The queue is round the block again, the sound as sharp as ever, but, you will be told, the Hassie is not what it was: 'Half of what you need,' you will be told, 'is a good club. The other quarter is the people who go there, and the other quarter is drugs.' Not so much of that in evidence at the Hacienda now. No dealers on the steps and in the niches up behind the DJ's booth. No Norwegian beer either, although the walls are still wet. Just another good club.

Matt Greenhalgh is 19 and is deciding what to do with himself; meanwhile he writes club reviews for *City Life,* another gift from the *Guardian* to the city. Matt remembers, with the enthusiasm of a veteran, the 'summers of love' before the 'inner cities', the dealers and the guns moved in, before the world discovered Madchester. 'I always thought the Hacienda was a godlike place, unreal,' says Matt. 'It will never be like that again,' you will be told. 'Everyone was mellowed, and taking drugs on a massive basis. There was a massive feeling of togetherness.'

The long-gone flares, said Matt, had started up on the terraces of Maine Road: 'City fans are always doing stupid things because their team's so crap.' City fans still hated United fans, and the other way about. Nothing turned off a Manchester soccer fan so much as scenes of Liverpool and Everton getting on together, standing together. City fans call United fans 'Munichs'; some United fans call themselves 'Young Munichs'. This is another side of Manchester, the brutal Northern jokes which have kept the favourite son, Bernard Manning, in work for so long.

Matt's sister Claire, an art student now living in Brixton, said: 'The one thing it's all about is attitude. There's an attitude up here. It's rough, down to earth, no trying to be anyone.' Funnily, though, there was no shorthand nickname for Mancunians, no equivalent to Scouser or Brummie. That's why they didn't have as much of an image. But Claire had spotted a new T-shirt slogan in the Hassie: 'Manchester, dodging the bullets and the rain.'

The Hacienda is part-owned by Tony Wilson, or Anthony Wilson, local Granada Television presenter, chairman of the most famous local independent record company, Factory Records. Tony is Sixties Cambridge with Salford vowels, and he has the widest suit shoulders in the North-west. Tony went to pick up a friend reading Bret Easton Ellis in her coupé outside and led the way to the Granada canteen.

Tony said that Manchester was coping better with the recession than the South. He said there had been a feeling in the Eighties that the South was where nice people lived and the North was cloth caps. Now people realised there was a better quality of life in the North and only footballers' wives from Luton didn't want to come to Manchester. Tony said the guns were about fashion. Handguns had replaced trainers as accessories. It was vanity, vanity was part of life. What was the answer? 'The answer is the end of poverty,' said Tony. 'You get rid of poverty and you get rid of the gangs. It's fairly straightforward.'

At the back of Granada is the entrance to the studio's tour, with a back-lot re-creation of a New York street scene. Some ladies from Waihi, New Zealand, were dancing to 'Lily of Laguna' with a Michael Jackson look-alike and a girl dressed as a cop, toting an imitation gun. The tour, featuring the *Coronation Street* set, has attracted more than one million visitors in two years; it was the sole purpose of the New Zealanders' visit to Manchester. This is the flash new Manchester, urban heritage, clever museums, visitor-friendly.

Granada has plans to convert an old warehouse across the road into a 'themed' hotel; Granada has plans for 'Media City', leisure, retail and offices on the banks of the much derided Irwell, following the pattern set in Salford Quays, Manchester and Salford's version of London Docklands. Granada will clearly remain a presence whatever happens to the franchise.

Media City is one scheme; there are others, warehouse conversions, glass towers, old offices into housing, ancient and post modern, glittering schemes, solid schemes to spark and sustain regeneration, launch a thousand glossy brochures, prompt as many meetings. The Central Manchester Development Corporation, with £150 million to spend over six years, has attracted £450 million into the centre; the development corporation at Trafford Park, the world's first industrial estate, has attracted £400 million and created 2,500 jobs. A regenerated Manchester Ship Canal Company has reopened the upper reaches of the Canal, and is leading redevelopment along its banks. (The Ship Canal was another Manchester snook. Frustrated with the Liverpool docks monopoly, Manchester simply moved the Atlantic.)

A new £80 million concert hall is being built for the Halle. The British Council is coming to new headquarters. A new rail link is being built out to Manchester's most modern pride, the airport (principal proprietor: Labour-controlled Manchester City Council) where traffic has quadrupled and profits increased from under £2 million to £42 million in 10 years, and where a £570 million terminal is now under construction. Buzz, buzz.

Everyone is being very brave about the recession. Some will tell you that Manchester is coping pretty well because there's nothing much more to lose in the way of traditional industry: between 1965 and 1981, employment in the textile industry here fell by 70 per cent; between 1981 and 1984, manufacturing as a whole declined by no less than 15 per cent. Some will also tell you that the much vaunted increase in the financial sector is mostly from branch offices of London concerns; they will also tell you that Manchester has gained because Liverpool 'has simply fallen off the map'.

There are worries about the effects of the Channel Tunnel, and worries about some of the speculative developments at Salford Quays and Trafford Park. Estate agents talk about 'time scales' of development 'moving out' from 1992–3 to 1994. Not good, regeneration-wise.

But there is always the Olympics: a successful bid would mean £2 billion of direct and indirect investment; 50,000 jobs; prestige, glamour, attraction. Whatever happens, Manchester is getting three new sporting venues which will be built in advance of the decision in the hope of influencing it. Laugh at that.

Bob Scott helps run most of Manchester's theatres, including the Opera House and the Palace; he also runs the Olympic bid, and he can talk. Bob Scott talks infrastructure, amenities and image. Manchester is not the glamorous choice, he says, but it is, 'in a funny way, the romantic one, the idea of a city motivating itself to reclaim former glories'.

Scott has the affection of an adopted son, a southern relish for the city's muscularity, lack of insularity, brassy self-confidence, and lack of reluctance 'to say bollocks' to patronisers and pretenders. He worries about drugs and guns, but contents himself with the thought that a reputation for a bit of edge rather than for bland provincialism has never done a city any harm. Look at Amsterdam. And what about Atlanta?

The criticism of all the shiny glass and clever conversion in the city centre is that it does little for the surrounding inner city areas, for Moss Side and Hulme next door, and Cheetham Hill to the north, another place of drugs and disaffection. The Cheetham Hill gangs are said to be one step up from the youngsters of Moss Side. Their methods, though, seem pretty similar. Earlier this year, a Cheetham Hill gang leader, White Tony Johnson, was shot dead. Again, charges have been brought.

Cheetham Hill used to be the Jewish quarter of Manchester, until they moved out to preferable Prestwich. Along Bury New Road and Cheetham Hill Road, Asian clothing businesses have taken over, their names striving, with that customary note of desperation, for appeal: La Fashion, Instyle (Manchester). One is different. This is The Legendary Joe Bloggs Incorporated Company, just near to where they are rebuilding Strangeways. Joe Bloggs makes street fashion clothing, and his hoardings are to be seen on the perimeters of most televised football matches.

Joe Bloggs is, in reality, Shami Ahmed, a 28-year-old Pakistani and another good talker. 'I came up with Joe Bloggs because it was very British.' All his clothes are made in Britain. 'People thought it was anti-fashion and anti-snobbery, that's why I thought it would work.' Ahmed started Joe Bloggs in 1986, neatly coinciding with (he would say leading) the rise of Madchester. He made the flared jeans, but no more. Now it's T-shirts that light up in the dark, ankle stranglers, T-shirts that change colour with the weather.

'We've put Manchester on the map as far as fashion is concerned,' says Ahmed, who left school at 16 and now has a Bentley turbo, a Ferrari Testarossa and an impatience with people who complain about lack of employment activities. 'When people think of London they think of Buckingham Palace; when they think of Manchester they think of Joe Bloggs. Competition is the wind that blows, that makes you fly higher. Nobody gives anybody a chance. Nobody will open the door for you, you've got to open the doors, climb the ladder. People expect too much. Give more and expect less; you perform better.'

Down the road, at Emperor House, Shonn Bros sell fancy goods. The business was started by Michael Shonn's grandfather, who arrived from Russia with nothing. The Olympics would be very good for Shonn Bros: all those souvenirs. Michael is proud of Manchester and has been a great fan of Napoleon since he was 12, hence Empire House. He has sympathy for people in Moss Side: 'I know you get guys who cause trouble, but there's no hope. You can't blame people on Moss Side. They're black and they can't get work. Where do they go? They've got to live.'

Further into Cheetham Hill, a group of Asian boys – Israr, Imran, Naame and Majid – were about to go off and kick a football around. Israr wants to be a vet; his father was a lawyer in Pakistan and now is a driving instructor. Naame thought the only way to make real money was with drugs. Israr's elder brother, 'a role model', they said, came by, bouffant hair, street fashion clothes, talking in Asian rap about the nation of Islam.

Bank holiday Monday. A rare slice of sunshine fell on Salford Quays, on the canalside houses and apartments, the Volvos and Mercedes, the sign advising against swimming in the canal. 'You don't fall in twice,' they say round here. Karen Cobbin, 29, hotel sales manager, and David Loft, 30, financial services consultant, from Brighton, were sitting on their patio doorstep. They liked Manchester; the people were more friendly, not so worried about what other people had got. Mind you, Karen had never seen mushy peas before they came here. Did she eat them now? 'God, no, definitely not.'

In Moss Side, the annual carnival was passing off in perfect peace, policemen were dancing and, in the words of another newspaper, the evil crack barons were hiding in their lairs. In the centre of the city, the Whit Walks, the traditional church procession, had just passed, and the pavements outside the pubs on the east side were thronged with older people, standing, drinking and laughing, a curiously time-warped, newsreel sort of sight.

More than £9 million has been spent on the environment and housing of East Manchester in the last 10 years, there is another £4 to come, and it looks as if it needs it.

In Miles Platting, in Fr Dominic Kirkham's presbytery at Corpus Christi, they are trying to renovate the community spirit, trying to get people to react to all the initiatives, liaising, pushing. There is the treasurer of the local Labour Party, a shopkeeper, a Post Office union official, and Maureen, who calls herself just a housewife and has started organising football training because that's what the kids want. There is a project to reopen the giant, listed mill that dominates Miles Platting, put workshops in, make amenities, opportunities. They want to start a community security service. They have got some money but they need more.

They want more help from the magistrates, the government, to sort out the local rotten apples, the vandalism and the drugs. They take you on a tour of the renovated housing, the burnt-out precinct, show you the mill close up. Fr Dominic says people who have just been factory fodder are beginning to think for themselves. They have formed a community assembly, a development trust. There is optimism and energy and no apologising. Very Manchester. 'You get so used to people telling you you're one step up from the gutter that you start to believe that you can't do anything,' says Maureen. 'But we can.'

Just to the east of Moss Side is Victoria Park, once a private estate of mansions, toll gates and keepers in uniform. The merchants have gone and their mansions are now mostly university buildings or flats. The inmates of a council hostel are playing bowls on the fine front lawn that once belonged to Sir Henry Platt. Two elderly ladies frown politely as they try dutifully to think of things that are better about Manchester today. Eventually they come up with less soot and more trees in the city centre, which have brought birds. The other day they had heard a mistle-thrush in Deansgate.

In Hulme, where male unemployment and empty properties vie at around 40 per cent, Charlie Baker, 27, shows the way round the giant Sixties estate of concrete barracks and walkways, the high rise Crescents designed, in a sad fancy, after Nash. Families found them impossible and were moved out, leaving old and young people, people with problems, mental problems, drug problems. In one part of the dereliction, young travellers are camped, their old vans and coaches parked around. The City Council has entered a plan to redevelop Hulme in Michael Heseltine's inner city challenge.

Charlie fears a new model development with a new model community and worries about what will happen to the people of Hulme. He wants to keep the Crescents. Charlie thinks that Hulme has developed an alternative community, unique in Britain. It has a spirit, he says, like the famous anarcho-alternative areas in Amsterdam or Kreuzberg in Berlin. This is Charlie's vision and he will argue it.

Walk down Piccadilly, London and ask about Manchester, what the name conjures, and you will get nothing, good club scene (twice), Manchester United. Two people, when prompted, knew about the guns and drugs. A South Korean in a Scotland the Brave T-shirt refused to comment. No one mentioned the rain.

There is a monument outside the mighty Town Hall celebrating Manchester's pre-eminence as the world's first nuclear free city. The inscription has grown old and faded now and some people mock the memory, recalling that the Manchester economy is well supported by the North-west nuclear industry.

Graham Stringer became leader of the city council in 1984 at the age of 34 and is still there, despite the odd hysteria over gay funding and trips to Nicaragua and a small spat with Militant. He arrived for confrontation and stayed for damage control; he is on the board of the development corporation; and he is the biggest employer in Manchester, which would no doubt intrigue the nineteenth century.

Ask him about Manchester and he has nothing pat, no slogan. But he talks about beating London for the Olympics bid, and he talks about the excitement and the pride in the city the night that United brought home the European Cup Winners Cup and Pavarotti was appearing at the G-Mex exhibition centre. The place had really been buzzing, and people in dinner jackets had been mingling with people in red and white scarves. Councillor Stringer had liked that.

Very Manchester.